LIFE IN LANGUAGE

CLASS 200 NEW STUDIES IN RELIGION

A SERIES EDITED BY Kathryn Lofton AND John Lardas Modern

ALSO PUBLISHED IN THE SERIES

Promiscuous Grace: Imagining Beauty and Holiness with Saint Mary of Egypt
Sonia Velázquez

Slandering the Sacred: Blasphemy Law and Religious Affect in Colonial India
J. Barton Scott

Earthquakes and Gardens: Saint Hilarion's Cyprus
Virginia Burrus

Awkward Rituals: Sensations of Governance in Protestant America
Dana Logan

Sincerely Held: American Secularism and Its Believers
Charles McCrary

Unbridled: Studying Religion in Performance
William Robert

Profaning Paul
Cavan W. Concannon

Making a Mantra: Tantric Ritual and Renunciation on the Jain Path to Liberation
Ellen Gough

Neuromatic: Or, A Particular History of Religion and the Brain
John Lardas Modern

Kindred Spirits: Friendship and Resistance at the Edges of Modern Catholicism
Brenna Moore

The Privilege of Being Banal: Art, Secularism, and Catholicism in Paris
Elayne Oliphant

Ripples of the Universe: Spirituality in Sedona, Arizona
Susannah Crockford

LIFE IN LANGUAGE

Mission Feminists and the Emergence of a New Protestant Subject

INGIE HOVLAND

The University of Chicago Press
Chicago and London

The University of Chicago Press, Chicago 60637
The University of Chicago Press, Ltd., London
© 2025 by The University of Chicago
All rights reserved. No part of this book may be used or reproduced in any manner whatsoever without written permission, except in the case of brief quotations in critical articles and reviews. For more information, contact the University of Chicago Press, 1427 E. 60th St., Chicago, IL 60637.
Published 2025

34 33 32 31 30 29 28 27 26 25   1 2 3 4 5

ISBN-13: 978-0-226-83829-8 (cloth)
ISBN-13: 978-0-226-83831-1 (paper)
ISBN-13: 978-0-226-83830-4 (e-book)
DOI: https://doi.org/10.7208/chicago/9780226838304.001.0001

Library of Congress Cataloging-in-Publication Data

Names: Hovland, Ingie, author.
Title: Life in language : mission feminists and the emergence of a new Protestant subject / Ingie Hovland.
Other titles: Class 200, new studies in religion.
Description: Chicago : The University of Chicago Press, 2025. | Series: Class 200: new studies in religion | Includes bibliographical references and index.
Identifiers: LCCN 2024033901 | ISBN 9780226838298 (cloth) | ISBN 9780226838311 (paperback) | ISBN 9780226838304 (ebook)
Subjects: LCSH: Dons, Henny, 1874–1966. | Dons, Henny, 1874–1966—Language. | Norske misjonsselskap. | Women missionaries—Norway—History—20th century. | Women missionaries—Civil rights—Norway. | Women missionaries—Norway—Biography. | Women missionaries—Norway—Language. | Feminists—Norway—Language. | Feminism—Norway—Religious aspects—Protestant churches.
Classification: LCC BV3703 .H68 2025 | DDC 284.1092 [B]—dc23/eng/20241004
LC record available at https://lccn.loc.gov/2024033901

For Sophia and Simone

CONTENTS

Introduction: Unlearning Protestant Dematerialization 1

    1   Listening 27

    2   Speaking 53

    3   Writing 78

    4   Reading 103

Conclusion: A Material-Discursive, Multiple Protestantism 130

Acknowledgments 139
Notes 141
References 165
Index 179

INTRODUCTION

Unlearning Protestant Dematerialization

One cold Friday evening in October 1920 in the Norwegian capital Kristiania (later Oslo), Henny Dons proudly welcomed a small crowd to the inauguration of the Mission School for Women. The inauguration was held in the living room of the new residential schoolhouse, a stately three-story building on a corner facing a park. Dons was in her midforties. In her youth, she had wished to travel as a missionary to the mission station Eshowe among the Zulus, but she had been prevented by a lung sickness and had instead turned her attention to supporting the global Protestant mission while remaining in Norway. This evening, she addressed the small, festive audience in the living room. We do not have pictures from that night, but from other photographs we know Dons wore full-length, many-layered dresses, with her hair neatly pulled back in a bun; she had an upright posture, a rounded face, and a steady gaze.[1] Standing in the new Mission School for Women, she detailed how the Ladies' Committee had been formed twenty years earlier, in 1900, with the aim of establishing a school for young women who wished to become missionaries overseas. Dons had chaired the committee for the past decade, and now, in 1920, their desire for a school had finally been fulfilled. The school was formally owned by the Norwegian Mission Society (NMS), an organization that sent Norwegian Lutheran missionaries overseas to Zululand, Natal, Madagascar, and China. NMS was the largest Christian organization in Norway outside the Lutheran state church, and, as Dons implied, it was significant that the organization had allowed this new space for women to be created.[2]

Dons did not mention in her speech that NMS already owned another Mission School. The other Mission School was not located amid the tall apartment buildings lining the streets of the capital, Kristiania, but in Stavanger on the west coast—a town of small white wooden homes and steamships in the harbor, the stronghold of Norway's evangelical Bible Belt. This Mission School had admitted young men as students since 1843. It was located a short walk from the NMS head office, where a small group of men met to make decisions, including the organization's general secretary, Lars Dahle. Dahle had received some requests from young women to be admitted to the Mission School (for men), but he found these requests preposterous.[3] In one of the letters that figured into the very long, back-and-forth negotiations over a Mission School for Women, he connected these requests to the women's rights movement. Certain "women's issues women," he commented critically, using the term closest to *feminist* at the time, "wish to abolish all difference." He warned: "I fear this is an underlying thought also for *a few* of the women who say that of course it is just as necessary to have mission schools for women as for men."[4] This was no minor matter; any formal connection between mission-supporting women and the political women's movement would, in his view, cause "*foundational damage* to our mission."[5] Nevertheless, the Ladies' Committee managed to establish a Mission School for Women after holding committee meetings for twenty years. It helped that Dahle retired in 1920, that the women agreed NMS would have sole ownership of the school, and that they relinquished to NMS the right to appoint a management committee to make all major decisions.[6]

Dons, diplomatic to a fault, did not hint at any of this protracted negotiation in her speech at the opening celebration. Instead, she stepped aside so the male pastor who chaired the school's management committee could speak. He said the school had grown out of the guidance of the Holy Spirit regarding "woman's place" today, and he called to the front seven young women who had enrolled as students to welcome them (two more would join them that year). Afterward, those present were offered a cup of tea to mark the occasion. The next morning the students returned to their lessons, which they received six days a week around the dining room table in the schoolhouse.[7]

This book is about Henny Dons and the Lutheran "mission feminists" in Norway in the first decades of the twentieth century. What has been dubbed the mission feminist movement by later scholars refers to a collection of disparate activities of some Lutheran women who were influenced by the early twentieth-century women's movement in northern Europe and who actively sought to raise the status of women in Protestant circles, especially in mission organizations. One of the organizations they worked in and on was NMS. Notably, these women had already gained the right to vote within NMS in 1904, almost a decade before women in general were allowed to vote by the state of Norway in 1913. Further representational changes followed as women were allowed to be elected to the regional committees of NMS in 1916, Dons was hired as the first woman in a paid position in the NMS central administration in 1917, and NMS's Mission School for Women was opened in 1920. Finally, women were allowed to be elected to the NMS governing board in 1939, the same year Dons retired. Historical studies of the mission feminist movement have highlighted such public, institutional victories to which Dons and her peers contributed—votes, electability, education, and paid positions for women—and their democratizing ripple effects.[8]

As I have dived into the archival material left from Dons and her feminist colleagues, however, what has struck me about these women is something less visible as a historical event: their concern with language use. I have become intrigued by the many new language practices they began using as they explored new ways of speaking, listening, reading, and writing. For example, when Dons gave a speech as a woman to a mixed-gender audience in the Mission School for Women on its opening night, this was a new use of words. She and her colleagues expended enormous effort on establishing the small residential school in which nine young women would sit around a dining table to listen to lectures and ask questions, to read books and write essays. The process had been pushed forward by a handful of women who called themselves a "committee," complete with bylaws, agendas, minutes, and formal correspondence. These language practices were all new.

Their Lutheran mothers and grandmothers had not been able to listen, speak, write, or read in any of these ways. Rather, such language practices had previously been actively discouraged. Two generations earlier, in 1866, NMS printed a statement in its magazine explaining that when mission-supporting women gathered together without any man present, they should not "lead with words and work in the word [*føre Ordet og arbeide i Ordet*]" but should instead simply "work"—that is, craft with their hands.[9] However, around 1900, some women in this same pietistic Lutheran mission tradition began working with language in ways their mothers had not done. Instead of gathering to work on crafts (while chatting over coffee), Dons and some of her peers banned crafts in their new monthly meetings and instead sat silently and listened to one woman give a talk, for example about "heathen" women in Madagascar. One of them might present a devotion, and they might send off a female missionary to China by "giving" her a Bible verse. Some of them volunteered to lead girls' mission groups in which they read aloud from a book, written by a woman, about the "peace" the British Empire had afforded NMS's mission to the Zulus. In the evening, they might open their own Bibles and ponder the creation of the first woman, Eve, as they consulted a Bible study newly authored by a woman.

The topic of this book, then, can be phrased in two ways. The book examines the new language use of Henny Dons and her peers among the early twentieth-century Lutheran mission feminists in Norway. Another way of saying this is that the book examines the emergence of a new language user: a Protestant feminist subject who combined "woman" and "words" in new arrangements in her life as an ethical project. Dons and her peers made something that to my mind was significantly creative. However, it is clear that it was also significantly constrained, and in retrospect I am struck by the contradictory consequences of their linguistic experiments—both harmful and fruitful.

I explore this topic through a fragmentary linguistic biography of Henny Dons, a series of glimpses into how she used language in her life.[10] She lived from 1874 to 1966 and was active in and around NMS during the first four decades of the twentieth century. Her name is still remembered in this tradition. In 2009, signs were put up on the college campus that was formerly NMS's Mission School in Stavanger (today VID Specialized University)—the school Dons was not allowed to attend or teach at—designating one of the buildings with a new name: Henny Dons House. The building overlooks a cobblestone courtyard, next to a granite statue of Lars Dahle. While Dons's name has lived on, however, her voice, as I reconstruct it here, may come across as puzzling today. For example, while it might seem important today to emphasize her role in supporting women's right to vote, Dons never portrayed this as central to her own work. And while we might assume that her prominence would come with influence, she seems to have had only limited impact during her lifetime on most of the mission-supporting women across Norway and to have been sidelined easily by the male leadership of NMS during the last decade of her career. Thus, Dons's life shows some of the complications of the histories of modern feminism. Public feminist figures such as Dons may have achieved a widespread recognition that was at the same time curbed and precarious, and religious feminisms did not always fit neatly with the "first wave" of the women's movement. The students and faculty who today pass by the sign announcing Henny Dons House might find it quite strange to imagine the life of this woman who once used new language practices to stitch together—albeit with considerable difficulty—her two worlds of Protestantism and feminism.

Dons's life, then, offers us a doorway into some of the recent histories of our late modern moment. She was a Protestant woman positioned at a time and place in which the early women's movement was growing around the North Atlantic, alongside a broader process of liberal democratization in northern Europe, the so-called high age of the British Empire, and the exploding global Protestant mission movement. Her life presents a microcosm of these larger histories of Western nineteenth- and twentieth-century modernity as they were co-formed (though our scholarship often treats them as conceptually separate today): expanding North Atlantic formations of liberalism, feminism, imperialism, and global Protestantism.[11] Therefore, this book is both the story of piecing together scenes from one life and the story of how a broader shift was nudged into motion as a new relation between women and words came into being at the crossroads of certain modern histories.

But, most importantly, what Dons can show us reaches beyond her historical world. She can show us something about what the literary theorist Toril Moi (2017, 44), in her engagement with Ludwig Wittgenstein, has called "our lives in language." The anthropologist Veena Das (2020, xiii), in her own conversation with Wittgenstein, has similarly emphasized that we have a "life *in* language (not just *with* language)."[12] Thus, the following chapters provide not just a series of glimpses of Protestant language use in Dons's life—her listening, speaking, writing, and reading—but also explore what this tells us about her Protestant "life in language": how her use of words constituted who she and others thought she was and what emerged as important for her in her relation with the world. Put another way, she can illuminate how Protestant language use was part of what made her a new Protestant feminist subject and part of what constituted her new ethical project of Protestant feminism. Her language use, subjectivity, and ethics wove together, and it is this interwoven phenomenon that I wish to capture as "life in language."

What characterized this Protestant life in language? I have spent a long time searching for conceptual tools to answer this question. Our current anthropological conversation on Protestant language use suggests that when Protestants use words, they seek to separate these from materiality, striving for intentional, sincere speech anchored in an interior, sincere self. As I will examine below, this striving is referred to as a "Protestant language ideology" (or "Protestant semiotic ideology"), a system of ideas that drive Protestants' motivations toward dematerialization (e.g., Keane 2007). The result is assumed to be a type of mentalistic Protestant individual who is centered on self-formation and whose Weberian "Protestant ethic" runs alongside and through the disembodied, iconoclastic narratives of Western modernity. This longing for dematerialization, it is argued, brands all Protestants, regardless of gender (or other social markers). In the broader study of religion, this assumed Protestant orientation toward interior belief at the expense of materiality is sometimes referred to as the "Protestant bias" (e.g., Meyer 2010). The scholarly conversation on Protestantism, then, often posits that not only Protestant language use but also Protestant subjectivity and ethics are driven by a craving for dematerialization.

However, in my research on Dons's life, I have struggled to apply the lens of an assumed Protestant desire for dematerialization. Dons's Protestant life in language was instead shaped by her desire to join material elements with linguistic ones. In particular, she seems to have forged strong connections between her use of words and her material, female body, to the extent that I will describe her use of words as woman-word operations; these operations were material-discursive. In her view, this language use was shaped not just by herself but also by forces and figures beyond the self—God and Satan, imagined women figures around the world, biblical characters—that worked in and through her. She enacted her ethical project of Protestant feminism in the midst of this shifting collection of beings. Her subjectivity and ethics were not only, or even primarily, anchored in a singular, sincere self, but instead appear in slightly different material-discursive configurations in different situations, reaching beyond the self. In this sense, her life in language took on a changeable quality, a capacity for internal multiplicity.

Therefore, in this book I argue that Dons's Protestant life in language—the series of woman-word operations that wove together language use, subjectivity, and ethics in her life—was characterized by being both material-discursive and multiple. In other words, when we look at Dons's Protestant life in language, we do not see a striving for the ideal of dematerialization, as today's scholarly conversation on the "Protestant bias" would lead us to believe; rather, we see a life in language constituted in operations that were composed of both material and discursive elements in intra-action. It was material-discursive. Moreover, we do not see language, subjectivity, and ethics rooted in a singular self or a singular system of ideas, such as a "Protestant language ideology"; instead, we see a multiple subject with a multiple ethical project, if by "multiple" we can conceptualize an entity—a Protestant woman using words—who is both composite (partly composed of forces and figures beyond the self) and protean (appearing in different forms across different sites).

As I follow this line of thought through the following chapters, my broader objective is to help reorient our scholarly conversation on Protestantism away from the assumed Protestant story of an individual, interior self who yearns for language, subjectivity, and ethics to be dematerialized. I think we will gain a more realistic understanding of Protestantism—and of our contemporary, modern world that Protestantism has helped form—if we shift toward understanding Protestantism as a story of material-discursive multiplicity. This will allow us to better engage with larger questions, such as: Why is it that Protestantism has grown up in tandem with what we call modernity over the past five centuries and has remained enmeshed with this modernity even through the accelerations of the past two centuries? What can account for Protestantism's ability to proliferate into such a dizzying variety of groups that exist in close relations—whether friendly or hostile—with some of Western modernity's most far-reaching projects in the nineteenth and twentieth centuries, including intensified forms of democratization and colonization, liberalism and feminism?

I suggest that the reason is not, as the prevailing scholarly picture assumes, that Protestantism drives a desire for dematerialization, matching the desires of modernity. As I hope to show in the following chapters, a close examination of a modern Protestant woman's life in language causes this picture to fall apart. Instead, a more plausible reason for Protestantism's mutually constitutive relation with modernity lies in Protestantism's unusual ability to combine linguistic and material forms in a variety of changeable configurations, offering the flexibility needed to sustain modern megaprojects over long periods of time and large territories, including projects of liberalism, imperialism, and feminism.

THE PROBLEM OF WOMEN USING WORDS IN CHRISTIANITY

Let me share a memory that shows my own family's entanglement in the story I will tell.

It is summer in southern Norway. My sister and I, home from college, are visiting our grandmother.

"I sat like this!" our grandmother exclaims, laughing as she pushes herself forward on her chair until she is balancing precariously on the very edge of the seat. "The teacher told me later she'd been concerned I would fall off!"

My sister and I laugh too, as our grandmother remembers herself in her midtwenties attending NMS's Mission School for Women. Now she is in her late seventies, perched on the edge of her chair in demonstration, and we are the ones in our midtwenties, sinking into the comfortable upholstery in her living room.

"The school that Henny Dons made happen," she instructs us in a defiant tone, "when the Mission Society didn't want to educate women."

I try to imagine my grandmother at the Mission School for Women in January 1950. She was a Norwegian-Lutheran nurse preparing to become a missionary wife in the French Colony of Madagascar. She was aware that just a few decades earlier, women in NMS had not been allowed to be "educated": they had not been told to read textbooks about Protestant mission history or listen to lectures about the New Testament. Yet she chose to balance on the very edge of her seat, apparently not sure, at first, whether her body belonged in a space with these kinds of weighty words—words about Christian history, about the Bible. My grandmother's emphatic instruction to her granddaughters—"the school that Henny Dons made happen"—came alongside her physical demonstration of the situation's underlying puzzle: how to combine a Protestant woman's body with words.

My grandmother and Henny Dons are not the only women in Christian history who have run into difficulties when trying to use words. In fact, the vast majority of Christian communities over the past two thousand years have experienced the phenomenon of women using words as a problem, imposing regulations on women's speaking, listening, reading, and writing. Christian communities have explained this to themselves in a number of ways, including through Paul's directive in the New Testament: "Let your women keep silence in the churches: for it is not permitted unto them to speak" (1 Corinthians 14:34), echoed by the rule laid out by the author of 1 Timothy that women should "be in silence" since the original woman, Eve, was created second and sinned first (1 Timothy 2:12–14).[13] And in the two thousand years since those statements were written down, the combination of women with words has frequently been regarded as risky in Christian settings across traditions: Orthodox, Catholic, Protestant, Pentecostal.

I start with biblical words because one of the challenges of understanding women's lives in Christianity, especially in Protestantism, is the challenge of describing the extent to which, for someone like Henny Dons, certain words shape life. More than that: certain words create life, give life, and are life. However, starting with biblical words might also be misleading, because it might imply that if only biblical words could be properly understood, then Protestant women's use of words would no longer present a problem. In my view, this is not how Christian words work in the world. This is one of the differences between my project and the field of feminist biblical scholarship, a field that at times takes a normative tack as feminist biblical scholars engage in close readings of biblical texts—such as the account of the creation of Eve, or Paul's letters to early Christian groups—to articulate how women in these texts have, in the scholars' view, been misconstrued by male authors and exegetes (e.g., Kartzow 2009; Trible 1973). While these careful readings have informed my understanding, I do not raise their normative questions of how the Christian Bible *should* be interpreted or what Christian feminism *should* be.

Instead, I am interested in the descriptive questions of ethnography: How does this problem—the problem of women using words in Christianity—work in lives? What happens when women combine with words in, for example, a particular Protestant situation? Of course, my distinction between normative and descriptive approaches does not quite hold in practice, since ethnographic description, like close reading, rests on evaluative judgments about what to notice and how to organize it. The distinction I am making is more one of emphasis: I do not wish to emphasize whether the mission feminists' language use falls under someone else's definition of "Christianity" or "feminism." Instead, I start with an ethnographic interest in what they said and did in their everyday social worlds and how this constituted what to them was "Christianity" and "feminism."

Though I am concerned here with Protestant feminists, even a moment's reflection will show that the problem of women using words stretches far beyond Christian communities. During my research for this book, two feminist voice-fragments have persistently returned to me, both evocatively attempting to grasp the magnitude of the problem. The first is the observation by the French philosopher Luce Irigaray ([1977] 1985, 68) that the feminine has "no possible place" in Western discourse. She adds that, in the male-dominated European theoretical tradition she engages, "the masculine sex" and ultimately the figure of "the father" holds "the monopoly on value" ([1977] 1985, 73). The second voice-fragment is a poem by speculative fiction author Ursula K. Le Guin (1993, vii) in which she conjures the clamoring voices of women readers:

> It's allowed. It is allowed, we are allowedSILENCE!
> It *is* allowed—it *is* allowed—it *is* aloudSILENCE!
> It *used* to be aloud.

SI-EEE-LENTSSSS.
I-EE AM THE AWE-THOR.
REEED MEEE IN SI-EE-LENT AWE.

>But—it's *aloud*–
>it *is* aloud–

[...] DO•NOT•NO•TRESPASS•KEEP•OUT•SILENCE!

Irigaray's reference to "the father" and Le Guin's use of "AWE-THOR" hint at the subtle influence of the figure of the Christian Father, the author-creator-God, in Western canonical discourse, while at the same time painting the problem of women using words as a broader, enduring problem in the history of Western Europe and in this tradition's settlement of North America.

It is admittedly difficult to bridge Irigaray's philosophical universalization (women have "no possible place" in language) or Le Guin's artistic expression ("KEEP•OUT•SILENCE!") to my ethnographic attention to particulars. But their observations about women's place in language continue to return to me, because in a roundabout way they connect to various women's experiences around the North Atlantic until today. Though women are typically stereotyped as being more "talkative" than men, a much more circumscribed picture emerges once one starts to dig into the issue. In the contemporary United States, where I am now based at a large university, colleagues periodically remind me of research in disciplines such as political science or management studies, in which controlled group experiments indicate that unless women are in a supermajority in a work meeting they speak less, are interrupted more, are less able to assert influence, and, if they do, are perceived differently than assertive men (Karpowitz and Mendelberg 2014). Meanwhile, disciplines such as communication studies may gather women's experiences through surveys, such as my colleagues across the quad who have examined voice—in this case, the ability to speak one's mind—in mother-daughter relationships in a context where girls may be socialized to self-silence, or, as I might put it in this book, to take up less space (Arroyo, Woszidlo, and Janovec 2020).

These are only a few of the many ways we might try to think about the far-reaching problem of women using words: by asking philosophical questions, through imaginative poetry, in controlled group observations, or by distributing surveys. We could add many more approaches, from literary close readings to theatrical stagings, from experiments in psychology labs to the careful transcripts of sociolinguists, since the problem we are dealing with is multiheaded, reoccurring across disciplines in different guises. But let me instead turn to the specific approach I will use.

In this book, I explore the problem of women using words in one Protestant tradition from my perspective as a cultural anthropologist in the archive. I start from the observation that Dons and her mission-feminist peers found that words did not operate in the same way for them as for their male colleagues. And yet, or perhaps precisely because of this, they focused intensely on language use. I will follow the problem of women using words as it was lived by Dons in her gendered Protestant life, intersecting with other lives, in this particular setting of early twentieth-century northern Europe, asking: How did the problem work in her life? What happened as she and her peers used words in new ways? This is a different scale of analysis than the micro level of a conversational moment in which a girl is subtly encouraged to self-silence, or the macro level of a Western canon that revolves around the masculine as its universal norm. Instead, this book's scale of analysis is the meso level of a life in language.

ETHNOGRAPHY IN THE ARCHIVE

I first encountered some of the archival materials from Henny Dons and her colleagues one day when I was walking across the cobbled courtyard of the leafy college campus of the Mission School in Stavanger (today VID). The school houses extensive archival collections, and I was in the midst of reading through nineteenth-century letters from Norwegian missionaries in Zululand. That day, one of the archivists was meeting a woman in the courtyard who pulled behind her a small wagon stacked with cardboard boxes. As I joined them, the archivist excitedly explained to me that these were documents saved by the Female Teachers' Mission Association from the early twentieth century. I became curious, and on one of my later trips down to the large archival rooms in the basement, behind the heavy fireproof doors, I asked about the new boxes and was allowed to explore them. Intrigued by what I found, I continued to follow the trail of these female teachers, including Dons, from one archival file to the next.

I grew to love the times I sat on the floor down there in the archives, next to the rows of tall industrial shelves crammed with endless boxes, my eyes growing red and itchy from the archive dust. I lifted out folder after folder and was amazed again and again at the documents these women had chosen to save: committee correspondence and personal messages, notebooks filled with handwritten meeting minutes, newspaper clippings, pamphlets, lesson plans for female mission students, Dons's notes for talks she gave to women's groups, a typed and unpublished book manuscript. I sorted through the correspondence between these women and the male leaders (to whom they remained loyal) in NMS, which had been saved in NMS's archival collection. I paged through tall stacks of mission periodicals that might tell me about the women. I browsed the racks of old books in the tucked-away corners of the Mission School's library to find Dons's published mission history, her collection of Bible studies, and her children's books still on the shelves, ready for me to borrow.

I began collecting and going through all these materials as an anthropologist in the archive. There are many similarities between anthropologists and historians who work ethnographically with archival materials. For example, we are often highly attentive to people: we slow down our reading to grasp glimpses of what the everyday world looked like to these people, and we pay attention to what they paid attention to, working with the grain of the sources. At the same time, we remain aware that the sources have been produced under certain circumstances and for certain audiences, and so we attempt to read between the lines, working against the grain, bearing in mind that the people who wrote, handled, and saved these documents had their own purposes for telling some stories and not others. However, there are also some differences between the disciplines of anthropology and history. In practice, these are not so much neat distinctions as spectrums along which anthrohistorians—both anthropological historians and historical anthropologists—might place themselves (see, e.g., Kalb and Tak 2005). I outline two of these differences here that I have used to delineate my own approach. They center on how I, as an anthropologist, assemble a context and a conversation.

First, assembling a context. In both anthropology and history, details are considered valuable, and these details are only deemed understandable to us, in a different lifeworld, if we can arrive at an understanding of their "context." However, the discipline of cultural anthropology, perhaps more so than history, pushes scholars toward thinking of context less as a world to be found and more as a methodological decision to be made. As Andreas Bandak and Jonas Jørgensen (2012, 449) put it, rather than speaking of "what the context . . . is" when we study Christianity, we might speak of "how this 'context' is produced" in Christian situations and in our framings of them.

As I sift through, arrange, and frame the materials from and about Dons, some contextual elements are pulled to the foreground, some are relegated to the background, and some are left out of the frame.

While there are many contexts in which Dons and the mission feminists could be situated, I have decided to frame them as particulars of four larger processes. I discuss these four contexts in the chapters below. In chapter 1 on *listening*, I focus on the evangelical context—especially the historical shifts of NMS as it grew out of the second-wave evangelical revivals—that can help us understand the opportunities this presented for women to gather in groups. In chapter 2 on *speaking*, I move on to the context of the bustling city of Kristiania around the turn of the twentieth century, including the varied women's movement(s) that emerged there among middle-class women. In chapter 3 on *writing*, I widen my lens to take in the conjunction in northern Europe between support for the expansion of overseas Protestant mission, the "high age" of the British Empire, and the changing place of white women in this new global context. In chapter 4 on *reading*, I add the final contextual layer, namely what we today think of as the "first wave" of feminism around the North Atlantic, which focused especially on women's suffrage. Together, these four processes—the evangelical revivals, the busy city of Kristiania, the global shifts of mission and empire, and first-wave feminism—provide my assembled contexts for the life of Henny Dons.

Second, assembling a conversation. Which sources and scholars do I draw into my text as I consider Dons's life? While historians might lean toward assembling a conversation about the specific historical period and place they are studying, anthropologists often proceed by turning their collected details into an example or a case of something—such as a social phenomenon, pattern, or experience—and convening a conversation about this something (Højer and Bandak 2015).[14] Thus, whereas historians might typically visit a number of archives to collect a wealth of sources about their time and place, anthropologists may be content with only one archive—as long as it provides a rich example.[15] As before, it is impossible to make a hard-and-fast rule, but I have found it helpful to consider the different strengths of these contributions. If I had been interested primarily in the historical and geographical setting of Dons's life, I would have collected sources and drawn together scholars that could help us understand early twentieth-century Lutheran Norway. But, although I have spent much time considering this period and place, I have not made it the primary focus of my conversation here. Instead, I am interested in Dons's life as an example of a Protestant woman using words, a social situation that recurs in many other times and places beyond early twentieth-century Norway. Therefore, I have delved into only a few archival collections but have drawn together conversation partners from far afield to try to understand what we can learn from this particular case—that is, from this Protestant woman's life in language.

PROTESTANT DEMATERIALIZATION?

It has taken me a while to collect these conversation partners. Or, more accurately, it has taken me a while to unlearn how we commonly see Protestantism in the study of religion: as a tradition preoccupied with separating belief from materiality, with disenchanting the world, with cultivating sincere, interior individuality—in short, with dematerializing language, subjectivity, and ethics. This view, which positions Protestantism as a building block of nineteenth- and twentieth-century Western modernity, has been baked into our canon through, for example, Max Weber's tying together of Protestant sects with asceticism ([1905] 2002) and Marcel Mauss's argument that these same Protestant sects helped create interior selves ([1938] 1985, 21). Since then, scholars of religion have increasingly argued that Protestantism has shaped not only our understanding of things and persons but also our very understanding of "religion," leading to a tendency to mistakenly analyze all "religions" through a lens that centers interior belief and decenters materiality. This critique has become so well known that it can be encapsulated in a shorthand: "the Protestant bias."[16]

In my own subfield, the anthropology of religion, an influential expression of this prevailing view of Protestantism is the notion that Protestants are shaped by a specific "language ideology"—that is, a system of ideas about language.[17] This has given rise to the argument that "the Protestant language ideology" (or "the Protestant semiotic ideology") pushes Protestants toward the goal of speaking sincerely as individuals without being encumbered by material forms (though in reality, the argument continues, this cannot be done, so they fail; in the end, the ideology is impossible).[18] If I were to think about Dons through the lens of this prevailing view, I would see a presumed singular whole—a Protestant woman using words—and I would look, perhaps, for her expression of an interior, sincere self or for her techniques of untying this self from material forms. I would look for clues indicating how she attempted to dematerialize her use of words, herself as a subject, and her ethical engagements.

But Henny Dons has helped me, slowly, to see Protestantism in a different way. If we return to the Mission School for Women that cold Friday night in October 1920, we might gradually notice this different picture. As we step into the warm living room, we see Dons speaking. She does not seem to say everything on her mind, but the main points of her tactful speech, cloaking unspoken truths, are recorded by another woman in a notebook that is later carefully saved. Dons has placed herself in the living room of the schoolhouse, tying her speaking body to a place, to a gathering of bodies. She gains authority from the crowd that listens to her, from the fact that a male pastor speaks next, from the trail of committee paperwork leading to this moment, from the visible line of the bodies of seven women students who are called to the front. If we tiptoe out of the living room and down the hallway to glance around Dons's bedroom,[19] we might see one or two of the letters she frequently received from women missionaries, which she liked to read out loud at the Female Teachers' meetings. We might see one of the notebooks she kept, filled with handwritten notes for her talks about what she perceived to be the plight of "heathen" women, the "place" of Christian women, or the creation of the first woman. We might see her well-thumbed Bible, in which I could safely wager that she had many times read the line describing Jesus's incarnation: "And the Word was made flesh, and dwelt among us" (John 1:14).

Returning to the living room and taking it all in, perhaps we can start to see a picture in which Dons and her feminist colleagues worked actively in and with material forms, tying their words to notebooks that could serve as concrete records, to typed papers, to groups, to the bodies of women, to a room in a house. Rather than aiming to stand apart from material forms, they specifically wanted words to combine with women's bodies, without indicating that they were seeking to dematerialize these bodies or the many other forms with which they became entangled in this process. These Protestant women thought words, bodies, and places were closely connected, in the same way they thought there was a close connection between "the Word," flesh, and dwelling.

Therefore, I have searched for conversation partners who would help me consider how to give equal analytical weight to both the women's words and their embodiment, to their use of both imaginative and material forms, showing that these often combined into women-word operations in which these Protestant women—contrary to the prevailing scholarly view of the Protestant language ideology and the Protestant bias—did not wish to separate language from materiality. I have wanted a method that would allow me to lay out the many discursive and material elements of Dons's language use and move from one to the next, without having to make these many elements fit the scholarly idea of dematerialization.

In working with these desires, I have found myself drawn to an unlikely pairing: Ludwig Wittgenstein and feminist new materialism. I turned to Wittgenstein's philosophy of language because of a certain double movement in his thinking: a passionate attraction to seeing language as inextricable from life forms and an equally passionate shying away from unitary wholes.[20] At the same time, I have found that new materialism—and especially feminist new materialism—can help turn these passionate insights into more practical tools. I focus on two such tools here: the "material-discursive" phenomenon (Barad 2008, 141) and the "multiple" phenomenon (Mol 2002).

A MATERIAL-DISCURSIVE LIFE IN LANGUAGE

One of Wittgenstein's remarks to which I have returned many times is reported by his student and friend Maurice O'Connor Drury as part of a conversation between them in Cambridge in 1930. Wittgenstein had asked Drury to read aloud the opening chapters of Sir James Frazer's *The Golden Bough*, and I imagine Wittgenstein may have been leaning back in the deck chair he kept in his rooms in Trinity College while Drury read from Frazer's analysis of rain ceremonies, fire festivals, and the ritual killing of the priest-king. All these religious rites, Frazer proposed, were scientific attempts to have an effect on the world, though they were based on erroneous ideas of how the world worked. Drury remembers Wittgenstein disagreeing strongly: "On the contrary," he interjected, the people in question had already demonstrated scientific achievements in other ways, such as metalworking or agriculture. The religious rites, Wittgenstein elaborated, were "not mistaken beliefs" but rather "the need to *express* something; the ceremonies were a form of language, a form of life" (Drury 1973, x; see also 1981, 134–135). This book about Henny Dons is in many ways a reimagining of this remark by Wittgenstein: when we look at an instance of what is called "religion" (such as "Protestantism"), we are not seeing a mistaken system of ideas or an impossible ideology, but rather "a form of language, a form of life."

Wittgenstein's *Lebensform* (life form), usually translated as "form of life," only appears a handful of times in his writings and has been much debated.

In Wittgenstein's remark to Drury, he seems to evoke "life" as something that is done or that happens dynamically, which anthropologist Knut Christian Myhre (2018a) describes as Wittgenstein's "deep pragmatism." This is also the case in remarks in his *Philosophical Investigations:* "And to imagine a language means to imagine a form of life" ([1953] 2009, §19); "The word 'language-*game*' is used here to emphasize the fact that the *speaking* of language is part of an activity, or of a form of life" ([1953] 2009, §23).[21] In a related remark on "natural history," Wittgenstein combines social and physical elements: "Giving orders, asking questions, telling stories, having a chat, are as much a part of our natural history as walking, eating, drinking, playing" ([1953] 2009, §25). Here human use of language occurs jointly with forms of physical actions, social interactions, and natural objects in one lively natural history—giving orders and walking, telling stories and playing. Das (2020, 256) has succinctly summarized this central problem in Wittgenstein by saying we are "equally . . . embodied creatures and creatures who have a life in language."[22] This gets to the heart of the matter: through all the instances of Protestant language use in Dons's life, she is a creature who has a life in language, and this is an embodied life. It seems to me, then, that Wittgenstein's "life form" points to the problem of how to bring together the range of forms that constitute language use, from physical and biological forms to historical and social ones (Moi 2017, 54–61). The "form of language, form of life" in which Dons took part had as much to do with her body as it did with her linguistic practices and social interactions, and these features occurred together in her natural history, or her life history, to cause multiplying complications. I am interested in these complications here: How can I describe her form of language as a form of life?

Wittgenstein was, as far as we know, not at all concerned with women's language use, let alone feminism.[23] Nevertheless, he can help us think about questions surrounding women, bodies, and language in new ways, especially, in my view, if we extend his concepts into today's conversation on feminist new materialism.[24] Wittgenstein would not have agreed to this extension, so this is not so much a reading of his work as a rereading, as I place him in a new, material-feminist conversation.[25]

Feminist new materialism is particularly concerned with how to address materiality, including the materiality of bodies, in response, for example, to the separation between (allegedly natural, material) sex and (allegedly cultural, discursive) gender that has emerged in liberal feminist theory. This liberal separation has been an attempt to resist the image of women as being particularly tied to bodies (as opposed to, for example, reason). However, the feminist new materialist conversation works against this separation and wishes to explore ways of incorporating the experiences and effects of the material in women's lives, and all lives.

For example, physicist and feminist theorist Karen Barad (2008, 141) has imagined that our bodies might be thought of as "material-discursive phenomena." Such phenomena are produced, Barad (2008, 141) suggests, through "iterative intra-activity" between materiality and discursive practices that mutually constitute each other. From my perspective, and stretching Barad, I think of Dons's body using words in life as a material-discursive phenomenon, akin to Wittgenstein's form of life. I should note, however, that in Barad's (2008, 137–139) view, "discursive" does not refer to speech acts, conversations, written words, or linguistic concepts but rather to the conditions that enable these practices. To think otherwise would, according to Barad, commit the mistake of representationalism; that is, it would mistakenly ascribe causal capacity to our minds and their ideas. While I am indeed concerned with decentering the perceived significance of ideology, I also think an analysis of Dons's Protestant life will be richer if it captures the dynamism of how she worked with words and words worked with her. Therefore, just as I am extending Wittgenstein, I am also extending Barad (and feminist new materialism): I use the term "discursive" in a stronger sense, encompassing not just the grounds that make linguistic actions possible but also those linguistic actions themselves, the words involved and how they were heard, spoken, written, or read, as well as the concepts they conjured and their effects.[26] In fact, though most new materialists might disagree, I think new materialism is particularly well suited to illuminating human language use in this sense.

I suggest, then, that Dons's life in language was a presumed whole—a Protestant woman using words—that we can open up. Once we do so, we see that this apparently singular whole contained a series of woman-word operations composed of intra-acting discursive and material elements. It was important to Dons that she, as a woman, used words, and in her view, her body was an important part of this linguistic situation. She sought to tie her body and words closely together in a variety of configurations. In my Wittgensteinian version of feminist new materialism, this Protestant woman using words was a form of life, combining her material body and discursive actions, assembling biological life forms with social ones, joining linguistic interactions with historical formations. She lived a material-discursive life in language.

A MULTIPLE LIFE IN LANGUAGE

I have debated whether to use the term "multiple" to describe Dons's life in language, since the term may convey plural lives in language, and I do not think Dons's life in language can be described as plural lives (or as many Donses). However, I have decided to use the term "multiple" because I think the designation "a multiple life in language" can help to capture the internal multiplicity of this life. In this sense, Dons's life in language was a changeable composite. It was a single phenomenon (a life in language) that was nevertheless not singular; it was composed of many elements, and their configuration changed slightly each time it was enacted. Let me outline two descriptions of a multiple entity that have helped me think through such internal multiplicity: Wittgenstein's remark on the word *games* and Annemarie Mol's ethnography of atherosclerosis.[27]

Wittgenstein concentrated intensely on everyday examples of "ways that one operates with words" ([1953] 2009, §1). He found it misleading to imagine that a particular word—such as *games*—had an abstract meaning apart from its operative uses. Instead, he sought to follow the word from one instance of use to another:

> Consider, for example, the activities that we call "games." I mean board-games, card-games, ball-games, athletic games, and so on. What is common to them all?—Don't say: "They *must* have something in common, or they would not be called 'games'"—but *look and see* whether there is anything common to all.—For if you look at them, you won't see something that is common to *all*, but similarities, affinities, and a whole series of them at that. To repeat: don't think, but look! ([1953] 2009, §66)

In other words, Wittgenstein argues that we cannot understand a word by approaching it as one presumed whole. Instead, we understand it by looking closely at an instance of use, and then another, and then another, and so on. This "look and see" method results in what he called "a sort of collection of examples": "How are we taught the word 'God' (its use, that is)? I cannot give an exhaustive systematic description. But I can as it were make contributions towards the description; I can say something about it & perhaps in time assemble a sort of collection of examples" ([1977] 1998, 94). Wittgenstein further suggests that when we look at uses of a word and assemble a collection of examples, we may find a series of affinities among them that can be thought of as "family resemblances": they are like the similarities that "criss-cross" among family members in "build, features, colour of eyes, gait, temperament, and so on and so forth" ([1953] 2009, §67). When we attempt to understand a word, then, such as *games* or *God* (or *Protestant* or *woman*), we find ourselves attempting to understand its multiple uses and their family resemblances.

Again, this line of thought can be deepened by extending it into feminist new materialism, this time into the work of science and technology scholar Annemarie Mol. As far as I know, Mol does not see her work as influenced by Wittgenstein, yet half a century after him she also explored the idea of internal multiplicity. She is not concerned with language, but with the body; her book *The Body Multiple* (2002) is a study of the disease atherosclerosis in and around a Dutch hospital. Mol wishes to describe how one presumed whole in the medical field—a body with atherosclerosis—is itself multiple, enacted differently across different sites. To understand this body, she takes a spatial approach, moving from one space to the next—from a physician's consulting room, to a medical staff meeting, to a lab, to a surgery table, to published statistics. In the consulting room, a ward staff member may listen to a man talking about the pain he feels in his leg when he goes shopping, and a while later, down a different hallway, a surgeon and radiologist may argue over which percentage of lumen loss they can deduce from an angiographic image of the patient's leg arteries (2002, 13–15, 73–74). The digressive conversation about everyday chores belongs in one site, and that site is closed when the next site is opened around a static image that demands a decision. Mol (2002, vii, 84) argues that her description of a body with atherosclerosis across different sites does not present plural bodies, nor does it present a series of different perspectives on a singular, undifferentiated body. Instead, it presents a multiple body, a series of enactments that constitute the body slightly differently in each site. Although it is a single body, it is neither singular nor plural. The body, she says, is "more than one, and less than many" (2002, 82).[28]

Mol wrote about bodies rather than language, but I wish to place her insights together with Wittgenstein's to examine woman-word operations. The type of multiplicity they each describe can be transformed into an analysis of Dons as a phenomenon—a Protestant woman using words—that was more than one and less than many, composed in many instances of use and enacted slightly differently in each one. However, to fully describe the multiplicity of Dons's Protestant life in language, I extend the idea of multiplicity further still: into the territory of both language use and language user, into the territory of Dons as a subject with a project.

A vital facet of Dons's life in language, as I think about it here, was her and others' perception that she was a woman subject. But when I say she was a "woman," how am I operating with that word? Extending Wittgenstein's thought, it seems to me that if we consider all the instances of use of the word *woman*, we will not find affinities that connect all. But we can look at what is called a "woman" in a specific time and place to trace a figure that incorporates some (not all) of a number of crisscrossing features. There may be bodily features coded with the word *female* that have resemblances and differences across varied instances of "woman" and that change within one instance of "woman" over her life course. Mol would remind us that the "woman" body is enacted differently across sites. The body interacts, or intra-acts, with crisscrossing discursive concepts, specific to times and places, that take hold in the "woman's" styling of her bodily features, her bodily comportment and affects, her desires and ideas, her experiences and relations. I could continue adding further elements, but let me pause here. The point I want to draw attention to is how this begins to present a woman subject who is a shifting circuit of physical, discursive, and imagined elements. This woman subject is multiple, both composite and protean: she is constituted by a shifting collection of parts, and she is enacted differently again and again. This woman subject is a single phenomenon, a woman, but she is not internally singular: she is "more than one." And yet she is not plural or many women: she is "less than many." In my view, Dons, as a woman subject, was "more than one, and less than many."[29]

Another vital facet of Dons's life in language, as I explore it, was her use of words as ethical operations as she reacted to, conceptualized, argued about, advocated for, and sought to spread Protestant feminism.[30] I will call this ethical engagement an ethical project.[31] By using the term "project," I wish to evoke the combination of language and materiality that occurs in our projects—the combination of imagined aims and concrete work that goes into the desire to do something and the many tangible ripple effects of that doing. A project is a creative process of trying out something without being able to exactly predict a certain outcome, a series of actions that require some effort and may be adjusted midway. A project draws together several ideas, supplies, technologies, and stretches of time that do not always align precisely with each other. We have our projects, we share projects, and we live in others' projects. In calling Dons's language use an ethical project, then,

I nod to its material-discursive character (it required imagination, but also materials), and, perhaps more unusually, I remain open to those instances in the chapters that follow in which this project emerges as internally multiple (its instantiations do not align precisely). As I examine the many aspects of Dons's ethical project of Protestant feminism, I do not describe it as split up into plural projects, such as many Protestantisms or many feminisms. I think it is more accurate to say she engaged with an ethical project—Protestant feminism—that was single but not singular; it was multiple, both composite and protean, involving many constitutive elements and enacted differently across different sites in her life. Dons lived with this project and also in it, as it extended beyond her.

The lens of project ethics leads to a different ethical analysis than the one that often accompanies the prevailing scholarly picture of Protestantism. The anthropological terms that cluster around Protestant ethics frequently tend toward interiority and individuality, ideas and ideals, intentions and immediacy. The terms lend themselves to a focus on the Protestant self, sometimes modified as the sincere self, and evoke images of self-cultivation. In this view, the Protestant ethic is best analyzed through the lens of virtue ethics: Protestants are taken to be sincere individuals focused on a mentalistic or dematerialized self-formation.[32] Instead, I suggest Dons's life in language can illuminate how Protestant subjects and their ethical projects are enacted in material-discursive, multiple circuits that move beyond the self. Dons was a multiple subject with a multiple project.

FOUR CHAPTERS, FOUR MAPPINGS

Wittgenstein ([1953] 2009, 3e–4e) suggested that when we study language use in life we are traveling "criss-cross" over a terrain and we end up with "a number of sketches of landscapes." We reject some of our sketches as "badly drawn or lacking in character," and we add new sketches as a point is "approached afresh." Our "half-way decent" sketches are "arranged and often cut down, in order to give the viewer an idea of the landscape." He elaborated in one of his Cambridge lectures: "I am trying to conduct you on tours in a certain country. I will try to show that the philosophical difficulties ... arise because we find ourselves in a strange town and do not know our way. So we must learn the topography by going from one place in the town to another, and from there to another, and so on" (1976, 44). Wittgenstein observed that this meandering process leaves out much but leads to a certain topographical understanding. The result, he said, "is really just an album"—an album that may allow the viewer to draw connections between one sketch and another, between one place and the next ([1953] 2009, 3e–4e). I think of his crisscross method of interpretation as a method of mapping.[33]

This method of mapping resonates with feminist new materialism, which is particularly attuned to "cartography rather than classification" (Dolphijn and van der Tuin 2012, 110). Feminist new materialists such as Barad or Mol are interested, for example, in mapping how various elements intra-act within a material-discursive phenomenon or in mapping different enactments of the body in sites around a hospital. In this sense, both Wittgenstein and feminist new materialists gravitate toward thinking spatially. In both cases, their mapping methods aim at a certain type of understanding: not the type of understanding produced through abstracting a classificatory system (and answering the questions: Why? What is the reason?), but the type of understanding that comes about by moving from one site to the next (and answering the questions: How? What are the connections?).

In the following chapters, I am oriented toward this cartographic understanding of Henny Dons's life in language. I follow Dons and her words from one site to the next and map the various configurations that emerged. Let me outline each chapter, or each mapping. They describe four instances of language use across Dons's life span: an instance of listening, of speaking, of writing, and of reading.

Chapter 1 focuses on listening. The chapter begins in a living room in Kristiania in September 1902, where the young Dons, in her twenties, had helped gather a small handful of her women teacher colleagues to form a Female Teachers' Mission Association. They agreed to meet each month to support the mission. However, they were adamant that they should *not* meet to make crafts to sell at "mission bazaars"; instead, they would sit still and listen intently to a lecture. What were they doing? I suggest that Dons and her colleagues perceived themselves to be responding to calls from "mission fields" and figures around the world, and that they sought to listen with proper affect because they thought this would affect the world. In short, I argue that Dons and her peers used this instance of Protestant listening to generate a responsive relation to their world—a world that formed the "conjured context" (Abram 2017, 28) for their meetings.

Chapter 2 considers speaking. It opens in July 1911, when Dons, in her midthirties, was invited to speak to a large, mixed-gender Christian audience. She was given a lectern to stand behind on a grassy hillside immediately outside a church, under heavy clouds that threatened rain. Unlike the male speakers who had preceded her, as a woman she was not allowed to speak inside the church building. I suggest that Dons's speaking can be understood through the space produced by, for example, her words, her sound, the lectern, and the audience. This particular space of speech was made possible because of (and sometimes despite) historical trajectories, such as the early women's movement in the city of Kristiania and the history of women's talk in NMS. I argue that in this instance of Protestant speaking, Dons embodied a voice that was thrown together as these trajectories momentarily combined in her gendered, speaking body.

Chapter 3 examines writing. I discuss three mission histories authored by Dons: a children's book, a short book on women and mission, and an unpublished manuscript. Dons wrote these in the 1920s and 1930s, from her midforties to her midsixties. Her texts were circulated to Christian groups of girls, young women, and female mission students, introducing them to the history of Protestant missions, sometimes in relation to the women's movement and sometimes in relation to the British Empire. However, I have been puzzled by the discrepancies between these texts, and I have especially wondered why Dons excluded women from two of the histories. I argue that these instances of Protestant writing provided a productive infrastructure for Dons's ethical project of Protestant feminism, but that the breaks in the infrastructure formed a project enacted as only partially connected in the world.

Chapter 4 describes reading. I focus on three readings of the creation story of Eve and Adam that occurred over the course of Dons's life, and I discuss Dons's changing interpretation of the creation account up until her late seventies. Dons repeatedly worked to relate and re-relate Eve and herself to women's "place" of being created second, or of being a secondary creation. I consider how her reading shaped her as a religious feminist subject, an ongoing situation she thought of as "being created woman." She conceptualized her biblical reading as taking place within a dense, connected web of discursive, material, human, and more-than-human elements and forces, placed within the vast span of creation. I argue that in this instance of Protestant reading, the religious feminist subject, Dons, was constituted through a series of bodily-discursive intra-actions.

Together the chapters gradually assemble a series of sketches of Dons's Protestant life in language. The purpose of assembling these mappings is to avoid foreclosure, or to practice holding open the presumed whole of a Protestant woman using words. Another way of saying this is that the aim is to "open up," in Mol's (2015, 58) sense of the term: "I tried to open up how 'woman' is shaped in biology and medicine." In my material-feminist extension of Wittgenstein, I wish to open up a Protestant woman using words and map the different woman-word operations that came about in the life of Dons, moving from one site to the next, then to the next, and so on.

A MATERIAL-DISCURSIVE, MULTIPLE PROTESTANTISM

The argument of this book is that when we open up Henny Dons, a Protestant woman using words, we see a series of woman-word operations weaving together language use, subjectivity, and ethics into a Protestant life in language, and this life in language is characterized by being both material-discursive and multiple. Dons shows us that her use of words was thoroughly life-embedded and embodied, constituted through discursive and material elements. Her life in language was composite, formed of many entities collected together, and it was protean, taking on a slightly shifted form each time.

In the conclusion, I will consider how holding open this presumed whole—a Protestant woman using words—can also help us hold open a larger presumed whole, namely Protestantism. In my view, once we place a close analysis of a woman's language use at the center of our picture of Protestantism, the prevailing scholarly picture of Protestant dematerialization falls to pieces. While the current scholarly conversation suggests that Protestantism presents a system of ideas that pushes Protestants toward a preoccupation with dematerialization, this does not fit the practices of actual Protestants, such as Dons. Her life shows us that Protestantism is not a singular story of individual selves who seek belief, interiority, and sincerity while shunning material forms. And her life is part of a five-hundred-year history in which it has been impossible to separate the discursive and the material in Protestant communities, as these groups have paid intense attention, for example, to the question of which gendered (and otherwise marked) bodies can use which words, in which ways, and in which places. Thus, Dons presents an alternative and more realistic picture of Protestant life: this life has long been embodied-linguistic, enacted among material and discursive elements handled with roughly equal consideration, though in configurations that vary from site to site. This picture of Protestantism does not lend support to the idea that Protestants are primarily guided by a dematerializing "Protestant language ideology" or that scholars exhibit a "Protestant bias" if they prioritize belief over materiality, nor does it show us a "Protestant ethic" of mentalistic self-cultivation. The longer I have worked on this book, the more I have begun to think that "Protestantism" has become a cipher in our scholarly shorthands. As scholars, we are the ones who have dematerialized Protestantism; Protestants have not done so.

This in turn leads to a much bigger question: How has Protestantism contributed to shaping what we call modernity and modern persons? Protestantism has developed alongside and in close relation—both affable and antagonistic—with Western modernity over the past five centuries, and there have been many intensifications and proliferations of this relationship in the nineteenth and twentieth centuries, in infinite variations across the globe. The current scholarly conversation suggests that at the core of this relationship lies a Protestant desire for dematerialization, which holds an affinity for the desires of modernity.[34] I agree with one aspect of this argument, namely that it is possible to say we moderns are all a little Protestant now, but I disagree that this is because of a dematerialization drive. Instead, the material-discursive and multiple properties of Protestant lives in language may have helped form some of the far-reaching correspondences between Protestantism and Western modernity.[35] While painting history in overly broad brushstrokes always leaves something to be desired, it can at least provide questions: Are there affinities between the flexible material-discursive composition of Protestant language use and the widening range of material-discursive configurations that has become possible in modern lives? Are there correspondences between the adaptive multiplicity of Protestant ethical subjects and the multiplicity required for the ethical megaprojects of Western modernity—such as liberalism, imperialism, democracy, or feminism—that can only be sustained so long as they remain changeable? While the study of one life in language cannot answer these questions, it can provide an example to prompt further questions about Protestantism and its many impacts on—and instantiations in—moderns as we know ourselves today. Therefore, the broader objective of this book is to help reorient the scholarly conversation on Protestantism toward an understanding more attuned to its material-discursive multiplicity.

01

LISTENING

In September 1902, five young Norwegian women, all teachers, gathered in a living room in Kristiania; they took notes to record their decisions, including one sentence that simply read: "Never bazaar." They had invited around fifteen of their women colleagues, but only five showed up. Although they felt discouraged, they still resolved that—as had already happened in Sweden—they would form an organization called the Female Teachers' Mission Association (Lærerindernes Missionsforbund, or LMF).[1] One of the women was Henny Dons, twenty-eight years old. We know she was short in height and left an impression on those around her; earlier that year she had been described by an older mission feminist, Bolette Gjør, as "a powerful, energetic little person."[2] I imagine Dons in her teacher friend's living room, leaning forward on the settee, in keen discussion about how to shape their new organization.

The five young women agreed to meet on the last Saturday of each month to support the growing Protestant mission to save the "heathens" across the world. And they agreed that their next meeting in October would not be in a living room but in a church hall. They knew there were already thousands of Lutheran "mission women's groups" (*missionskvindeforeninger*) across Norway, in which women came together every month to work on handcrafts such as spinning, sewing, or knitting. These groups periodically sold their crafts, often at "mission bazaars," and donated the money to the mission—most often to the Norwegian Mission Society (NMS). However, the female teachers in Kristiania felt strongly skeptical of this. They were not opposed to crafts per se, but they did not want crafts at their new gatherings, prompting the statement in their minutes: "Never bazaar."[3] In this chapter, I wish to pause at this moment of decision and ask: Why did Dons and her teacher colleagues choose to bar crafts?

Taking an ethnographic approach to their monthly mission meetings, I show that by removing crafts, the women assembled sound and silence in a new way, and this new soundscape in turn enabled them to listen. Rather than the traditional hum of spinning wheels and the rhythmic click of knitting needles, they wanted the sound of one voice speaking while the women in the room were silent. I suggest that they thought this type of listening was a better response to calls from various figures—from God and missionaries, from women in Norway and in faraway lands. Moreover, they maintained that if their responsive listening was carried out with the right affect, it would produce effects on these figures around the globe. For example, their listening in Norway might increase the blessing among "heathen" women in Madagascar, thus contributing, in their view, to the salvation of the world.

The theme of response was evoked already in their first meeting in the living room in September 1902. Dons later recalled they had discussed a biblical passage, 1 Corinthians 1:26–29, because "we five thought these words fit us in particular."[4] Maybe one of them opened her Bible and read the passage out loud as the other four listened:

> For ye see your calling, brethren,
> how that not many wise men after the flesh, not many mighty, not many noble, are called:
> But God hath chosen the foolish things of the world to confound the wise;
> and God hath chosen the weak things of the world to confound the things which are mighty;
> And base things of the world, and things which are despised, hath God chosen,
> yea, and things which are not, to bring to nought things that are:
> That no flesh should glory in his presence.

I study these lines by Paul as I wonder why the five young women in 1902 felt this passage fit them "in particular." The passage begins by summoning its readers, or listeners, to attend to their "calling." It clarifies that those who "are called" are "chosen" by God. And then it lists the types of things God has chosen: "the foolish," "the weak," "base things," "despised," and "things which are not." Perhaps the passage allowed the five women to articulate two seemingly contradictory sentiments at once. On the one hand, it allowed them to perform humility as young Protestant women. It gave them a way of claiming that their unusual actions—coming together in a living room to draw up bylaws for an all-women Christian organization that would ban crafts—did not arise from their own choosing, but from God's choosing: they were called. But at the same time, this lent not just apparent humility but also a great sense of importance to their meeting, and to them; they were called, and they had responded.

Response has not been a prominent category in studies that address Christians' engagement with God and other entities that transcend the here and now, whether in religious studies or in the anthropology of religion. Instead, a widely cited analytical concept has been a more clearly active one, namely mediation. Mediation might briefly be defined as the practices Christians undertake to make their invisible God "present." The mediation turn has been highly productive in its emphasis on the affective, bodily, and material qualities of Christian practice—what Birgit Meyer (2010, 2011) has called "sensational forms."[5] At the same time, it seems to me there are reasons to query this relatively concentrated focus on the "problem of presence" (Engelke 2007). I have suggested instead that Protestant Christians' engagement with the transcendent is more accurately described as an unstable multistranded relation—that is, a relation made up of many moving strands. Christians' desire to mediate God's presence is one of these strands—and it is an important one. But I think there are also other strands, some of which may include critique, refusal, witness, absence, immediacy, failure, repetition, and hope/waiting (Hovland 2018).[6] Here, I explore response as yet another strand in Protestant relation-making—a strand that encompasses a complicated mixture of passivity and activity, reception and creation.[7]

A response presupposes a prior state, action, or speech act—such as a "calling"—as well as the respondent's listening and generation of a state, action, or speech in turn, as a secondary event in the sequence. Through this, a relation is created or recreated. Since this experience of responding is everywhere apparent in ethnographic descriptions of Christian communities, I have wondered why we have not developed scholarly conversations around the category of response or related categories such as listening, reception, or being called. Perhaps the reason for this neglect is that listening and responding have seemed too secondary, reactive, or even inactive. In the neighboring field of linguistic anthropology, James Slotta (2023) suggests that listening has largely gone unnoticed because it has fallen into the shadow of speaking; while the ability to speak effectively has long been associated with voice, capability, ethical agency, and social significance, the act of listening has been assumed to be passive. Slotta (2023, 4–5) argues that, on the contrary, listening is a social action that "requires care" because it both promises rewards and poses risks—such as, for example, the risk of listening to the wrong people. Listening can tie together language use, subjects, and ethical stakes in ways that are experienced as highly consequential in people's lives.

In this chapter, I focus on listening and responding as categories that arise from the material under consideration and allow us to gain a richer understanding of what Dons and her mission-feminist peers in Norway thought they were doing. They developed a new "genre of listening" (Marsilli-Vargas 2022) or, as Ludwig Wittgenstein ([1953] 2009, §23) would put it, a new "language-game," which wove together linguistic innovation—using silent listening in all-women's meetings to respond to calls—with their understanding of themselves as subjects and their ethical project. They associated the need to respond with urgency and agency; for them, it constituted a form of ethical relation with the world.

This ethics of response is not limited to this particular Protestant tradition. Amira Mittermaier refers to a similar orientation among Sufi Muslims in Cairo. For her interlocutors, the understanding that dreams might come from an "Elsewhere" highlighted "the ability—or obligation—to respond. The recognition that agency does not rest exclusively with the individual dreamer does not mean that responsibility is *displaced* onto other agents... Responsibility rather can come *through* the dream" (2012, 261). Among the Norwegian women, the ethics of response began to encompass not just a transcendent Elsewhere in the singular (as perceived by Mittermaier's interlocutors) but also relations with several other types of Elsewheres they imagined as groups or places, such as "heathen women" or "Madagascar" or "the whole world."[8] They used a specific term to refer to such areas: *out there* (*der ute* or *derute*). The female teachers attuned themselves to calls from God as well as from "mission fields" and figures "out there." And, like the Sufis in Cairo, they thought they had a responsibility to respond to these entities beyond themselves, thus relativizing their own individual ethical agency. Mittermaier (2012, 249) suggests that instead of thinking of this as merely an ethics of agency or of action, we might think of it as an "ethics of passion," in the sense of "being acted upon" and "embedded in webs of relationship."

Why, then, did the young, energetic Henny Dons and her teacher friends think it was important, as they responded to being "called," to record the decision "Never bazaar"? I argue that when they started holding meetings centered on listening instead of crafting, their new listening practice allowed them to generate a new responsive relation to the world. I develop this argument by first describing the crafting meetings of the traditional mission women's groups, from which Dons and her colleagues wished to differentiate themselves. I then examine the new listening meetings that Dons and her teacher colleagues in Kristiania began holding, and I especially consider how the women perceived themselves to be responding with right affect to fields and figures "out there" who "called." Finally, I turn to the question of how we might map this particular woman-word operation of listening, and I suggest we can map it as a relation to the world that stretched across scales from "hearts" to women's meetings to "the whole world."

CRAFTING MEETINGS

Come Over and Help Us! is the informal title of a painting that has been a central image in the history of NMS.[9] The life-size painting depicts Africans on a beach, looking toward a sailing ship (behind which the sun is rising) and greeting it with outstretched arms. An angel hovers above. Different black-and-white versions of the same image formed the front-page banner of NMS's magazine, *Norsk Missionstidende* (*Norwegian Mission Tidings*), for more than seventy years (1883–1911 and 1925–1966). Mission friends looking at the painting knew it represented the ship bringing missionaries to other lands, to the African figures stretching out their arms. It captured well, in a single powerful image, the evangelical revivalist perception of being "called."

Protestant overseas missions were still a relatively unknown activity in Norway in the early nineteenth century, but this changed with the second-wave evangelical revivals. These revivals were an enthusiastic movement that swept through the Protestant populations of northern Europe at the turn of and into the early nineteenth century; they spanned the North Atlantic and in the United States became known as the Second Great Awakening. They reached Norway in the 1790s, when the wandering preacher Hans Nilsen Hauge inspired the pietistic Haugean movement, and they spread and intensified through the 1820s to the 1840s. The revivals ignited a wish for Christian commitment to be a more affective, active part of everyday life and emphasized the need to be converted and to convert, or to "be saved" and to "save." Some Norwegian Lutherans became concerned in a new way for others across the globe, in particular for whether these others would be "saved." At this time, the religious landscape in Norway (as in the other Scandinavian countries) was dominated by the Lutheran state church, the Church of Norway, which was integrated into the state government and designed to encompass the state's geographical territory—that is, to encompass virtually the entire population of the country. The large bureaucracy of the state church did not make much move toward the evangelical idea of "saving" people through missions. However, some of its members—touched deeply by the revivals—decided to form their own lay "mission groups" (*missionsforeninger*) outside the church structure, while still remaining church members. In their new mission groups, they would be able to focus on the urgent salvation of people far away.[10]

In August 1842, sixty-five of these new mission groups sent representatives to a gathering in the town of Stavanger on the windblown west coast, and together they established the Norwegian Mission Society (Det Norske Missionsselskab) with the aim of sending Norwegian missionaries overseas.[11] An (all-male) governing board was formed, and a (male) secretary was appointed who would live in Stavanger. The grassroots of the organization consisted of the many local mission groups. These groups were attended by both men and women who came together for regular meetings to hear mission news and devotions. Each group could send a (male) delegate to vote in the NMS general assembly. (No woman attended the general assembly as a delegate until Bolette Gjør acquired a delegate's ticket fifty years later, in 1892.)[12] The groups also sent financial donations to Stavanger so the secretary could start a Mission School to educate prospective (male) missionaries.

Very soon a second type of group emerged alongside the mixed-gender mission groups. This second type was referred to as "mission women's groups" (*missionskvindeforeninger*) and consisted of only women. One of the first of these was founded in the early 1840s by Gustava Kielland, a pastor's wife in Stavanger.[13] Kielland accompanied her husband to a public meeting about Protestant missions, and in her later memoirs she recounted: "What I heard there made a deep impression on me. I became so shameful and sorrowful that I had had such lukewarm thoughts about the mission cause."[14] She felt strongly that she needed to respond.

Kielland immediately invited four other women to hold a mission meeting with her at the parsonage, one day each month. They sang one Christian song together and then turned to the handcrafts they had brought with them. Children were present. Kielland described the meetings as follows: "It was often difficult to read aloud or talk together during the meetings because the spinning wheels spun, the carders rustled, the knitting needles and sewing needles moved quickly in busy hands."[15] The women took a break for coffee and sandwiches and, during this relatively quieter time, one of the women would read aloud a story or pamphlet related to the mission. Then they talked with each other about the story—or about home matters. Soon, up to thirty women were joining in the monthly mission meetings at the roomy parsonage. Periodically, they sold the crafts they made at social sales events, which in later decades became known as mission bazaars, and donated the money to NMS.

The mission women's meetings had surprising success. Only six decades later, by the turn of the twentieth century, the number of mission women's groups had grown to between three thousand and four thousand, spread across all of Norway. By comparison, the number of mixed-gender mission groups was just over nine hundred.[16] Although the secretary in Stavanger kept track of the mixed-gender mission groups so they could send delegates to the NMS general assembly, he did not keep track of the women's groups; they were not part of the formal organizational structure of NMS. However, each time he received a donation from a women's group, he printed a receipt in the organization's magazine *Norwegian Mission Tidings*. As these pages of receipts show, NMS soon became financially reliant on the women's groups, and by 1900, around 75 percent of the organization's income came from their donations (Tjelle 1999, 181).

Kristin Fjelde Tjelle (1999, 175) has observed that in practice this was the largest (loosely) coordinated women's movement in Norway at the time. The groups typically adhered to a common meeting time, namely the first Monday morning of each month, or sometimes the first and third Mondays.[17] The size of the groups varied from a handful to more than a hundred members, but Tjelle (1990, 108) estimates that on average each group probably had around twenty-five members, so by the turn of the twentieth century it is likely that around seventy-five to one hundred thousand women were involved from all parts of Norway—or 7 to 9 percent of all Norwegian women at the time.[18] The mission women's movement bridged upper- and middle-class divides as well as the urban-rural divide with apparent ease, appealing to farmwives and women on smallholdings in Norway's extensive rural areas, to rural and urban middle-class women (including wives and daughters of craftsmen, traders, or teachers), to upper-class women (such as wives and daughters of civil servants, clergy, businessmen, or sea captains), and to certain working-class women who carried out the domestic work of seamstresses, cooks, or housekeepers in charge of servants (Tjelle 1990, 26–27, 60–83). The groups did not, however, usually accommodate the lowest social classes of the working poor, such as the women who labored as the lowest-ranked servants or as workers in the new industrial factories around Kristiania.[19] Scholars who have studied the mission women's movement in Norway have argued for its significance as part of the cultural trend toward broad-based democratization, given the large number of women involved in self-organized groups from different social classes across the country (Norseth 2007; Skeie and Norseth 2003). Here I take up a related anthropological question: What did the women themselves think they were doing?

Ethnographers of meetings have suggested that meetings do not just assemble words, papers, bodies, ideas, and activities. They also, "by definition" (Brown, Reed, and Yarrow 2017, 13), refer to something beyond themselves—what Simone Abram (2017, 28) calls the meeting's "conjured context." Moreover, meetings officially tend toward organization, although this does not mean that they are per se organized or that unorganized matters are always resolved (Brown, Reed, and Yarrow 2017, 15, 23). What did the meetings of the mission women assemble? And what did they tend toward organizing? Which affects were put together to achieve effects? One bundle of associations they moved toward organizing was that between Norwegian women, crafts, affects of response and responsibility, and faraway "heathens." Bolette Gjør later recalled her participation in a mission women's group in the 1850s as follows: "I sat as if in a church, and the work seemed to me so holy. With happy wonder I had to ask: Is it really possible that these stitches I am now knitting will contribute to saving souls in heathen lands?"[20] This was a new way of using needlework. Many decades later, Dons (1925a, 17–18) commented that because most women in the nineteenth century had little opportunity "to use their abilities in outer action beyond the purely domestic," these first mission women's meetings must have felt like "something of a revolution in the women's world." Although the meetings were often held in homes and centered on homecrafts, their new assembling of crafts with worldwide concerns about salvation tended toward a new organization that went beyond the "purely domestic." The women oriented themselves toward a new "conjured context," namely "heathen lands."

Another bundle of associations the meetings assembled were those of particular sounds and silences. The meetings created a "sonic-scene" in which sounds became intertwined with layers of affective and political concerns (Kasmani 2017). One layer was the actual sounds of the craftwork, the children, the coffee, the conversation, and a story being read aloud. At another level, there was the question of whether the meetings were, metaphorically, sufficiently quiet. For example, Bolette Gjør recalled that some people criticized these noisy women's meetings for running counter to "a woman's quiet conduct,"[21] echoing the words of the author of 1 Timothy in the New Testament: a woman must "be in silence" (1 Timothy 2:12). In other words, the new evangelical mission movement prompted the question of what it meant for women to be quiet in a new context as they started to gather in Protestant meetings without men.

In fact, it seems some women may have tried to hold different types of mission meetings in which they primarily read and prayed and thus were indeed (literally) more quiet, but this proved far more problematic. At a regional NMS assembly in Trondheim in 1866, one of the discussion items concerned the women's groups and, in particular, what it was appropriate for women to do when they met. The male delegates at the regional assembly agreed it was good that women came together to work on crafts to be sold to raise money for NMS. However, the assembled men recorded statements, later printed in NMS's magazine, that women should not "lead with words and work in the word." Instead, women had "a particular skill with hands," and women's groups ought to focus on "acts of hands, the collective work of hands." Specifically, women should not gather without men, the delegates stated, to "read and pray."[22]

One example of how this edict played out in practice can be found in some recollections by Bolette Gjør. When she was a young woman in the 1860s, she and her sister Rikke decided to invite the nearby mission women's groups around their town, Hamar, to a large joint meeting, thinking that this time they would meet without crafts. Gjør later recalled that people were "stunned" at this "unwomanly" proposal. The sisters, not easily defeated, sought to counter the criticism by rearranging the seating in the proposed meeting so the women would not sit "on rows of benches like the men" but instead "in groups around small tables." They also conceded that the women would bring their crafts, and they invited the local male bishop to hold a devotion. With these adjustments, the meeting was deemed sufficiently womanly to go ahead.[23] The gathered women kept their hands busy with crafts, chatted with each other around their small tables, and heard the word of God from a man.

We see here that women's "silence" was understood in different ways. The New Testament texts that encourage women to be quiet sometimes refer to literal silence (women not making a sound) and sometimes to metaphorical silence (women submitting to men).[24] But only one of these themes seems to have been picked up in the evangelical Lutheran milieu around the mission women's groups in Norway, namely metaphorical silence. Therefore, despite the initial questioning, it gradually became broadly acceptable for Christian women to gather around humming craftworks and converse together (perhaps pausing briefly to listen to a short story, or a devotion given by a man), while it was still uncommon for Christian women to gather for the purpose of quiet prayer. The consensus that emerged among Norwegian Lutherans in the late nineteenth century was that the sound the women made was not in itself a problem. Thus, the mission women managed to establish a new type of affective-political "sonic-scene" in their noisy, innovative gatherings, while still remaining within the larger framework of metaphorical quietness. This opened up new possibilities. Most interestingly for this discussion, it enabled the women to respond with affect to the world beyond their homes: to "heathen lands" and to God's "call" for them to help with the "mission cause." But the more intriguing turn in the history of the women's meetings came in the early twentieth century when five female teachers decided to change this format.

LISTENING MEETINGS

In 1902, when Dons helped establish the Female Teachers' Mission Association (LMF), the *Come Over and Help Us!* picture was still on the front page of NMS's magazine. Dons later echoed this message when she wrote that it was not just the "heathens" on the African coast who were calling; rather, "*Christ* is calling those women who have received his salvation" (Dons 1925a, 7; italics mine). In response to this perceived cry, the women in LMF began holding meetings on the last Saturday evening of each month.[25]

LMF proved popular. In 1917, it had reached one thousand members, 20 to 25 percent of all female teachers in Norway at the time (Tjelle 2002, 70–71). It also became influential. LMF members paid an annual membership fee and were sometimes asked for additional donations. These women, who controlled their own money, were part of a new demographic that had begun to emerge in Norway toward the end of the nineteenth century, as some urban middle- and upper-class women began taking up paid employment outside the home as trained teachers or nurses. Their step out of middle- and upper-class domesticity was eased by the fact that most of them were unmarried; for example, in 1910, 90 percent of female teachers in Norwegian towns were single (Tjelle 2002, 80). NMS also began employing a few single women as paid teachers, nurses, or midwives in the schools and clinics they ran in South Africa and Madagascar. In fact, when the female teachers in LMF collected money, they did not simply send it to a mission organization (as the traditional mission women's groups did), but they instead entered into negotiated agreements with the organizations—primarily NMS—so their donations would support the salaries of some of these female missionaries overseas.

I focus here on the LMF group in Kristiania (later Oslo), which had 229 paying members in 1927 (LMF 1927, 72–78) and kept handwritten minutes of its meetings. Each monthly meeting may have been attended by twenty to forty women, and their "annual feast" was usually attended by around a hundred women.[26] Dons took on the role of "chairman" for the LMF group in Kristiania from around 1905 to 1927 (in addition to being LMF's national leader from 1905 to 1946).[27] In her capacity as "chairman," she often chaired the monthly meetings (and even if not chairing, she was always present, unless hindered by illness or travel).

What was different about the LMF meetings? Instead of coming together in a home, the LMF women seem to have usually met in a church hall.[28] They did not bring crafts, and they did not arrange bazaars. This was not because they were categorically opposed to crafts or the idea of bazaars. In fact, when Dons later became employed by NMS as their children's secretary, she helped establish a Home Crafts Circle in 1918, in part to encourage women to work on crafts "in their spare time at home" and then sell the items at a mission sale and donate the money to NMS.[29] Similarly, Lina Lerheim, Dons's colleague and a "female traveling secretary" who traveled around to speak to NMS's various groups, stated in a lecture to some women's groups that each woman should keep a "mission craft" at home on which she could work "in small quiet moments."[30] But crafts were not brought to the LMF meetings.

Moreover, in the LMF meetings there was conversation between the women only at certain specified times. The meetings usually opened with a collective song and a prayer. A woman (or sometimes an invited man) then gave a lecture on an aspect of the history of Christian mission or on a Bible passage, while the assembled women sat still and listened. Sometimes one of the women read aloud news from female missionaries or missionary wives in Zululand (South Africa), Madagascar, Santalistan (India), or China—either from a letter or from published pieces in mission magazines. In this way, the women kept up with news from various mission projects overseas, especially those in which Norwegian women were closely involved, such as the boarding school for girls operated by Johanna Borchgrevink in Antananarivo, Madagascar, or the leprosy colony run by Marie Føreid a little further south, close to Antsirabe. The meeting minutes occasionally record that the teachers enjoyed coffee, tea, and sandwiches. Finally, there was always a "prayer time" at the end of each meeting as one of the women prayed aloud while the others joined in silently.

The LMF format was different from the traditional mission women's groups, and Dons tried to influence the traditional meetings later in her career. When employed by NMS in 1917, she sometimes visited the traditional women's groups that gathered around crafts and conversation. However, she thought there was room for improvement. For example, in one letter to the general secretary of NMS, she pointed out what seemed to her a lack of "understanding and interest" in the mission cause in the traditional mission women's meetings; a few years later she reported that these meetings lacked "life and energy."[31] Rachel Lange, a female traveling secretary in NMS, also regularly visited the traditional groups and reported the same observation: "Many of the leaders in our women's groups do not have the boldness to ... pray aloud ... [There is] often a lot of talking, in many places they talk so that they almost cannot bear to be silent even when one is standing there and telling them about the mission ... [What they want is:] Drinking coffee, raffle tickets, a lot of talking, first, last and in between. Yes, it is sad in many places, unfortunately!"[32] In other words, Henny Dons and Rachel Lange, who were familiar with the LMF meeting format, described the traditional groups as assembling sounds and silences at the wrong times: the women were seen as talking constantly when they should have been listening quietly, but then being quiet when they should have had the boldness to pray aloud. Their conversation, while lively and energetic, did not display the *right* affective "life and energy."

To explore this different understanding of affect in more detail, let me give two examples of meeting minutes that are broadly representative of the LMF group in Kristiania. The first is from March 1913.[33] The meeting was chaired by Dons. This time, a male missionary had been invited to speak, and the minutes record, in abbreviated sentences: "Missionary Østby lecture on the work on Madagascar's western coast. Spoke grippingly about a trip with the native evangelists to wild bandit tribes." The missionary described how, even among these "bandit tribes" such as the Sakalavas, "hearts and doors were open" for the gospel, and the minutes add: "Prayer for the *Sakalavas* was especially laid on our hearts."

However, the women in the meeting were not just concerned with their relation to faraway Madagascar. They were also mindful of their relation to groups of women and Christians in Norway. Dons announced that a Miss Ragnaas would represent LMF at the upcoming national meeting of the

Norwegian Women's National Council, and the group then selected Miss Essendrop to travel as their representative to the NMS general assembly (which had been opened to women delegates just under a decade earlier, in 1907). The same Miss Essendrop then provided some "warm and heartfelt" words based on their "prayer text"—a selected verse from the Bible—to introduce their concluding prayer time, speaking "about *the work of the Holy Spirit*, about 'the decisive hour' for every single person and now for the whole world."

What did this meeting assemble, and what did it tend toward organizing? The "conjured context" of the LMF meeting in Kristiania in 1913 assembled a world. First, there was the space often referred to in the minutes as "out there."[34] In this case, the story from "out there" came from Madagascar, where some people were seen as "wild" but also as possible candidates to join the worldwide community of Christians. Second, the meeting assembled organizations—the Norwegian Women's National Council and NMS. Third, there was the transcendent space of the Holy Spirit, as well as the associated space of "the whole world." By meeting, these Protestant women perceived themselves to be connecting to the transcendent divine, but they were also connecting to multiple other characters and areas: to other women, to other Christians, to imagined figures on the other side of the world, and to the idea of "the whole world." The meeting conveyed that a different world was possible, not just in terms of turning non-Christians into Christians but also in terms of turning Norwegian women into important actors whose "decisive hour" mattered on the world stage. The LMF women were elaborating here on their evangelical sense that they needed to live with another possible space always in view (Hovland 2016, 348). They assembled a different, hopeful world map of divinity and humanity. This hopeful map was overlaid on the actual world map, critiquing it and seeking to change it.

The second meeting I will consider took place in May 1918. This meeting too was chaired by the "chairman," Henny Dons. The woman who recorded the minutes chose to elaborate more fully on the meeting's atmosphere:

> 25th May 1918: ... The Norwegian flag brightened up between fresh spring flowers, at the chairman's place stood a couple of delightful roses, and when she came to chair the meeting she was received most heartily. For it happened to be the case this time that our chairman was celebrating her birthday on precisely the LMF day, and we so wanted to show her our devotion and gratitude ... Miss Dons thanked us, very moved, and gave a talk based on our prayer text John 3:27–36 about this: *How can we through*

our mission work in LMF help each other to grow in our Christian life? It is about *growing*—also when it comes to the work that we have taken upon ourselves out there. The stronger and more heartfelt *our* personal Christian life and prayer life is, the richer will be the help and blessing for them *out there*. There is a constant back-and-forth between them and us . . . let us try to *help* each other! Let us make use of the personal connection and try to . . . share more with each other also of the *personal* experiences in our Christian life . . . Strongly and intently she then laid this question on our hearts: *"Are you a take-it-for-granted Christian, or do you know what it is to be saved?"* . . . Miss Helga Kristiansen, whom we are sending to Santalistan, was with us probably for the last time before her departure . . . we bid her farewell and will promise to follow her too with our thoughts and prayers.[35]

Here we see even more clearly that these women were not just assembling a world; they were also seeking to affect this world. They believed that the more intimately they felt, shared, and knew they were saved in Kristiania, the more "heathens" would be brought to the same salvation "out there." In this context, their own efforts to put together the right affects—in a shared, emotional orientation toward salvation—must have stood out as a great responsibility. Perhaps it seemed to the LMF women as if the fate of at least part of the "heathen" world was resting on whether they, in their meetings, were able to be "heartfelt" Christians. And their heartfelt Christianity would manifest itself in Christian listening.

LISTENING TO A WORLD THAT CALLS

In June 1912, Henny Dons led a guided conversation in the Kristiania LMF meeting on the following topic: "From all the mission fields it is said that there are far too few female workers. A letter was mentioned, just received from Miss Ofstad [a mission worker in Madagascar], in which this was stated firmly."[36] Not only did the LMF women assemble a double-layered world map, a hopeful world map overlaid on the actual one, they also assembled a map of cries and calls from around the world—from "heathens," from female mission workers, from "the mission fields," from Christ. Somewhat counterintuitively, to do something in response to these calls, they replaced crafts with listening.

It is sometimes difficult, diving into the archival fragments from around a century ago, to imagine what the world looked like to the mission feminists. Hillary Kaell's (2020a) concept of "Christian globalism" may help us understand some of what was going on. She uses the concept to describe how some Christians in North America over the past two centuries have worked to imagine and make real the world as a globe. In this view, the world as a whole, with a common global humanity, can form a significant part of someone's personal lifeworld. Therefore, Kaell (2020b, 818) suggests, we will better understand the historical world of these Christians if we closely examine "histories of global aspirations, imaginations, and relations," histories that include other figures around the world, such as "heathens," as well as figures that are other-than-human and more-than-human, such as angels, the dead, or God.

In this vein, we can gain a glimpse into the world of Dons and her peers—both their imagined globe and their particular Christian lifeworld—through the figures with which they populated it. For example, we have already encountered the imagined figure of Africans reaching out their arms in the NMS banner called *Come Over and Help Us!*, as well as stock figures such as "wild bandits" in Madagascar. After NMS was established in the midst of the evangelical revivals of the 1820s–1840s, several other Lutheran mission societies were formed in Norway in the wake—and occasional resurgence—of the revivals over the next decades, and Dons and her peers regularly referred to these organizations by informal labels indicating the people they wished to evangelize. With its primary focus on Africa, NMS was known as "the Heathen Mission"; the women also referred to "the China Mission," "the Santal Mission," "the Israel Mission," "the Sami Mission," "the Home Mission" (evangelizing in Norway), and "the Seamen's Mission." These, then, were some of the characters of the women's world—characters to which they related.

Dons also worked with a distinction between Christian women and non-Christian women around the world. In her pamphlet on "Women's task and work in the mission" (1923b), she represented the non-Christian woman, "our sister out there" who is "crying out to us" (1923b, 8), through several figures distributed around the globe: the "heathen" woman, the "Muhammedan" woman, the Chinese woman, the Indian woman, and the Jewish woman. Dons argued that for these non-Christian women to be "won for Christ," they must "see Christ lived in the life of women" (1923b, 10). In her view, this was a task for all Christian women, not just those sent abroad as missionaries, because women in Norway needed to support the work through love, understanding, prayer, sacrifice, and donations: "There is the deepest connection between the work here at home and the work out there" (1923b, 10). She urged her contemporaries: "Are you praying for these women? Do you cry to God day and night for all these women who are still fighting for their right?" (1923b, 9). She ended with a final question: "What is your response today?" (1923b, 10).

Dons and her LMF colleagues thought it was of utmost importance to respond. Against this background, the change from crafting to listening that they embraced might appear surprising; it might appear to be a change from a more active response to a more passive one. However, the LMF women do not seem to have thought of it that way. Rather, as mentioned above, in Dons's view the traditional crafting groups were the ones lacking the right kind of energy, producing sounds and silence at the wrong times. The LMF women assembled a new organization of sounds and silence that must have seemed to them more energetic, or, in my academic terms, more properly affective and therefore effective. Instead of the constant stream of sounds in traditional meetings—from wool carders and coffee cups, chatting and busy hands—the LMF meetings cultivated the sound of one woman's voice, or occasionally a man's voice. The bodies that were listening were still, without needles in their hands. This outline of listening, as it is framed in the meeting minutes, likely reflects something of the "genre of listening" (Marsilli-Vargas 2022) that had developed in the group. Based on the minutes, we do not know whether all the women in the meeting actually listened in this focused way. Nevertheless, the ideal seems to have been a listening that might be described as bodily, affective concentration and response: the women ought to intently hear what was said, and then feel something. As the minutes sometimes put it in their idealized description, the words spoken were "laid on our hearts."[37] This listening presented a complex combination of active passivity or passive activity.

The women's attention to their "hearts" might easily lead us to conclude that their response to the world expressed a desire to dematerialize their language use and ethical project, especially as they shifted away from crafting. But once we start to look more closely, we see that they assembled a range of material elements around their new genre of listening. Their listening meetings allowed them to swap out one form of materiality, namely crafts, with other forms of materiality, such as notebook and pen, Bibles and lecture notes, lists of prayer topics, a different soundscape, a spatial arrangement that enabled a single voice to be heard, and a different use of bodily comportment and affects in the space. While crafts had traditionally been associated in their milieu with women's submissive silence, the female teachers deployed their bodies in a new affective woman-word operation of listening they associated with a new silence—one that was, in their view, able to generate a responsive relation to the world that would be truly impactful. Therefore, I think their new meetings show the importance to these Protestant women of selecting different forms of materiality that could constitute their material-discursive lives in language so they would have effects, as they saw it, around the world.

The women's responsive listening also allowed them to rework ideas about authority. Whereas the traditional women's meetings were often held in homes or local assembly houses and cultivated a soundscape that evoked associations with the domestic sphere, the LMF meeting in Kristiania was instead held in a church hall, with a type of speech and listening that evoked the interactions of a formal, public sphere. In many ways, LMF meetings were modeled on school classrooms, in which LMF members as teachers spoke with authority to an audience. They were also modeled on the Lutheran church service (with which the women were very familiar), in which a male pastor spoke authoritatively to an audience. In fact, the LMF women sometimes alluded to this similitude by saying, for example, that LMF was "called to priestly service for Him."[38]

It seems that by organizing their monthly meetings around listening quietly to authoritative speech, these women were forming public relationships between themselves, rather than domestic relationships. This created quite a different affective-political "sonic-scene" than the traditional women's meetings. As mentioned earlier, the traditional meetings largely existed within the common expectation that Christian women ought to be quiet. The traditional women's groups fit this expectation, paradoxically, through their emphasis on *noisy* crafts. The LMF meetings, on the other hand, in many ways aimed to challenge the notion that Christian women ought to be quiet—for example, by supporting women mission workers and elected representatives. But they did so, again paradoxically, by emphasizing the importance of *quiet* listening. They claimed the "quiet" injunction for themselves but wielded it with public authority. Thus, their listening represented a reinterpretation of the injunction for Christian women to be silent. By embracing women's literal silence in a new way (requiring still bodies in a meeting of only women), they were able to stage a powerful rebuttal of women's metaphorical silence.

However, the LMF meetings did not completely adopt the male-dominated church model of public silent listening and of authority. They added an idealized understanding of a "feminized" affective atmosphere. For example, as mentioned in the minutes above, the women decorated the room with "fresh spring flowers" and "delightful" roses. They used expressions of personal devotion to Dons, who allowed herself to be "very moved" by the beauty and intimacy of the meeting, and this response was then recorded in the minutes. The intimate moment became officially recorded intimacy. The minutes also use adjectives to describe the atmosphere that the recorder wished to emphasize; the events in the meetings are regularly referred to as "beautiful," "amazing," "delightful," "wonderful," "lovely," "peaceful," "rich," "atmospheric," "enjoyable," "cozy," and "festive."[39] In other words, the women's listening occurred not just in the context of public relationships among themselves, in which they took on "male" authority. These relationships were also placed within a particular "feminized" affective environment, owned by the women. This allowed them to produce a new type of Christian women's authority that enabled them, in their view, to work with God as they responded to him and to the calls they heard from around the world. The women's listening to the world, then, led to changes in their relations among themselves and in how they presented their relation to others. And from their perspective, these changes were not primarily anchored in their own volition; in their view, they had been "called" to respond.

LISTENING AS WORLD-ENCHANTMENT

Was this focus on Christian listening unusual? In certain respects, it was not. Ethnographers have described other examples of Protestant and Pentecostal listening, such as the American charismatic evangelicals who desire to hear God's voice through training their absorptive capacities (Luhrmann 2012), the Ghanaian Pentecostals who "soak" in God's word through repeated listening to recorded sermons (Reinhardt 2014), or the British conservative evangelicals who seek to practice attentive listening in church as well as "personal" listening when reading the Bible (Strhan 2015). In these cases, scholars have described the listening of the Christians as oriented both toward self-cultivation and toward God. For example, Anna Strhan (2015, 109) argues that the conservative evangelicals she studied in London seek to form a "listening 'I'" that is not wholly self-determined but still works to form certain virtues. Strhan (2015, 65–67) offers a finely tuned description of this listening as a particular Foucauldian technology of the self (e.g.,

Foucault 1978). She builds on Charles Hirschkind's (2006, 12) description of "ethical listening"; Hirschkind argues that Muslims in the Islamic revival movement in Cairo listen to cassette sermons as a means of cultivating a pious sensorium around the self and pious virtues in the self (such as humility). In addition, Strhan suggests, the ethical self-formation that the London evangelicals seek through listening stands in an ambivalent relation to the autonomy of the rational subject of the Western Enlightenment. The evangelicals embrace this autonomy yet also desire to be receptive to another, namely God, in their self-formation.

But there is a difference in the listening practices that developed among the Lutheran female teachers in Kristiania that makes me hesitant to interpret these primarily as a technology of the self, or a certain type of self-cultivation, within the frame of a Foucauldian poststructuralist virtue ethics. The women's listening was meant to transform their *responding* to figures around the world (including God) into *affecting* these figures around the world (including God). In other words, in their view the listening had distributed effects that went beyond their own Christian selves. An understanding had developed among the LMF women that by listening to calls from fields and figures "out there" using a particular affective combination—quiet concentration, an intense response, a sense of obligation—they would affect the fields and figures "out there." As the minutes above put it: "The stronger and more heartfelt *our* personal Christian life and prayer life is, the richer will be the help and blessing for them *out there*."[40] Another way they phrased it was: "God is willing to give, if we will receive."[41] They thought that if LMF women received, then God's giving would occur not just in the LMF group but also—more crucially—in other parts of the world. Thus, the women felt responsible for responding to the cries they heard. In their view, their listening was a response that forged affective ties between themselves and others and would allow God to work through these ties. Their listening would direct God's blessing to places near and far; it was a new kind of aural affect that would flow through global connections to help convert "the whole world."

Against this background, I have found the LMF women's listening closer to a different Protestant example that can help reorient us away from listening as a technology of self-cultivation to a technology of world-enchantment. Joe Webster (2013, 217) argues, in his description of how conservative Protestant Brethren in Scotland listen to different forms of speech, that as they listen to "a powerful sermon, a moving testimony, an exciting 'Godincidence' ... these 'technologies' cast their spells"; the effect of the listeners' entwinement with these technologies is that in listening they conflate "speaker with word with

God (or the devil)." Webster (2013, 220) describes this as a process of using language "to enchant the world"—and to try to change it. For example, when the Scottish Brethren sit in their meeting hall and listen to gospel preaching aimed at the "unsaved," Webster (2013, 90) suggests that this "physically absent category of the 'unsaved' was, for my friends, more real ('real' in the sense that it directed action in the world) than the audience sitting facing the preaching." Similarly, the listening developed by Dons and her teacher colleagues in Kristiania was a technology of world-enchantment. They too, like the Scottish Brethren, used listening to map the world (including the absent but "more real" figures who inhabited it) and to generate relations and responsive action at different scales, from their "hearts" to "the whole world."

THE DIFFICULTIES OF FEMINISM

As I was going through some of Henny Dons's documents one day in the Mission Archive in Stavanger, in the windowless basement with the rows and rows of archival boxes, I was half-listening to two archivists standing by a table in the next room and sorting out old lantern slides. The slides depicted the work of NMS in South Africa in the early twentieth century and had in the past been shown to mission groups in Norway. One of the archivists was reading aloud the slide captions and chuckling at some. While she was herself an employee of NMS, the presentation of the mission a century earlier clearly seemed outdated to her.

"The missionary is preaching," she read, "about Jesus." She laughed softly at the thought that the captioner felt the need to specify the preaching was about Jesus. Another one: "The missionary is preaching to the wild heathens." This time her chuckle turned into a sigh. I walked into the next room and the archivist made space for me at the table, lifting up slides for me to see. She told me about an image she had come across earlier that juxtaposed two photographs. The one at the top depicted some African youth, and the one under it showed an African girl in a white dress. The youth at the top were labeled "Heathen youth," and the girl was labeled "Christian girl." Underneath the two photographs, a caption had been added: "Who do you think is prettier?"

"What? Can you imagine!" the archivist exclaims, having repeated this caption. She straightens up and looks at me. I nod slowly.

"I feel it here," I say, and hold my hand to my stomach.

"Yes," she says, holding her stomach too, "It's quite . . ."

She does not find the right word and her sentence trails off. We stand there for a brief moment, hands on stomachs, before turning back to the slides.

After a while, I return to my old documents, but the archivist calls me over again at a particular lantern slide.

"Look at this, Ingeborg! It's Henny Dons!"

I come over and look closely. It is indeed a photograph of Henny Dons, taken on her trip to South Africa in 1928—the only time Dons traveled to see the "mission field." In the picture, she is standing up very straight next to a row of Zulu women. The archivist reads the caption out loud: "Henny Dons hands out bars of soap for Saturday cleaning." She half-smiles in bemusement, then shakes her head at the words.

The history of Henny Dons and the mission feminists in Norway is entangled with histories of difference, of colonized territories, of positioning "heathens" as other, of ranking women. These historical realities can at times feel like a gut punch to contemporary feminists, whether inside or outside NMS, as when recounting the question "Who do you think is prettier?" At other times, it can feel like all that is left to do is sigh with disappointment at the caption "wild heathens" or shake one's head in disagreement with the phrase "hands out bars of soap," knowing how closely this was tied to the idea that African "heathens" were "dirty" and African Christians needed help becoming "clean." And sometimes it may seem easier to simply say that Dons and her colleagues were not feminist.

Other scholars have mostly resisted this, for various reasons. For example, Karina Hestad Skeie (2015a, 345–346), in her research on Norwegian women in the Norwegian Lutheran China Mission Association at the turn of the twentieth century, has argued that the presence of contradictions does not rule out the presence of feminist concerns, and she suggests these women carried out a "feminist project in practice" alongside other "seemingly contradictory practices." At the same time, Skeie is careful to emphasize that in her view this feminism can only be stretched so far. Other scholars too have provided nuanced discussions of the feminist impetus of Dons's contemporaries in Lutheran Norway and have argued that recognizing this as "feminist" helps situate the influence of religion on the sociopolitical development of feminism in northern Europe.[42] I agree with this concern. At the same time, I think we can go further than this.

I too have chosen to call Dons and her peers "mission feminists," and I too consider this an important label to use. While Dons used neither our current term "feminist" nor her contemporary term "a women's issue woman" (*kvindesagskvinde*), she did insist, when she was seventy-two years old, that "this question" of women and Christianity had been a lifelong one for her: "Ever since my early youth," she wrote, "when I became a personal Christian, until I am now over 70, I have worked with this question: Women's life and service in the congregation."[43] Dons typed out this sentence as part of a response to a male pastor who had printed an opinion piece in the Christian newspaper *Vårt Land* (*Our Country*) arguing that women could not be pastors. Dons replied: "As a Christian woman, I read the Bible with completely different eyes than You as far as it applies to the woman." She stated she had to "find her way" to what the Bible taught her "so that I could find my place as a Christian woman. And I received a specific calling from God to help other women find their place." Dons went on to remind the pastor that there had been a women's "struggle" since the 1880s to gain "the right to education, work, and equality, in collaboration with the man, both in the home, in society, and in the church" and that over the years she had been surprised and saddened to experience that the men of the church were often "the least understanding, yes, the most fanatic opponents, when it came to women's fight for their crystal-clear rights as humans." When she read the Gospels' depiction of Jesus, she continued, she found: "Everything he says and everything he does applies equally to women and men." In this book I use the term "feminist," then, in part to reflect Dons's own presentation of her work with questions surrounding women's "life," "service," "place," "struggle," "fight," and "rights."

At the same time, I also use the term "feminist" here because I wish to make the connection between the historical mission feminists and feminisms today. I wish to add to the conversation on feminism and its many histories and definitions by thinking of Dons and her colleagues as exemplifying some of its difficulties. These are difficulties for me precisely because my feminism today—in writing this book, for example—would likely seem difficult to Dons. She would disagree with me that she was conjuring a world or using listening as a technology of enchantment. She would disagree that she was evoking the figure of "the heathen woman" in "Africa" as a stereotyped foil for Lutheran women in Norway. And she would disagree that one of the effects of her listening was at times to render this African figure mute while she and her colleagues in Norway used the figure as a springboard; they gained an expanded use of words precisely in responding to what they referred to as the former's "call." Dons's life in language shows us that our North Atlantic histories of feminism have been formed, in part, through this interweaving of feminist language use with the relational difficulties that accompany the notions of listening, responding, and responsibility.

MAPPING: PROTESTANT LISTENING AS A RESPONSIVE RELATION TO A WORLD

Let me return to one of the first decisions Henny Dons and her four teacher colleagues recorded in their minutes in 1902, which they carefully saved for later readers: "Never bazaar." Tracing the importance of this decision, we are able to see that the LMF women agreed with the traditional mission women's groups that it was necessary to respond to the calls they heard—the calls from God, from Christ, from the mission fields and figures "out there." But they thought that working on crafts together in a meeting was not the proper response. The traditional groups, in their view, did not assemble sound and silence well. These groups emphasized metaphorical quietness, such as subservience to male authority, rather than literal quietness. Instead, the LMF women experimented with literal quietness, arriving at a new use of language. They found that meeting as women, sitting still together and listening intently to gripping words, was the proper affective response to the cries and calls from around the world, and thus more effective. They broke with and also reclaimed the expectation that Christian women should be silent. They allowed one woman at a time to speak aloud, with authority—thus challenging the expectation of metaphorical silence. But for the other women in the meeting, they emphasized the importance of literal silence. More importantly, they recast what it meant to "be in silence."

How might we map this instance of Protestant language use? I have argued that the women's Protestant listening generated a responsive relation to a world—or to their world. The act of responding always needs something to precede it, a prior conjured context, and the women's meetings were a way of responding, as they saw it, to God's "call" and to figures "out there." The women reworked the world map, listening to the cries and calls they heard, and paid attention to what they thought of as far-reaching connections between themselves and these other calling figures. More precisely, I suggest that we can map the listening of Dons and her peers in the form of a responsive relation they perceived to stretch across scales from their "hearts" to their women's meetings to "the whole world"—or from the most "intimate" to the most "immense," to adapt Kaell's terms (2020a, 3). They produced this linguistic innovation by assembling specific bodies, affects, and objects in a meeting place that was theirs, arranging themselves in certain bodily comportments while sitting together in a room in Kristiania, and this material-discursive technology allowed them, in their view, to wield an impactful silence that would connect with and affect themselves, the calling figures, God, and the world. What we see in this Protestant woman-word operation of listening, then, can be thought of as one "of the infinite ways language enters life," to borrow Talal Asad's phrasing in his engagement with Wittgenstein (Martin 2014, 12); the women's new "form of language" constituted a new "form of life" in the world (Drury 1973, x).

In thinking of the women's listening as a relation, I am also inspired by feminist new materialism, especially by the anthropologist Marilyn Strathern's interest in the relations that compose forms in the world and how these relations divide and multiply at different scales.[44] Strathern does not think that persons (or other individual figures) are conceptually distinct from their relations; she argues instead that figures are composed of and through their multiple relations. In the same way, it seems to me that the form of Dons as a listening Protestant woman was composed of and through her multiple relations, enacted at different scales. In her listening, she emerges as a composite subject. At the scale of a meeting room, we see her together with a group of women listening with heartfelt concentration to another woman one Saturday evening. In their view, this relation was at the same time replicated at a larger scale, as the collective of Lutheran female teachers in LMF in Norway were listening to "calls" from around the world, such as from "heathen" regions in Madagascar. And the relation was replicated at a smaller scale as each woman was urged to listen to God and give her own affective response in her "heart." When Dons listened in the LMF meetings together with her colleagues, she was a Protestant woman subject, a body-word nexus in that moment, who was composed of these multiple relations.

The concept of response also highlights the complicated ethical agency that these women perceived themselves to be working with—God's, others', and their own. Yes, they were *with* God, but from their perspective they were also responding by working *for* God, by allowing God to work *on* them, and by opening themselves so God could work *through* them in other places and peoples—in Madagascar, Santalistan, Zululand, China, and "the whole world." The relation we see here was based on an understanding of ethical agency that went beyond the self, as the agency of the listening woman (able to respond) was simultaneously taken to be the agency of the callers (able to elicit a response). Thinking more carefully about the ethical aspect of this orientation of response thus allows us to consider a larger bundle of agencies in these Protestants' engagement with the world (cf. Mittermaier 2012, 252). It also allows us to see how, in their view, the LMF women were affecting God. Although their God was all-powerful, they thought he still wished them to *receive* so he could *give* in a series of changing engagements: God called them, they called missionaries, the non-Christians called them, they called God, God called them again. In other words, their ethical project of Protestant feminism was not, in their view, primarily anchored in their individual selves but instead was a project enacted through a collection of assembled figures; the project shows us a type of collective ethical agency, an agency of call and response. In this sense, it was a multiple, or composite, ethical project, constituted by many forces and figures to which Dons and her peers connected but that also extended beyond them.

AFTERWARD

So, we might ask: Did the women's listening work? From their perspective, it likely did. Up until World War II, the Protestant worldwide mission grew, as did the number of people in Africa and Asia who identified as Christian (although these two historical events do not have a simple cause-and-effect relationship). In Norway, the LMF women and their allies did manage to create more public space for women in Christian organizations.

On the other hand, an outsider might notice that the LMF women's listening did not work in one important respect: the vast majority of the traditional mission women's groups across Norway did not adopt LMF's understanding that listening was the most proper response to the mission call. Perhaps the traditional groups felt uncomfortable with the idea of one woman speaking and others listening silently, which evoked associations to male-dominated public space and authority. Or perhaps the affect of concentrated listening LMF demanded was experienced as too intense, especially compared with the relaxed atmosphere of the traditional gatherings around crafts, coffee, conversation, and raffle tickets. Or perhaps the traditional women had a sense that the most Christian response to "heathen" calls was simply tangible action: make crafts, raise money.

Although LMF continued to exist, its impact on NMS receded strongly after World War II, echoing the overall contraction of the women's movement in northern Europe at the time. Today, the common perception of mission women's groups in Norway resembles the traditional conversational crafting groups more than the intently listening LMF groups. While women's groups today may set aside some time to pray or listen to a devotion, they may also bring some knitting, eat cake, and chat over coffee. They still hold lively and noisy mission bazaars, where they raffle tickets to sell homemade crafts and baked goods, and then donate the money to NMS. The particular listening meeting that Henny Dons helped to develop in her LMF circles in the first decades of the twentieth century—in which women experimented with a new assembling of bodies and words, sounds and silence, God and the world, women and authority, decisions and effects—is no longer prevalent in this Lutheran tradition.

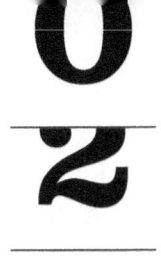

SPEAKING

The heavy clouds threatened to bring rain. The organizers of the Mission Summer School in July 1911 were anxious that Henny Dons's talk might be derailed, but they invited her to come up to the lectern on the hillside, in an open area scattered with a few leafy trees. Dons, thirty-seven years old, looked out over a few hundred people. "I have been given the task of speaking about *unity*," she began, her practiced teacher's voice ringing out over the assembled crowd; "it is a task marked by responsibility and difficulty."[1] As she was speaking, she was able to look directly at the white-painted wooden church at the foot of the hill, framed by the fjord and the dark blue mountains beyond, knowing she was forbidden from speaking inside it because of Paul's injunction in the New Testament: "Let your women keep silence in the churches: for it is not permitted unto them to speak; but they are commanded to be under obedience" (1 Corinthians 14:34). She spoke for around twenty minutes from the hillside before bringing her talk on unity to an end with a final sentence urging the need for the Holy Spirit "to burn us clean."[2] It had not rained.

As I look back at this scene just over a century later, I wonder how to understand Protestant speaking. In the anthropological conversation on Protestant language use, speaking has often been analyzed as an expression of a "Protestant language ideology" (or a "Protestant semiotic ideology") that works toward a certain type of dematerialization; from this perspective, a Protestant seeks to speak sincerely and freely, in tune with an individual interior self, without being encumbered by material forms (Keane 2007).[3] If I were to view Dons speaking outside the church through this scholarly lens, her speech might be thought of as an instance of the Protestant sincere speaking self, an attempt to truthfully express her interior state. Standing alone behind the lectern, she might be seen as a representation of Protestant individualism. Perhaps her speaking might be thought of as an attempt to be unencumbered by her female body, to stand apart from this material form. Her individual, sincere speech might then be thought of as a type of ethical agency separating her from her body. But I do not think this was what was happening.

The scholarly conversation on Protestant speaking has not usually incorporated gender as a significant analytical factor.[4] However, like Dons's Lutheran community in early twentieth-century Norway, most Christian communities throughout most of Christian history have perceived there to be a particular risk associated with the speech of women in specific Christian places. For example, Christian communities, including Protestant ones, have often enforced rules preventing women from speaking inside a church or from speaking in public about the word of God. Most Protestant communities over the past five hundred years have not, in fact, wished to separate speech from bodies, but have rather insisted strongly that the two are inseparable. Since this runs counter to the prevailing scholarly view of a "Protestant language ideology" that drives Protestants toward dematerialization, it has raised the question for me: What would an analysis of Protestant speaking look like if we took gendered bodies into account, placing them at the core of our analysis, as Protestants have often done?

If we take Dons's gendered body into account when considering her speech on the hillside, our analysis might shift away from tracing connections between Protestant speaking, sincerity, interiority, dematerialization, and individualized ethical agency. Instead, what frames Dons's speech for me is a broader set of connections that intertwine her speaking with space and place. In this instance, Dons's speaking cannot be kept separate from her subject position as a woman, which again in this instance cannot be separated from her body, the physical space it took up and the physical places it could be in and under what conditions, her social "place" in the Protestant community, and the broader question of whether she could have a "place" in language at all (Irigaray [1977] 1985, 68). The woman and her spoken words became a combined operation in the world, a body-word operation, producing a voice that was placed and took up space, that created an alternative Protestant place on a hillside, and that experimented with a "place" in Protestant language. Therefore, I suggest that her speaking does not so much tell us about subjectivity and sincerity as it tells us about subjectivity and space.

One of the terms I will use to explore this relationship between speaking, subjectivity, and space is "voice." This term is regularly invoked in conversations on feminist theory, in part because of its versatility: it manages to combine material sound with discursive meaning and linguistic action with political impact. It has often been used to refer to a type of agency, positing women as beings with a certain individual or group identity out of which they "have" a voice (or, if they do not "have" it, out of which they need to "gain" a voice)—and it is almost always assumed to be beneficial in some way to the woman who has it.[5] It is only recently that some feminist work has begun to raise questions about this view (e.g., Coddington 2017); we might ask, for example, why a voice is often thought of as wielded by an autonomous self, or why having a voice is automatically seen as desirable, whether in personal or political life.

Therefore, while I draw on the versatility of "voice," I depart from much of the previous usage in feminist theory, instead exploring voice as a type of place—a dynamic place that is continuously being produced. I am inspired here by feminist new materialism, especially feminist geographer Doreen Massey (2005, 149), who has argued that a place is a "throwntogetherness."[6] A place, Massey (2005, 151) says, happens when entities with different trajectories cross each other's paths and form a momentary place through their combination: "an ever-shifting constellation of trajectories" coming together on purpose and by chance. Reflecting the difficulty of distinguishing cleanly between place and space, Massey allows them to blend into each other. In this chapter, I repurpose Massey's "throwntogetherness" to my historical case and trace some of the historical trajectories that met, or were thrown together, in Dons's speaking voice on the hillside in July 1911. Which trajectories constellated to create this moment of speech? How did they come together in Dons's voice? What type of constellated place was formed? I am interested in how we might lay out the components of such a thrown-together Protestant voice.

I argue, then, that one way of understanding this instance of Protestant speaking—Dons's speaking on the hillside outside the church—is to see her as embodying a thrown-together Protestant voice. Her Protestant speech had more to do with a constellation of historical trajectories of women, bodies, and words than it had to do with the immediate expression of a sincere self, and it stood far from a desire for dematerialization. This mapping leaves us with a different conceptualization of how spoken words and ethical agency relate in Protestant Christianity. Rather than thinking of voice primarily as individual ethical agency, I here think of voice as a throwntogetherness, and I explore this thrown-together meeting point—the moment of trajectories merging in Dons's speaking body—as the point at which collective agency came together in her voice in one instance. This ethical agency was beyond her control as an individual; at the same time, it constellated in her voice in that moment. From this perspective, the voice coming from Dons's body can be understood as a point of analysis for the distributed components that came together to produce a momentary ethical subject enacting one moment in an ethical project—in this case, one instantiation of Dons's ethical project of Protestant feminism.

Let me begin by describing the scene of Dons speaking, paying attention to how this scene stitches together speaking and space. I then examine two trajectories that met in Dons's speaking voice, as I hear it: first, the trajectory of Dons's path through the early women's movement(s) in the busy city of Kristiania at the turn of the twentieth century; second, the trajectory of tension surrounding women's talk in the Norwegian Mission Society (NMS). These trajectories were thrown together in a particular configuration in the gendered, speaking body of Dons on the hillside outside the church in July 1911.

A LECTERN ON THE HILLSIDE

The Mission Summer School in July 1911 was the first of its kind in Norway. It was organized by Norway's Mission Study Council (Norges Missionsstudieraad), a committee formed the same year and of which Henny Dons was one of the founding members. The Summer School was held at Framnæs Christian school (today Framnes) on Norway's western coast, on the downward-sloping incline of the mountains toward the broad, majestic Hardangerfjord. Dons likely took the train from her home in Kristiania, on Norway's southeastern border, across the mountains to the Summer School, since train tracks had been extended to the western city of Bergen just a few years earlier—a concrete sign of Norway's expanding industrialization. I imagine Dons sitting by the train window, herself a concrete sign of social changes: an unmarried female teacher from the upper middle class, thirty-seven years old, traveling to speak in public to a mixed-gender Christian audience.

The Summer School drew around five hundred youth who gathered for five days, from Monday to Friday, to be inspired by lectures about Protestant mission, to listen to biblical devotions, and to get to know each other in reading and discussion groups. They held communal prayer meetings during the light Scandinavian summer evenings with "determined, purposeful prayer for specific, listed topics."[7] The focused prayer had a "powerful, gripping effect," one participant reported afterward in the magazine of the Female

Teachers' Mission Association, *Missionshilsen* (*Mission Greeting*), adding: "For example, when we walked home Tuesday evening after praying for China, some of us said to each other: 'I bet they felt our prayers out there this evening—,' such power and force was there over the prayer meeting that night."[8]

When it was Dons's turn to deliver her plenary talk on Thursday, the Summer School had already heard sixteen plenary speakers. These sixteen had all been men, and they had all spoken inside Vikør Church (today Vikøy), the main venue for the Summer School's plenary gatherings.[9] Dons was the only woman plenary speaker on the program. However, it was illegal for women to speak inside the churches of the state church, the Church of Norway, at this time. The organizers of the Summer School had asked the Norwegian government's Department of Church and Education—the governing authority over the church—for permission for Dons to speak inside the church building, but the department had declined, instead sending back a reminder that this was "not permitted."[10]

A young Norwegian man who worked as a preacher for the Norwegian Lutheran China Mission Association, Knut Rettedal, was a participant at the Summer School that year. Forty years later, he wrote an essay titled *Woman's Place and Right in the Mission Work*, in which he recalled the moments before Dons's speech in 1911. He recounted that the organizers had "erected a lectern [*reist en talerstol*]" on the hillside by the church so Dons could deliver her talk outside (Rettedal 1951, 36). But the weather looked uncertain, and they were worried: "Would the rain hinder the meeting outside, and the law hinder the meeting inside?" The young Rettedal jokingly suggested to one of the male theologians present that if it started to rain, the five hundred or so participants could bench themselves inside the church while Dons stood on the steps immediately outside the church door; she could then deliver her talk to a man standing immediately inside the door, who could shout it out to the crowd inside the church, sentence by sentence. The theologian was not amused, Rettedal reported. Fortunately, he added, God withheld the rain and Dons was able to start speaking "from the lectern on the hillside" (1951, 36). Rettedal's use of the word *talerstol*, which can be translated as *lectern*, indicates that something more had been provided than simply, for example, a chair for Dons to stand on; perhaps an actual lectern had been taken out of the church. In Norwegian, the word *talerstol*, when used in a church context, may also sometimes serve as a synonym for *prekestol*, which translates as *pulpit*, so that Rettedal's sentence contains some ambiguity: Dons began speaking "from the lectern [or pulpit] on the hillside."

Dons began by invoking the "responsibility and difficulty" of speaking about unity within "God's kingdom," especially among Christians involved in mission.[11] It is not surprising that she highlighted the difficulty of this topic. In Norway, the Lutheran state church had long held a legal monopoly on organizing Christian life, but the decades leading up to Dons's speech had seen many changes: Christian organizations outside the state church were granted the legal right to exist in 1842, NMS was established the same year amid the evangelical revivals, and since then several more Lutheran mission organizations had sprouted up—the Israel Mission in 1844, the Seamen's Mission in 1864, the Santal Mission in 1867, the Home Mission (Lutherstiftelsen, turning into Indremissionsselskabet) in 1868, the Sami Mission (at first Finnemisjonen) in 1888, the China Mission in 1891, and a second Home Mission (Vestlandske Indremissionsforbund) in 1898. They were all competing for financial supporters. It was in this context that Dons spoke severely about Christians' "lack of unity," saying they stood "divided, separated, yes often in open warfare amongst themselves," and that this was "not just a lack, a weakness, but *sin*."[12] But, she acknowledged, "unity" was difficult, and was something Christians needed to "grow up to and into."[13] Moreover, in her view, unity did not mean similarity; Christians should not all have the same opinions or work in the same way. While she could smoothly have included a comment at this point about relations between women and men in Christian organizations, she did not broach the topic at all. In later writings, she strongly emphasized Paul's phrase in the New Testament: "there is neither male nor female: for ye are all one in Christ Jesus" (Galatians 3:28; e.g., Dons 1928, 65). But in her talk at the Summer School, forced to speak outside because she was a woman, she did not raise any questions about unity between women and men.

Instead, continuing her talk under the dark gray clouds, she moved on to broader conceptualizations, saying: "Jesus's *ideal of unity* is, first, something infinitely wide and all-encompassing ... But second, Jesus's ideal of unity is also something very deep and thoroughgoing."[14] I wonder whether her explication of the intentions of Jesus perhaps crossed the line, for any of her listeners, from speaking to preaching. In addition to being forbidden from speaking inside church buildings, women in Norway in 1911 were also forbidden by law from "preaching" (that is, expounding on the words of the Bible to an audience) in any location, whether inside or outside a church.[15] As Dons's voice sounded out over the assembled participants, speaking about Jesus's ideal of unity, some of the listeners may perhaps have been able to perceive the lectern on the hill as an alternative pulpit. But in her final point Dons returned easily to the practical, as she reminded her listeners: "The work that is needed most of all, for all mission activity, is *the work of prayer*," and *"lack of unity hinders our prayer."*[16] In ending, she wove her own words together with biblical phrases, without giving the biblical references but instead counting on her audience's ability to recognize the images. She urged them to consider how they were "biting and devouring each other instead of loving and serving each other," and she admonished the crowd to let the Holy Spirit "burn us clean."[17]

I am interested in considering how Dons's speech came about in this instance, or what it came about despite. What type of voice was this? How can we understand this instance of Protestant speaking?

PROTESTANT SPEAKING AND SPACE

Simon Coleman has considered the effects of speaking among neo-Pentecostals in Sweden, including when they evangelize on the streets of Uppsala and invite people to church. In considering the effects of this speech, Coleman suggests that while not many people, if any, are converted by this particular action, the speaking does have an effect on the Pentecostal speakers themselves. He argues that their speaking is a way of externalizing a part of the self so it can reach out, or a way of constituting their identity precisely in the act of "extending it out into the world" (2003, 22; see also 2006, 178). Here I wish to pick up on the connections Coleman draws between Pentecostal Christian speech, self, and space and to extend this line of thought by considering how, from the perspective of feminist new materialism, Protestant Christian speech may relate to the coming-together of a voice simultaneously with the coming-together of a space.

Most obviously, the physical place of speaking mattered to Dons and other participants in the moment; it made a difference whether she spoke inside or outside the Vikør church building. The words that came from her body had to be differently placed than the words from the bodies of the men plenary speakers. Although the organizers of the Summer School wished for her talk to take place inside the church, her body—coded as *woman*—had a significant influence on her voice in that moment, a material reality that could not be avoided. The subsequent report in the magazine of the Female Teachers' Mission Association made a point of reporting the physical place in which Dons spoke, noting she "had to" deliver her lecture outside in the area under the trees.[18] Speaking and space were interlinked for Dons and her peers because the physical place of speaking was tied so closely to the social "place" or position of the speaker in the community.

Though Dons herself remained faultlessly diplomatic in her speech, she too noted her location. Around two decades later, she recorded some memoir reflections in which she recalled speaking outside the church at the Summer School in 1911. In her reflections, however, she wrote about this event side by side with another: in 1927, the law regarding women's speech in churches had been changed, and she was invited to speak from the pulpit *inside* the cathedral in Bergen.[19] She commented that the difference between these two events showed the significant shift in "the position of women" as "a preacher of God's word" that occurred between 1911 and 1927.[20] Elsewhere, she often spoke and wrote about the importance of "woman's place" in the mission (e.g., 1923b, 3–6; 1928, 84). Similarly, Rettedal's (1951) recollection of Dons speaking outside the church in 1911 formed part of his argument for why a new understanding of "woman's place" was needed in the mission work. Their tying together of the physical place of speaking with the social place of speakers echoed the arguments to which they were responding, which stated that women could not speak inside churches because of Paul's guidance in 1 Corinthians 14 that women must "keep silence in the churches" to be "under obedience." Paul too tied together the physical place of speaking (or not speaking) and the social, ranked place of the speakers. To know where to speak was to know your place.

The organizers of the Summer School nervously sought to create an alternative place for Dons's speech by bringing together her body and the sound of her voice with the object of the lectern, its positioning on the hillside, its proximity to the church building, and a gathered audience. I am interested here in how Dons's voice, circulating out of her body and into others' bodies, was intertwined with the creation of this alternative Protestant space. It reminds me of how Birgit Meyer, David Morgan, Crispin Paine, and Brent Plate (2010, 209) define the body to show its centrality to material religion: "A body consists of viscera, skeleton, musculature, and flesh, but also brain/mind, sensation, imagination, cognition, and the interface with the worlds around and within the body. The body enters integrally into every feeling, thought, emotion, and perception that human beings have." Building on this view, I see Dons's speaking body as a complex, made up of both material and nonmaterial elements, that is reaching out into the world—through her physical appearance in front of the audience, through the sound of her voice, through her words strung together into sentences—in ways difficult to categorize as inside or outside her tangible body. The place of her body, and the space she extended into as she spoke, helped produce a different Protestant place.

The instance of Dons's speaking at the Summer School in 1911 was an instance of words, bodies, and space or place intertwined; in this case, to speak was to work in, with, and on space. This voice-space was material-discursive, as the placement of Dons's speaking body merged into social placement, and the spatial reach of the sound of her voice merged into the creation of a religious place. Here I wish to explore this voice as a throwntogetherness, drawing on—and adapting—Massey's suggestion that a space is a throwntogetherness, a meeting of trajectories that come together in a moment, on purpose and by chance. What came together to make the voice of Dons speaking on the hillside?

FIRST TRAJECTORY: A WOMAN'S VOICE IN KRISTIANIA

The story of Henny Dons's speaking voice, as I tell it here, begins in Kristiania. The city of Kristiania (whose name was changed to Oslo in 1925) was the capital of Norway and its largest city. Henrikke Margrethe "Henny" Dons was born in its rural surrounds in May 1874, and her family moved into the city in 1883, when Henny was around nine years old. There was a great sense of change in Kristiania at this time, both physically and politically. There was constant new building activity. Moreover, the urban intelligentsia had become tired of the old political elites and, with support from the rural farming population, brought about broad democratizing reforms in the parliament in the mid-1880s—just as Henny's family found their way around the growing capital.

The shift in political climate presented a notable opportunity to ask new questions about women. The early women's movement was already underway in the United States, England, and France, where newly educated, middle-class women had launched campaigns for women's suffrage from the mid-nineteenth century onward, and these impulses were soon taken up in Scandinavia. The Norwegian Association for Women's Rights (Norsk Kvindesagsforening) and the Norwegian Association for Women's Right to Vote (Kvindestemmerettsforeningen) were established in 1884 and 1885, when Henny was ten and eleven years old, by groups of upper- and middle-class Kristiania women (Agerholt 1937). However, though the early women's movement is often depicted as centrally concerned with voting rights, in reality it spanned a tumultuous and decentralized assortment of new causes taken up by women who sometimes collaborated and sometimes worked at cross-purposes, both in Norway and in its broader North Atlantic context. In Kristiania, different groups of women became steadily more organized around a range of causes, including women's legal rights, women's educational opportunities, a range of socio-moral issues affecting women (from public health and hygiene through prostitution and temperance to homemaking), and the safety and pay of working-class women, especially in the new factories (Agerholt 1937). Norway's legal reforms of the 1880s also affected women, for example through the Married Women's Property Act, which granted some greater economic rights to married women. However, unmarried women still retained far more extensive economic and legal independence, and thus different categories of women—married or unmarried—were incorporated in different ways into this early formation of the Norwegian democratic welfare state (leaving the riddle for later twentieth-century feminists of how to secure equality for married women with children in a liberal democracy; Hagemann 2002).

Henny grew up in the upper middle class of the capital. Her father, Johannes Albrecht Dons, took the position of director of Oslo Hospital, Norway's oldest psychiatric hospital, and her mother, Johanne Marie (née Fleischer), could afford—and would be expected—not to engage in paid employment but to manage the household, including her seven children. Perhaps Henny was sometimes taken on trips into the bustling city center together with her siblings, to walk Kristiania's cobblestone streets in her layered dress and hat, past the tall rows of apartment buildings arranged around inner courtyards, the columns of the university, the lion sculptures in front of the parliament, the tram and its bell, and the occasional novelty of a slow-moving automobile. She probably only rarely met married women in her middle-class circles who were in paid employment, though many of them were likely involved in voluntary charity work. At the same time, she would have interacted with domestic servants, married or unmarried women from the city's working class; other working-class women took up employment, for example, in the city's new textile mills and match factories. Meanwhile, the majority of Norway's married women lived outside the capital, in rural, agrarian areas and scattered towns, with many working on family farms or smallholdings. However, these arrangements of women, marriage, employment, and respectability were changing even during Henny's teen years (Blom 1990). She did know a handful of middle-class women, most unmarried, who were employed with a salary outside the home—namely some of her teachers at Nissen's School for Girls (Nissens Pigeskole), one of the first schools in Norway to allow young women to take the "middle school exam." Henny took it in 1891, when she was seventeen years old.

Henny's experience over the next three years then changed the course of her life. She was offered domestic employment as a governess for a Dr. Bugge and his five children in Hardanger on the west coast. While there, she was invited to join a mission group for young women, and she also read letters to the Bugge family from their former governess, Ragna Olsen, who had traveled to Madagascar to work as a governess for the family of missionary pastor Røstvig (Dons 1952, 32–33). This introduction to the evangelical mission world made a deep impression on Henny. Just over a decade later, she pinpointed this as the time she became "a believer," one who wished to have her "life in God, to know him *personally*," elaborating: "How I could *encounter, experience* Christianity—that became the great life question for me. And God explained it to me more and more; so that when I left Hardanger in 1894, I knew that I belonged to God and wanted to serve him."[21] Henny Dons, twenty years old, moved back to the Kristiania area and enrolled at the two-year teacher training college Asker Seminar; she also joined a local mission women's group.[22]

Upon graduation, Dons began working as an elementary school teacher, and it was around this time she discovered the Young Women's Christian Association (YWCA). She must have stood out in some way from her peers, for already in 1899 she was asked by the YWCA secretary Marie Sinding to speak at the organization's Pentecost meeting for leaders. At the meeting, the twenty-five-year-old Dons walked up in front of the audience and gave a speech. These are the earliest recorded words of hers we have; they were so striking that they were written down. She told the assembled YWCA leaders: "Have you helped us? No. Women have only had to do with superficial things. Things that have to do with the soul, she has left to the man. We ask of you, woman: Take responsibility and leadership into your own hands" (Voksø and Kullerud 1980, 122–123). This was a daring theme for the young teacher to choose. Just four years previously, Sophie Pharo, the editor of the YWCA magazine *Vort Blad* (*Our Magazine*), had printed that one of the organization's goals was to foster true womanhood: "The true woman holds back, she is shy. She never speaks so loudly that she might draw others' attention to herself. The deep chord in her character is shy politeness and forgetfulness of self [*selvforglemmelse*]" (Voksø and Kullerud 1980, 121). This goal was not uncontested, however, because the YWCA secretary Marie Sinding envisioned a more active role for the young women around her. In her view, women ought to free themselves from an era of submission, and at the leaders' meeting in 1900 she reportedly stated that "the liberation struggle that we women must go through is more difficult than any man can understand" (Voksø and Kullerud 1980, 123). Henny Dons quickly gravitated toward Marie Sinding.

Around the same time, Henny Dons arranged to meet with Bolette Gjør, the pastor's wife who edited the women's magazine published by NMS.[23] I imagine the young Dons sitting on a sofa in the Gjør parsonage in Kristiania, explaining that she thought she had a calling from God to become a missionary overseas. The mission station Eshowe among the Zulus was especially on her mind. Perhaps she tried to talk through with Gjør the difficult issue of her father not supporting her desire, since he regarded it as "not sensible," though she had tried to explain it to him in writing and he understood "that he cannot be permitted to set himself against it."[24] She was planning to send a letter of application to NMS. I wonder if Gjør, in her sixties, recalled that she had herself had a calling to become a missionary when she was younger, but had at the time been brusquely told that single women could not become missionaries; they could only travel to the "mission field" if they married a male missionary. It had been an impactful experience for the young Bolette Gjør, and she later suggested she had "strangled" her own calling.[25] However, as she met with the young Henny Dons, she knew women's work opportunities were changing, and Gjør was a prominent feminist advocate for women's education and employment in NMS.

After the meeting, Gjør wrote to Lars Dahle, the NMS secretary in Stavanger, that Dons was "an unusually competent lady" and "very warm in her Christianity."[26] Gjør was impressed by her energy. She registered only one reservation: Dons "has joined herself warmly to Miss Marie Sinding," the YWCA secretary, and "in my eyes, this is no particular recommendation." Gjør explained that she disagreed with some of Sinding's interpretations of the Bible, and "when one adds Miss S's rather emancipated views on women's submission and her battle for women's liberation from man's violations, well, then it is no longer a very lovable form of Christianity." Nevertheless, on the basis of her "long conversation" with Dons, Gjør concluded that Dons made "a very good impression" and that the NMS governing board ought to read her forthcoming application closely: "I believe she is a force that will be able to accomplish something and that one must be careful not to cast away."[27]

All seemed set for Dons to exchange letters with the NMS board and to start preparing to travel as a young woman mission worker to the Zulus at Eshowe station in Southern Africa. However, her plans then came to an abrupt halt.

In 1903, at twenty-nine years old, Dons contracted a serious illness she referred to as "a lung sickness."[28] Her father paid for her to stay at Gjøsegaarden Sanatorium, a privately owned sanatorium that specialized in treating tuberculosis and other lung illnesses using the most modern cure known for these potentially lethal diseases: quiet countryside surroundings, an abundance of fresh air, walks, good diet, and hygiene (Jordåen 2006, 41–42). About halfway through her nine-month stay, Dons wrote to the chairman of the NMS board, "It looks like I will conquer the illness. But thereby I have not reached clarity concerning what God has decided for my future."[29] In the end, the circumstances surrounding her illness caused her to withdraw her application to become a missionary. She returned to her teacher's post in Kristiania.

In 1904, the thirty-year-old Dons knew for certain she would not travel to Southern Africa. She turned her renewed energetic capabilities to supporting overseas missions while remaining in Norway, and she seems to have committed herself fully to this future as she stepped into a series of significant leadership roles in rapid succession. Among the upper and middle classes of Kristiania, the early women's movement as well as the evangelical Protestant movement were movements of organizations—committees, boards, bylaws, agendas, votes, meetings, and minutes—and this was a social form Dons unreservedly embraced. So unreservedly, in fact, that as Lisbeth Mikaelsson (2002, 111) notes in her article about Dons's life, it is difficult to even gain an overview of all the committees and boards in which she became involved.[30] For example, in 1905 Dons was chosen to be the national "chairman" (*formand*) of the Female Teachers' Mission Association, the organization she had helped to establish along with some of her teacher colleagues in 1902; she served as national chairman for more than four decades, from 1905–1946. In addition, in 1905 she took on the role of chairman for the local chapter of the Female Teachers' Mission Association in Kristiania. Also in 1905, Dons was elected chairman of the board of Norway's YWCA, a position she held 1905–1917 and again 1932–1941 (Mikaelsson 2002, 115–116). In 1905, she also joined the Ladies' Committee (Damekomiteen), which was seeking to establish a Mission School for Women and in the meantime provided ad hoc courses in Kristiania every two years for a couple of young women at a time who wished to become missionaries. The Ladies' Committee was led by Bolette

Gjør, and when the elderly Gjør passed away, the leadership of the committee was handed to Dons in 1910.[31]

In 1910, Dons secured another board membership that, in retrospect, most clearly reveals her diplomatic skill. A few years earlier, Gjør had attempted to build a formal connection between the sprawling mission women's movement, which comprised thousands of small groups scattered across the country, and the political women's movement, which in 1904 had been organized at a national level through the Norwegian Women's National Council (Norske Kvinders Nasjonalråd), an umbrella organization for women's organizations in Norway.[32] In 1907, Gjør, in her seventies, created an organization she hoped could represent some of the mission-supporting women, the Mission Workers' Circle (Missionsarbeidernes Ring), with the aim of joining the Norwegian Women's National Council.[33] However, Lars Dahle, the NMS secretary, prohibited her from writing about this initiative in the women's magazine she edited for NMS, *Missionslæsning for Kvindeforeninger* (*Mission Reading for Women's Groups*), and the Circle largely failed to gain traction among mission women.[34]

Nevertheless, in July 1907, Gjør attended the national meeting of the Norwegian Women's National Council to request that the Circle become a member. Although some attendees voiced support for a closer tie with the mission women's groups, others were skeptical, likely reflecting the larger tension at the meeting between those who thought feminism—or "the women's issue" (*kvindesagen*), in the terminology of the time—should prioritize campaigns for women's legal rights, especially the right to vote, versus those who thought it should also encompass women's local organizing around socio-moral concerns such as public health and hygiene, social purity (against prostitution and trafficking), temperance, homemaking, and, now, religion.[35] In the end, the voting result was four votes short of approving membership for the Circle.[36] Gjør left on a train the same evening, deeply disappointed (Ebbell 1946, 178). A while later, she entered into a flurry of correspondence with NMS Secretary Dahle, who advised her that if Christian mission-supporting women were to become associated with the political women's movement in Norway it would cause "*foundational damage* to our mission."[37] In frustration, Gjør replied as forcefully as she could within the bounds of their letters: "When a movement occurs in our time that has not previously occurred in world history, then we cannot close our eyes as if this were something that did not concern us, but we have to look at it and ask: What are we to do here? To me it seems that it is God who speaks to us through this awakening of the women."[38]

Gjør passed away shortly afterward, in 1909. At the next meeting of the Norwegian Women's National Council in 1910, Dons attended on behalf of the Circle and reapplied for membership. Not only did her conduct at the meeting easily secure membership for the Circle (Ebbell 1946, 179), but the attendees also elected Dons herself to sit on the national board of the council (she received the highest number of votes of the new board members), where she served for nine years, first as treasurer and then as vice-chairman (Michelet 1946, 58; Mikaelsson 2002, 120).

The following year, in 1911, Dons was one of the founding members of Norway's Mission Study Council, the committee that organized Norway's first Mission Summer School that summer.[39]

This was one of the trajectories, then, that produced the moment of Dons's speaking on the hillside outside the church at the Summer School in July 1911: the early and growing women's movement(s) in Norway among upper- and middle-class, educated women in the busy, also growing, democratizing capital city of Kristiania. What was Dons's voice in this instance? It was the voice of a new type of employed woman—an urban, unmarried, middle-class teacher—coming together with the voice of a woman caught up in, and committed to, the passions and committees of the expanding Protestant mission movement. It was the voice of a young woman who was able to imagine the possibility of working overseas, even when her father disapproved. It was the voice of a teacher accustomed to the authority of speaking to an audience of children in her classroom, coming together with the voice of a woman in Kristiania who knew that other women were campaigning for the right to vote in national elections. It was the voice of a woman who could take a train on the new tracks across the mountains to the Summer School, coming together with the voice of a woman who, in her midthirties, had already repeatedly experienced that other women voted in favor of her leadership.

SECOND TRAJECTORY: A WOMAN'S VOICE IN NMS

"Too far!" Lars Dahle shouted, rising from his chair, and Emma Dahl ran from the room. Dahl was an unmarried female mission worker for NMS in Madagascar, on leave in Norway in 1895 and speaking with the NMS secretary. A few years earlier, it had become known that she (and likely other Norwegian and Malagasy women too; Nyhagen Predelli 2003, 230–234) was teaching about the Bible to both men and women inside church buildings in Madagascar. Lars Dahle, on behalf of the NMS leadership, had sent a stern warning to the Norwegian missionary group in Madagascar. He emphasized that women had no "ethical legitimacy" to instruct men about the Bible in meetings and that their conduct should be bound by the statements in 1 Corinthians 14:34 and 1 Timothy 2:12, which directed women to be silent in the churches (Nyhagen Predelli 2003, 227).

Line Nyhagen Predelli (2003, 228–229) has detailed the resulting feud between Dahle and Dahl, including Emma Dahl's illness (which was interpreted by her missionary colleagues as being partly caused by the secretary's letter) and her draft exegesis about women's right to preach, which she planned to send to him but probably never did. On leave in 1895, she met with Lars Dahle and told him she would not go back to Madagascar unless NMS changed its regulations. According to a letter she sent afterward to friends in Madagascar, reported in the missionary Theodor Olsen's diary, Dahle told her that if she did go back to Madagascar she would "turn crazy," and when she brought up 1 Corinthians 14 and women's right to speak, "Dahle became furiously angry, got up from his chair and shouted (!): 'Now, this is going too far!' And Ms Dahl ran out the door with her tears rolling and cried on her way to the mission school, at the mission school, at her cousin Mrs. Thorne, the whole day. She must have been somewhat hysterical, when she was in Stavanger."[40]

However, although Lars Dahle in his office in Stavanger attempted to maintain clear boundaries around women's speech, through shouting if necessary, the dispersed organizational form of NMS made it impossible for the leadership to fully control how speech was used in all parts of the organization. The Norwegian missionaries in Madagascar, for example, operated at a far remove from Stavanger, and it took a long time for letters to travel back and forth by sea. The thousands of local mission groups that constituted the grassroots of NMS, spread out across Norway, could not all be closely monitored from Stavanger either. What could the NMS leadership do to shape this amorphous organizational landscape? While they sent warnings to their missionaries, they did not feel this was an appropriate way of communicating with the many mission groups that provided the organization's finances. Therefore, they tried a more inspirational approach with the groups. Their most important tactic was to send speakers.

This led to something of a paradox. Some of the first instances of Christian women speaking to mixed-gender audiences in Norway occurred in these far-flung local groups, as NMS asked missionary wives and single female mission workers on leave in Norway to travel to the groups to tell stories from the "mission fields," as a way of distributing information and encouraging donations. It is ironic, as Nyhagen Predelli (2003, 231) notes, that toward the end of the 1890s NMS even paid Emma Dahl, who had again returned from Madagascar, to travel as an emissary to speak about the mission to large, mixed-gender gatherings. Secretary Dahle approved of this practice; it appears to have been distinct, for him, from the issue of women speaking in churches or from the women's movement more broadly. These distinctions became clearer when he forbade Bolette Gjør from publishing anything in NMS's women's magazine that advocated for organized collaboration between mission women and "the women's issue" (*kvindesagen*), as he and the men on the NMS governing board thought it would be unfortunate if NMS were perceived to support "women's liberation."[41]

If the speech experiments of Gjør, Dons, and Dahl and her peers generated tension with the male leadership of NMS, they also, and perhaps more surprisingly, stood in tension with many of the three thousand to four thousand mission women's groups that made up the bulk of NMS's grassroots support, as can be gleaned from editorial comments printed in NMS's women's magazine *Mission Reading for Women's Groups*. Almost as soon as Bolette Gjør took on the role of the magazine's first editor in 1884, she began printing occasional exhortations to the women's groups regarding how they should use their voices. She apparently did not think she could go so far as to encourage them to hold devotions themselves. But she did exhort them *not* to invite a man to read or to lead, as was often done, in her view, "in the country" (as opposed to in the city).[42] She observed critically that, in her experience, when women read out loud from her magazine in the local women's groups it was often done "softly and quickly" so that the mission stories did not "make an impression," in turn leading the women to have only "lukewarm hearts" for the mission. She argued that a woman in each group needed to read the material ahead of time, choose excerpts to read out loud, "pause" at interesting information and "draw attention to it," "alternate" between reading and retelling, and "bring about a small conversation."[43] It is unclear whether Gjør's directives had any effect. For example, one women's group wrote to the magazine in 1896 and specifically mentioned that they read and prayed themselves—though only if no man was available.[44] Some years later, in 1908, Gjør found that she still needed to repeat her exhortations, stating that "mission sisters" should be able to pray "with sound" when they met together. She maintained that this would lead them "closer" to the mission.[45]

Why did Gjør encourage the women to use their voice in this way—to lead the meetings, to read loudly and clearly, to pray with sound? As I worked through the archival material mentioning women's speech, I wondered whether the background for these statements was certain negative connotations surrounding "women's talk," not only inside church buildings but also outside them. There are hints of these connotations in NMS's women's magazine. For example, one women's group in western Norway that wrote to the magazine in 1887 included a comment about how critics labeled them: "We often hear taunts and insults and we are asked if we are now going to the gossip group, and more."[46] At least in this place, the women's group was known to some as a "gossip group." Meanwhile, Gjør too seemed to think of women's talk as being potentially problematic, as when she authored an unsigned editorial statement in the next issue stating that women do indeed waste "many moments" on "idle [*ørkesløs*] talk and activities that are not useful" and that their group meetings should offer a contrasting space in which "it will do you good to hear the Word of God and other good words."[47] She again directed her editorial statement especially at rural women in "our narrow, poor valleys," also cautioning them not to make excuses for why they could not attend the monthly group meetings.[48]

Gjør's opinion was shared by some others, especially women who, like her, lived in the city of Kristiania and felt affinity for the urban, middle-class women's movement. For example, in a large joint gathering of all NMS women's groups in Kristiania in 1914, a "lively discussion" was held about the need for women to "contribute" to the monthly group meetings so these could be "rich in content." It was stated that "women are so afraid of speaking" and that the reason for this "might politely be called spiritual reservation" but was in reality "fear of people." This fear needed to be "conquered." The participants framed the need to speak within a configuration of women and Jesus: "It is Jesus himself who calls us to work. And when he calls, he needs us—he wants to be in our bodies, speak with our mouths, and work with our hands." One attendee urged women's groups to become "independent" of the male pastors whom they frequently invited to hold devotions, and another attendee stated: "We must all be responsible."[49]

Similar sentiments were expressed some years later by the newly hired "female traveling secretaries" (*kvinnelige reisesekretærer*) in NMS. These were women, typically single and middle class, whom the organization employed from 1918 onward to visit NMS groups—the women's mission groups, the children's mission groups, and sometimes also the mixed-gender mission groups. The decision to permanently hire women to speak in public (as opposed to inviting women to do so on an ad hoc basis) was such a significant one that it had to be voted on by the NMS general assembly in 1918; it was approved (Voll 1977, 23). The handful of women who were hired were, like Gjør, often unimpressed by the traditional women's groups they visited in the rural areas. For example, in 1920 the female traveling secretary Rachel Lange recorded in her notebook that the women's groups were happy to receive her, but: "Many of the leaders in our women's groups do not have the boldness to hold a devotion, nor to pray aloud or read from God's word." Although there was "a lot of talking" in the groups, this chatter was not the type of speech that "warm Christians" could enjoy.[50] While in the previous chapter I outlined how the mission feminists found that the women in the traditional groups were not able to properly *listen*, here we see that they also found these women lacking in their ability to properly *speak*. A few years later, the female traveling secretary Lina Lerheim stated that she encouraged women's groups to come together for joint meetings, and she thought women ought to lead these meetings. Since they were not used to doing so, some of them should "practice," and the effect would be increased interest in the mission.[51]

However, judging by the continued urging of Gjør, Dons, and the female traveling secretaries, it does not seem as if they felt there was a significant change in women's speech in the grassroots of NMS during the early decades of the twentieth century. The traditional women's groups themselves do not, on the whole, appear to have been convinced. Even as late as the 1940s and 1950s, Dons continued to advocate for louder reading. In a training course for NMS female traveling secretaries, she told them it was "depressing" to experience "how badly" many people still read out loud from the Bible when they gathered in groups, and she encouraged the female traveling secretaries to set an example when they visited the mission groups by reading "clearly, loudly, and well" (1945, 13; see also 1952, 13).

Perhaps the hesitancy that Dons and her colleagues ran up against was an indication of the strength of the biblical injunction against women speaking in a church, its force emphasized by the NMS secretary's anger—"Too far!"—when a woman challenged it. During the first decades of the twentieth century, the majority of women in the grassroots of NMS may have felt the need to remain safely within this boundary and to not dabble in prominent speaking practices in their groups, even if they were physically gathered in a parsonage, a farmhouse, or a local assembly house rather than inside a church.

There is also another possible reason, namely that Gjør and other mission feminists themselves grappled with this difficulty, resulting in somewhat mixed messages about women's voice. For example, Gjør wrote a book for NMS's fifty-year anniversary in 1892, *Missionsbarnet* (*The Mission Child*). It is a fictionalized, semiautobiographical account of a young woman who felt she had a calling to become a missionary overseas but was told by a famous mission bishop that women could not become missionaries. She strangled her calling and remained in Norway, though she continued to support the mission. Gjør introduced the book in NMS's women's magazine as depicting "the mission life among women," including women's "mission thoughts" and their participation in women's mission groups. She said these things had often taken place "in silence and secret" and "have not previously been known or made public."[52] However, she chose to publish the book under a pseudonym, Margrethe. Although she disclosed herself as the author in NMS's women's magazine, she did not print her own name in the magazine until 1893, when she had edited it for nine years.[53] (This event provoked some strong reactions, such as from one well-known female missionary in Madagascar, Marie Føreid, who stated that Gjør's printing her own name as editor was "a dangerous consequence of the women's movement"; Ebbell 1946, 165.) Moreover, Gjør connected her book itself to quietness: "Let [the book] be among you in quiet mission hours."[54]

Similarly, in 1904, when NMS decided to grant women the right to vote in the mixed-gender mission groups, Gjør commented favorably on the decision in NMS's women's magazine, but clarified that this did not mean women would speak at mixed-gender mission meetings, since this was "not something to be desired or sought after."[55] Thus, her exhortations for women to speak in the women's groups stand somewhat at odds with her ambivalent references to women's silence, her own use of a pseudonym, and her explicit discouragement of women speaking when men were present. Dons too demonstrated this contradiction. While she did speak to mixed-gender audiences and could state bluntly in the YWCA magazine, "Let us make a clean break with our muteness," she also published a book on women and mission in which she praised the "quiet" spread of mission women's groups.[56]

Let me return to Dons's speaking at the Summer School in July 1911. A second trajectory that produced this moment was the trajectory of the thousands of mission women's groups across the country and the male-led organizational framework of NMS they supported. Dons's voice in 1911 was a voice speaking to both the male leadership of NMS and to the majority-women grassroots of the organization at the same time, as she wished both of them to relate differently to women's speech. Both the organization's leadership and its grassroots allowed her to speak, even listened to her, but could not readily find a place for her voice in other ways, as Dahle disavowed "women's liberation" and the mission women's groups largely seem to have shied away from prominent speech. When Dons delivered her talk outside the church at the Summer School in 1911, then, her voice could not be separated from Paul's voice in the background: "Let your women keep silence in the churches: for it is not permitted unto them to speak" (1 Corinthians 14:34).

In this context, it is telling that Dons ended her speech at the Summer School by stating that prayer is "the work that is most needed."[57] Dons and her colleagues often made this turn toward the importance of prayer, and perhaps this was, in part, their response to the ongoing ambivalence surrounding women's speech. Prayer was a type of speaking that could alternate between having sound and being quiet, between being noticed and unnoticed. Prayer was also a way of influencing events without overtly taking on leadership. Dons stood behind the lectern on the hillside knowing that a woman's body speaking from behind this makeshift "pulpit" was forming a new Christian place. At the same time, she used the last minutes of her speech to turn her audience's attention to prayer, to an alternative space for women's (and men's) speaking that could shift between visibility and invisibility, sound and silence, as needed.

MAPPING: PROTESTANT SPEAKING AS A THROWN-TOGETHER VOICE

Henny Dons speaking on the hillside next to the church at the Summer School in July 1911 was an instance of Protestant speech. While the scholarly conversation on Protestant language use has often drawn connections between Protestant speaking and sincerity, interiority, dematerialization, and individualized ethical agency to suggest that Protestants are sincere speaking selves, I have traced a different set of connections in this chapter. Although sincerity tells us something about Dons's Protestantism, we see more if we broaden the frame.

What was happening as Dons spoke? I have argued that when we look at this instance of Protestant speaking, we see Dons embodying a thrown-together voice, a dynamic space produced as trajectories came together in her speaking body in the moment. The scene of Dons's speaking is reminiscent for me of Veena Das's remark, in her discussion of Ludwig Wittgenstein, that we have a "life *in* language (not just *with* language)" (2020, xiii). Dons's speaking can be seen as a "form of life" in which her body and words cannot be separated (e.g., Drury 1973, x; Wittgenstein [1953] 2009, §19). This form of life, or life form, joins social forms with material ones, historical forms with linguistic ones (Moi 2017, 54–61). This woman-word operation was composed of material and discursive elements that are difficult to cleanly separate: Dons and her words, material circumstances and spiritual technologies, physical objects and political movements. There is Dons's body, newly given the opportunity to train to speak to an audience in a classroom. She had new role models to draw on—her own women teachers, mostly unmarried like herself. Unlike her foremothers, she had been through many committee meetings and expressed herself in formal correspondence. She drew distinctions between the sound of her voice as it entered into the world and the sound of the voices she heard in the traditional women's groups. She was aware of discussions around how the different sound quality related, for example, to womanhood, shyness, and Jesus. At the Summer School in July 1911, she was provided with a physical lectern of some sort outside the church, echoing the form of the pulpit inside. It seems to me that a feminist new materialist approach helps us better take into account the material-discursive character of this linguistic situation—or this linguistic space.

This has implications for how we think about the ethical agency of speech in Protestantism. I have approached Protestant speaking as a thrown-together voice, and though this voice instantiates a subject with an ethical project, this is not the same as the individual ethical agency envisaged within the scholarly framework of a "Protestant language ideology." Dons's ethical project was not primarily anchored in an interior, singular self that sought to speak unencumbered by material forms. Instead, when Dons and her mission-feminist colleagues spoke, they were composite subjects, assembled at the meeting point of several trajectories. For them, spoken words were inseparable from material bodies. They also thought of their own speaking as, for example, Jesus speaking through their mouths, and they linked speaking with objects and effects in the world, such as church buildings or being drawn "closer" to the global mission. They thought of their speaking practices as something new, made possible in part through a new instantiation of what they called "woman's place." There is an interesting overlap here between the mission feminists' own reflections on speaking and the feminist new materialist lens I use. While they would not share my theoretical vocabulary, they would likely agree with the notion that their speaking was an ethical process of working in, with, and on woman's place and space, and that the space produced was not made through individual agency. Rather, my analysis of voice as throwntogetherness would lie closer to their understanding of the collective production of a woman's voice, composed by a variety of trajectories, including their bodies, their places and spaces, their gatherings, and their relations with more-than-human figures. The speaking Protestant woman was a multiple subject, and her ethical project was not under her individual control; it was enacted in moments in which trajectories came together.

AFTERWARD

A few months after the Summer School in July 1911, Henny Dons traveled to Scotland to participate in a mission meeting for women with around two hundred participants, held in St. Andrew's church in Edinburgh. Dons was asked to report on the meeting to the magazine *Sambaandet* (*The Bond*), published by the Western Norway Home Mission Association. Dons reported that she had asked one of the women in Edinburgh if it had proved difficult to organize the meeting, since women would be speaking inside a church. She conveyed the woman's response: "No, we are done with that here. Is there really anyone who still seriously thinks that Paul's word to women in Corinth applies to women in our time?" Dons added her own comment in her report: "To preach the gospel is not perceived here to be a *man's right*, but a *human right*."[58] In the same year, Dons signed an open letter to the Norwegian government, together with Marie Sinding and four other well-known Christian women, to request that women be given the right to speak inside churches in Norway; the letter was printed in the feminist women's magazine *Nylænde* (*New Frontiers*).[59] And indeed, in December 1911, five months after Dons spoke on the hillside, the law was changed, and women were granted the right to speak inside church buildings so long as they were not preaching (Norseth 2007, 434). (Beginning in 1925, women were also allowed to preach the word of God, both outside and inside churches, except at Sunday morning services; Norseth 2007, 440.)

Dons remained committed to the work of public speaking over the next decades as she invested much energy in giving talks to Christian audiences. For example, in 1921 she wrote in her annual report to NMS that she had given more than a hundred talks in the preceding year.[60] And among the materials left from her in the archive of the Mission School for Women are six notebooks filled with closely lined, handwritten notes for numerous public devotions and lectures she gave.[61]

As I have considered Dons's insistence on women's speaking throughout her life in the face of tensions around her, there is a final question I have sometimes wondered about: What did she think, through all of this, that Paul meant when he said women must be silent in the churches? Dons herself readily acknowledged that she did not subscribe to the more liberal Protestantism that was gaining a foothold among some scholars and a few pastors in Norway (though not in the more conservative mission circles, including in NMS), which advocated for elements of a historical and critical approach to biblical interpretation.[62] For example, when Dons volunteered to teach a course on mission history to a few future female missionaries in Kristiania in 1910 as part of the efforts of the Ladies' Committee, the chairman of the regional NMS committee sent her a letter to inquire whether she adhered to "the 'modern' theological standpoint" (though he noted that the committee would be prepared to approve her teaching of the course even if her views were somewhat modern).[63] She replied briefly: "Jesus Christ is my savior and my Lord. The coming of God's Kingdom is what I pray and strive for"; she added that her personal theology was "to receive and use the entire grace [*bruke hele naaden*] in Christ Jesus."[64] The chairman was satisfied and approved her teaching.[65] However, he still had some more specific questions about her relation to biblical texts: Did she believe in the virgin birth of Jesus? Did she believe Jesus's body was both buried and raised—that his tomb was empty? Dons dashed off a brief, cursive note across the bottom of his letter stating that her response was "a complete and unconditional *Yes*" and sent the letter back to him.[66] She did not wish to associate herself with more liberal readings.

Yet I grew curious about Dons's somewhat unusual formulation—to "use the entire grace"—when I realized she used it again in a book she wrote almost two decades later, *Women of the Bible*. In it, she suggested there were two reasons women had still not been "set on an equal footing" with men in Christian communities: it was difficult for the man to give up power, and it was difficult for the woman to "start using the entire grace that is at her disposal [*hennes rådighet*] through Jesus Christ" (1928, 67). Perhaps, then, Dons placed herself in relation to Paul by evaluating how she, as a woman, could "use the entire grace" at "her disposal"; maybe this is why Paul's statement in 1 Corinthians that women should keep silence in the churches did not mean, to her, that women should keep silence in the churches. It seems likely that she indirectly indicated a possible justification for this rereading when she reported the words of the woman in Edinburgh in 1911, namely that Paul's guidance was specific to a local situation and did not apply to all women.[67]

At the same time, it is possible that Paul's reasoning still held some sway for Dons, because—as far as I know—she never directly stated that she supported women's ordination as pastors.[68] In retrospect, it seems obvious to make the connection between Norwegian Lutheran women speaking in new ways in the early twentieth century and the later question of women's ordination: the stained-glass ceiling. However, Dons and her mission colleagues almost never advocated for women's ordination and only rarely even articulated the hope it might happen. It is difficult to know, therefore, what Dons made of the ordination of the first woman pastor in the Church of Norway, Ingrid Bjerkås, in 1961, exactly half a century after Dons's talk from the makeshift pulpit on the hillside at the Summer School. When Bjerkås was ordained, Dons was about to turn eighty-seven years old. Dons was surely informed of the strong counterprotests surrounding Bjerkås's ordination, including the negative vote from a majority of the bishops' council of the Church of Norway (Tønnesen 2014). Perhaps she also noted that NMS did not consider following suit. The tension that had channeled through Dons's gendered, speaking body in July 1911 was strong enough that this took three generations; in 1990, the NMS general assembly voted to hire women who would preach from pulpits as ordained pastors (Mosevoll 1992, 217–220).

03
WRITING

Sometime in the 1930s, Henny Dons took her place at the head of the oak dining table at the Mission School for Women and organized her stack of typed pages on mission history. She was there to teach her weekly lesson, and she looked around the table at the group of about ten young Norwegian women who wished to become missionaries. They were nearing the end of the term; they had learned the names, actions, and organizations of Christian men who had engaged in mission over the past two thousand years. Sometimes when Dons taught this class, she added a final lecture at the end of the term on "the women and the mission." This time, however, she decided not to include the supplemental material on women. She had already left it out of her book manuscript on mission history.[1]

I have puzzled over this scene for a long time. Why did Dons exclude women when she lectured on mission history to young women who wished to become missionaries? Why did she exclude women when she used those lecture notes to compile a book manuscript on the history of Christian mission?

To try to understand this scene, I will explore it here as an instance of Protestant writing. Writing was an important activity in Dons's life, and she produced a copious amount of published and unpublished texts, especially in the 1920s and 1930s.[2] During this time—when she was in her forties, fifties, and early sixties—she was employed by the Norwegian Mission Society (NMS) as the organization's children's secretary, in addition to teaching weekly lessons at NMS's Mission School for Women. Her prolific writing produced objects—books, pamphlets, pages—that helped to enact her work as they circulated among various Christian audiences.

Among the many writings Dons penned, some were mission histories. In fact, she was the first woman in NMS to author books in this genre. The particular genre of a confessional "mission history" was a useful genre within

NMS, as it explained what NMS was doing. Thus, mission history was an important subject at the Mission School (for men) in Stavanger, and mission history texts were also distributed much more widely among the NMS grassroots. The mission might otherwise be somewhat difficult to conceptualize for supporters in Norway, who encountered "the mission" through crafting work in their mission groups, through bazaars to raise money, through magazine stories and lantern slides, or through traveling speakers urging them to "answer the call." Within this context, some male authors had published mission history books that circulated within mission circles and provided instructive overviews, such as *The Norwegian Mission Society, Its Origin and Historical Development, Its Work Fields and Its Workers* (Landmark 1889) and *A Bantu People and Christianity: The Norwegian Mission Society's Seventy-Year Zulu Mission* (Stavem 1915). The genre of mission history had become a shared activity within the NMS tradition, used both to inform and to inspire. Dons too was drawn to it in her writing life.

In this chapter, I focus on three of Dons's engagements with the genre of mission history: first, a children's book written for use in children's mission groups in Norway, titled *Africa is Waiting* (Dons 1920a); second, a short book meant to be read by youth individually or in Christian groups, titled *The Christian Woman and the Heathen Mission* (Dons 1925a); and third, an unpublished and undated book manuscript, likely typed around 1936, which was based on Dons's lecture notes for her class on mission history at the Mission School for Women and probably meant to be given the title *The Gospel's Way to the Peoples*.[3] As I have considered these three texts, lined up on my desk, I have been surprised by the differences between them.

Each of the three texts is a tangible remnant of Dons's ethical engagement as it appeared and circulated in the world. Of the language practices I am interested in—listening, speaking, writing, reading—her writing is the practice that produced the most concrete artifacts: typed pages and books that could be distributed to audiences far beyond her own desk and beyond the sound of her own speaking voice. Inspired by the work of Courtney Handman (2017, 2018, 2019), I suggest that Dons's written texts form a type of Protestant infrastructure. Handman (2017, 316) has proposed that an "infrastructural account" of Christian language use can help us better understand its operations and effects, including the effects Christian language use has when it acts in infrastructural fashion to form modalities of circulation—communicative paths between places or channels between entities.[4] In this sense, Dons's writing acted as infrastructure for her ethical project of Protestant feminism. This infrastructure was made up of the written texts, their material circulation in books and typed pages, and the social interactions that clustered around them as people read and used them. The infrastructure was enabling, as it allowed Dons's ethical project to spread tangibly beyond herself. But more than that, the infrastructure was also productive; Dons's ethical project lived in the world through this material-discursive circulation, and thus the infrastructure produced the shape the project took.[5]

Yet there seem to be breaks in this infrastructure. For example, Dons wrote the children's book to be used in Christian girls' and boys' groups, and the text indicates that she wanted the young children to learn about the British Empire but not about women's mission societies. However, in the second text, her short book on women and mission, she did the opposite: she wished to circulate information to young women about women missionaries but not about imperialism. I have especially tripped over the fact that in the third text she chose to teach women students about mission history at the Mission School for Women by describing only what men had done. Therefore, the question that became a problem for me, and sparked this chapter, was: How did Dons's writing, her Protestantism, and her feminism connect? Why do each of her texts summon different worlds—whether an imperial world of "Christian Europe" and "dark Africa" (as in her children's book), or a world transformed by the rapidly rising women's movement (as in her women's book), or a world simply filled with men (as in her unpublished manuscript)? What does this writing infrastructure tell us about her ethical project of Protestant feminism as it was enacted in the world?

In the anthropological conversation on Christianity, one possible way of resolving these questions would be to view Dons's three texts as separate ethical actions that prioritize different ethical values. From this perspective, we might say that Dons and her Protestant community were guided by an abstracted value structure, or a hierarchy of values, and that each of their actions aimed to realize the most important value in the situation (Robbins 2013).[6] A similar line of thought has occasionally been expressed in studies of the Norwegian mission feminists; for example, as I will return to below, Lisbeth Mikaelsson (2002, 122) has proposed that, while most of Dons's writing was "feminist," Dons's argument that non-Christian women were helpless because of original sin was "antifeminist." In short, these idealist approaches to ethics suggest that we might be able to read Dons's writings and then triangulate and classify a coherent system of values that drives them, ranking feminism above or below other values, such as, perhaps, imperialism or evangelicalism.

However, I am not sure that we gain a better understanding of Dons's ethical project of Protestant feminism by classifying each of her actions as either valuing or devaluing feminism, or by dividing her actions into those we judge to be feminist, nonfeminist, or antifeminist; we can only do this if we assume we know what "feminism" (and "Protestantism") is and then evaluate each of Dons's writings based on our own definition. Instead, I think we gain deeper insight into Dons's ethical project by following it from text to text, from site to site, and examining how it was enacted in her world. This lens—a project ethics lens—allows us to see that Dons was not so much working from an abstracted system of values as she was working *on* values; that is, she was producing and changing Protestantism and feminism as she was enacting them in the world across different sites. As I have followed Dons's project from one text to another, it emerges as a single ethical project—a project, as she saw it, of Protestant feminism—that was not singular but rather internally multiple.

As mentioned in the introduction, my thinking about internal multiplicity has been shaped by the approach of science and technology scholar Annemarie Mol. In her study of atherosclerosis in *The Body Multiple*, Mol thinks in "spatial" terms (2002, 25). She argues that a body with atherosclerosis takes on a "multiple" form as "matters, terms, and aims travel from one place to another" and the body is enacted slightly differently across different sites in and around the hospital (2002, viii). Mol's argument that the body is "multiple" thus conveys the "manyfoldedness, but not pluralism" of a body; the multiple body is neither plural (it is not many bodies) nor singular (it is not constituted of different perspectives on the same body; 2002, 84). This raises the question: "What is it to hang together?" (2002, 83). Mol suggests the multiple body hangs together through "partial connections," a term she borrows from anthropologist Marilyn Strathern ([1991] 2004; Mol 2002, 80). The many enactments of the body are partially connected—they are joined to each other even as they pull apart. Mol (2002, 82) elaborates: "They are partially connected, more than one, and less than many." I will stretch this feminist new materialist approach to consider Dons's ethical project, which it seems to me was also characterized by internal multiplicity, by being "more than one, and less than many." It was enacted slightly differently across each of the different texts and their circulations that formed the infrastructure for her project in the world. From one text to the next, the project emerges as partially connected.

As I examine Dons's writing in this chapter, then, I argue that this Protestant writing took the form of a productive but partially connected infrastructure that constituted her ethical project of Protestant feminism—a project thus enacted as partially connected in the world. Why did Dons sit down at the oak dining table in the Mission School for Women and refuse women a place in the history she taught? I suggest it was not because she was devaluing feminism to replace it with a higher ethical value. Instead, she was enacting her ethical project of Protestant feminism as a multiple project. Like Mol, I will take a spatial approach and follow Dons's ethical project from site to site. To develop this argument, I will describe Dons's three mission histories in turn: a children's book, a women's book, and an unpublished manuscript.

A CHILDREN'S BOOK

I imagine an NMS girls' group in the 1920s. Perhaps a mother in a rural community has volunteered to be the leader, encouraged by her friends in the local mission women's group—though she is already busy with her daughters, the household, the vegetable rows and chickens, and the neighbors. She is happy to receive a copy of Dons's (1920a) book written to help her, *Afrika venter: Barnebok om misjonen* (*Africa is Waiting: A Children's Book about the Mission*). The book is forty-eight pages long, including many pictures, and is divided into ten short chapters or "lessons." The mother reads the foreword, in which Dons suggests that she might read the book out loud to the children, one lesson at a time (1920a, 2), and she decides to hold the meetings in her home, as Dons advises (1919, 6). She invites a small crowd of her daughters' friends and acquaintances from the village and surrounding farms.

At the meeting, perhaps around twenty girls in the pinafores and long-sleeved dresses of 1920s Norway, hair in braids, congregate in her living room, squeezing together on the sofa and forming a circle on the floor. They are more than willing to loudly join in the Christian children's song the mother starts off with and then listen in anticipation as she recites a Bible verse, prays for the meeting, and records their names in a book (Dons 1919, 7, 13). She tells them they may work on the crafts they have brought from home—some embroidering, some crocheting—or take notes in a notebook during the lesson, because she finds herself fully in agreement with Dons's observation that children need something to do with their hands as well as their minds during the meeting (1919, 9).

The mother then begins with the first sentence of the "first lesson" of *Africa is Waiting*. "Africa has been called 'the dark continent,'" she reads out loud to the girls, "because it took so long before we in Europe got to know what life was like on this continent." She shows them the pictures on the first spread, including a photograph of two serious African girls carrying small siblings on their backs, standing in front of a grass house. The mother continues reading out loud: "The people of Africa are among those with the darkest skin in the world. And the darkness of heathendom is also thick and dense" (1920a, 4). She lets the girls study the map of Africa and teaches them the names Dons provides for major rivers and lakes, deserts, and people groups. Then they hear about the first European explorers and traders who "dreamed of becoming rich in Africa." But, the mother explains, "nobody thought of the poor people who lived there, and who were often treated in such a gruesome manner by the white people." She shows the girls some of the names "that tell us what the Europeans wanted in Africa": the Slave Coast, the Gold Coast, the Ivory Coast. "This is the great sin of Christian Europe against Africa," she continues reading; "Nobody brought the light of Jesus Christ." This light, she instructs the girls, is what Africa is waiting for, and she ends the lesson by asking them to raise their hand if they are able to answer Dons's questions: "Who will bring it? Will you? Will I? . . . What can you do? What will you do?" (1920a, 6).

Henny Dons became the first woman employed in the NMS central administration when she left her teacher's position to be hired as NMS's first children's secretary in 1917. I ponder what this meant to her as I look at a photograph from the NMS consultation meeting (*rådsmøtet*) in 1919, a meeting of all central decision-makers in the organization (Nome 1943b, 148). Dons was joined by two other women, Miss Hirt and Miss Ottesen, and they sit alongside forty-nine men in dark suits. In her new job, she worked to support NMS children's groups, in which children gathered every fortnight to learn about the mission. At the end of 1918, she reported 440 NMS children's groups; this number quickly doubled to somewhere between 900 and 1,000 groups a decade later.[7] Dons preferred boys' groups and girls' groups to meet separately, though this was not always possible because of a lack of leaders.[8] The work was skewed in terms of gender; in 1921, she reported 40 boys' groups out of a total of 740 children's groups, and on another occasion she observed that the majority of the groups were led by women.[9] In the archival sources, Dons appears pleased with this work; unlike the occasional critical remarks aimed at the mission women's groups, I have not come across such criticism of the children's groups. In fact, after a couple of years the children's work had gained such momentum that NMS appointed another woman, Anna Michelsen, to assist Dons, and when Michelsen stepped down due to illness in 1920, Julie Ellingsen took her place.[10]

Ellingsen and Dons lived at Pilestredet 83, a large, multistory house NMS first rented and then purchased in Kristiania.[11] The house's elegant facade presented a front door framed by iron columns under a series of thin, arched windows, overlooking a spacious park. The house also served as the NMS office for children's work. In addition, Dons regularly rented out the many rooms in the house, on behalf of NMS, to other Christian women.[12] The house became, in effect, a women's communal living and working space tied to the mission. It provides a counterpoint to the photograph of the NMS consultation meeting in 1919, in which Dons is difficult to find amid the rows and rows of suits. In contrast, the women's space of the large house fits within what Adrienne Rich (1994) has conceptualized as a long history of women living outside the expectations of heterosexual marriage, sustaining relationships with other women that, even if nonromantic, leave significant marks through domestic companionship, collaborative work, or friendship.[13]

In the large house, Dons and Ellingsen coordinated their efforts. Ellingsen focused mostly on supporting needlework, woodwork, and other craftwork in the NMS children's groups by distributing instructions, patterns, models, and materials. Dons focused on editing *Barnebladet* (NMS's *Children's Magazine*), arranging courses for the leaders, and providing written texts.[14] She wrote several books for them, such as *Africa is Waiting* (1920a), *China is Waiting* (1920b), and *Madagascar is Waiting* (1922), and collections of stories and guidance for the groups (1915, 1919, 1923a).

Let me return to what the young Norwegian girls in my imagined girls' group thought as they listened their way through the second lesson of *Africa is Waiting*. It is a long lesson on the transatlantic slave trade. Sometimes, Dons (1920a, 2) comments in her foreword, one lesson may be too long for the children and may need to be divided in two; she suggests asking the children what they remember from the first part before starting the second. In another book, she advises that children remember more if you "tell," "show," and "talk with them" in addition to reading (1920b, 3). Perhaps the mother follows Dons's advice and, as she begins the second part of the lesson on the slave trade, asks the girls what they remember from the first. If they do not remember the statistics and the location of trade routes, perhaps they remember the vivid and terrifying story Dons recounts about an African mother and her small children being captured at night and driven through the forest. When one of the young daughters is struck on the head and collapses from exhaustion, her hand is cut off to free her from the ropes and she is left to die, pleading with her mother to help her; the mother cannot break free of the ropes and clutches at her baby as one of the slave traders reaches to tear it away. In the girls' group, the Norwegian mother might remind the girls of Dons's words: "It is a terrible thing that *Christian Europe* has traded slaves in Africa" (1920a, 7), before reading the second half of the lesson on how Great Britain abolished slavery. What Africa is waiting for, the girls now learn, is that "we Christians must try to make good toward Africa the sin that has been committed against it through many, many centuries by Christian Europe," and Dons encourages her audience to adopt the prayer "forgive us our sins" as "a mission prayer" (1920a, 11).

The girls continue learning about the relationship between Europe and Africa in the next three lessons, which describe Protestant mission work in Southern Africa, with a particular focus on the work of NMS. In passing, they learn that the Dutch settlers, or Boers, did not treat Africans well. But, the mother reads, the British are now "masters" in South Africa, and this has made it easier for the mission as many new missionaries have arrived "and the light of Jesus [has begun] to shine in many places" (1920a, 13). Perhaps the girls are struck by what a Zulu girl is able to do: although she is early given chores to help her mother, she is a capable helper, and she can carry a jar of water on her head while walking easily and braiding a bracelet of grass at the same time (1920a, 22). However, there is a change as she matures and is "sold" into marriage. Perhaps the Norwegian mother talks with the girls about how Zulu mothers "love their children very much and care for them as best they understand," but apparently they do not understand that children should not always get their will, be dirty all over their bodies, nor be left alone in a hut with an open fire (1920a, 21). The Norwegian girls learn that the British defeated the Zulu king in 1879 and this brought "peace and quiet" for a few years, though it was "not easy" for the willful Zulu to "bow" and they "tried to revolt," endangering the missionaries (1920a, 23–24). The girls crane their necks to see the photograph of Zulus seated inside a church, and the mother reads that from 1900 onward there has been "peace and order" in Zululand under British rule, which has allowed the mission to progress (1920a, 24).

One of NMS's female traveling secretaries who traveled around to visit NMS's groups, Rachel Lange, noted approvingly that some children's group leaders let one child borrow the book they were reading each time. The child would learn a section by heart and recite it to the group at the next meeting.[15] I imagine some of the older girls borrowing *Africa is Waiting* in turn and memorizing sections from the next four lessons: on David Livingstone and on the missions in Uganda, the Congo, and colonial Sudan. When they arrive at the tenth and final lesson, on Muslims in North Africa, perhaps the mother begins by reminding the Norwegian girls that Muslims are "the

Christians' worst enemies" and Muhammad started a "holy war" against Christians (1920a, 39, 45), before a girl stands up to recite the story she has learned by heart about a Muslim bride on her wedding day: "Go over to the crate and lift the curtain that hangs over it, and you will see a sorry sight. A nine-year-old girl is squatting in the crate and staring at you. Her hair hangs matted, her eyes are swollen from crying" (1920a, 47). The girl-bride is desperate, exhausted, and after dancing for her new husband through the night, is beaten by him (1920a, 47–48). Perhaps the girls study the final photograph of a group of male African church leaders from across the continent before the mother allows them to ask questions about what they have just heard.

To end the meeting, the girls sing a closing song while passing around the "mission box" in which they may donate some of their pocket money (Dons 1919, 12). Finally, the mother instructs them to kneel around the living room, fold their hands, close their eyes, bow their heads, and pray "forgive us our sins"—the prayer that here meant they desired to help the "waiting" Africa.

PRODUCING PROTESTANT-FEMINIST SENTIMENTS

It is easy to see, a century later, how Dons's mission history for children fits into "the colonial library," as Gaurav Desai (2001, 4–5) defines it: "The set of representations and texts that have collectively 'invented' Africa as a locus of difference and alterity," a set of images that remain at once curiously routinized even as they are contested, and that together "*do* things" in the world. We recognize the all-too-familiar images as the young Norwegian girls are taught to associate "Africa" with darkness, lack, dirt, and ignorance; to associate "Islam" with enmity, cruelty, violence, and male dominance; and to associate "Europe" with Christianity, victory, peace and order, and an ability to repent for past sins. In the colonial library, Protestantism cannot be neatly untangled from these conjoined images, from race and empire. They constitute each other in a specific "form of life," to use Wittgenstein's term (Drury 1973, x), or, as David Chidester (2020, 43) puts it, "a form of life and a form of death."

It is perhaps less easy to see how Dons's mission history for children is feminist. Was it part of her lifelong exploration of the question of Christian women's place? The African women she presents in the book are helpless figures, in need of a Christianity preached by men. I have only mentioned some of these figures, but they are sufficient: the enslaved mother, the ignorant mother, the Zulu girl who grows up to be "sold" into marriage, the abused Muslim girl-bride. The Norwegian girls surely picked up on the underlying message: proper marriage and motherhood remain impossible for African women as long as they remain either "heathen" or Muslim. However, Dons is not concerned here to communicate the role of European women in this mission. She almost exclusively describes male missionaries, and all the book's pictures of church workers, both European and African, are of men.

At first, I wondered why she excluded her feminism when teaching young Norwegian girls about mission. As noted, Lisbeth Mikaelsson has taken this line of thought one step further. In general, Mikaelsson (2002, 2003) has argued for the importance of using the label "feminist" for Dons and her peers (such as the China missionary Marie Monsen). Mikaelsson adopts a broad understanding of what such feminism might encompass, to enable us to trace how religious women sometimes, though not always, challenged gender hierarchies. In one instance, however, Mikaelsson finds Dons to be "antifeminist," namely when Dons described non-Christian women as helpless and stated that this was part of the punishment women had to endure because of Eve's original sin, alleviated only by Jesus (Mikaelsson 2002, 122, commenting especially on Dons 1928, 9). This raises the question: Was Dons feminist in some writings but antifeminist in others? In the end, I have arrived at a different answer than Mikaelsson. Rather than divide Dons's writing into feminist, nonfeminist, or antifeminist ideas, I am instead interested in following the distribution of Dons's ethical project of Protestant feminism across its various sites. As Lisa Lowe (2015) has argued, we often tend to read the colonial archive and the liberal archive separately, as two histories, but we gain a far deeper understanding of global history from the turn of the nineteenth century onward once we read these archives together. Let me do so here, as it can help us see Dons's multiple project.

My context, then, is the complex configuration that occurred in northern Europe at the turn of the twentieth century, when the growing Protestant mission movement intersected with both the so-called high age of the British Empire and the expanding women's movement. On the one hand, Dons and her women colleagues saw themselves as standing in the midst of a large historical change as they kept track of the expansion of Protestant mission work both numerically and geographically around the globe. The bulk of Protestant missionaries were sent from northern Europe and North America to sub-Saharan Africa, India, and China, and the engagement of Scandinavian organizations in this new project situated the region within new transnational networks (Nielssen, Okkenhaug, and Skeie 2011).

The rise of Protestant missions at the time was such that when more than a thousand Protestant mission leaders—including the leader of NMS, Lars Dahle—gathered for the World Missionary Conference in Edinburgh in 1910, they adopted the confident "watchword": "The Evangelization of the World in This Generation" (Stanley 2009, 88).

These Protestant mission activities overlapped unevenly with the expansion of the British Empire in the nineteenth century and into the twentieth, and to some degree also with French colonization, in a long historical co-occurrence of Protestant mission and north European colonialism (see, e.g., Etherington 2005). Within NMS, the question of how to relate Protestant mission and colonialism had been the subject of heightened debate a few decades earlier during Britain's invasion of the independent kingdom of Zululand in 1879, the ensuing Zulu civil war in the 1880s, and the eventual formal British annexation in 1887. A majority of Norwegian missionaries in Natal and Zululand developed a theological justification for this specific act of imperialism, which historian Jarle Simensen (1986, 94) has labeled the "humiliation thesis." It was commonly expressed among the Norwegian missionaries in the argument that the Zulus had displayed such willful "hard-heartedness" toward the mission that God needed to "humiliate" them through a violent British invasion and victory for them to realize their need for the Christian gospel. A few Norwegian missionaries questioned the humiliation thesis during and after their wartime evacuation, but most stepped into their new role as theological cheerleaders for Empire, and the humiliation thesis became NMS's official line (Hovland 2013, 201–225). It was later repeated in the writings of Dons.

Dons's book *Africa is Waiting* weaves together descriptions of Zulu mothers allowing their children to be willful and a Zulu people who did not find it "easy" to "bow" to the British, but who in the end reached "peace and order" under British rule. Dons spelled out the same sentiment in theological terms in one of her lecture notes on mission history: "Lutheran Christianity, with its clear view of *sin* and *grace*, faces many challenges among the superficial and self-righteous [*selvgode*] Zulu people."[16] She repeated the same argument both before and after her seven-month stay with the Norwegian mission in South Africa in 1928,[17] showing that her interactions with Zulu Christians and NMS missionaries did not alter her view on the relation between Christianity and colonialism; the view must have been quite settled in the Norwegian mission in South Africa by this point. In fact, by the time Dons was writing in the 1920s and 1930s, she repeated it in such an offhand manner that it is clear it was no longer subject to questioning. In this case, she also mirrored the broader contemporary attitude in Norway, where the British Empire was glorified in history textbooks of the time (Reistad 2014). For Dons, a Norwegian Lutheran woman in the early twentieth century, British imperialism had become not only right but also thoroughly routine.[18]

The spread of Protestant mission and the violence of the British Empire occurred alongside an expansion of women's roles in northern Europe. The women's movement gathered pace. The mission began offering opportunities for single, middle-class (or aspirational middle-class) women to be respectably employed with a salary as teachers or midwives, say in Zululand. And knowledge of the growing mission world also presented new opportunities for married middle-class or farming women in Norway to gain access to an expanded world, an outlook of "Christian globalism" (Kaell 2020a) that could bring with it a sense of their significance. While mission-supporting women in Norway might seem to be on the periphery of the Empire, then, they and other women around the North Atlantic contributed wittingly and unwittingly to larger transnational processes as they knitted together faith, race, nationalism, political and religious expansion, and their own changing status as women (Halvorson and Hovland 2021; Hill 1985; Okkenhaug 2003).

Here I am particularly interested in holding onto the difficulties this world presents to us today, such as the difficulties of understanding how both feminist and Protestant histories have been formed. In this case, the imperial occurred in tandem with the liberal—such as the emphasis on universal human dignity, abolition, and rule of law. The Norwegian girls squeezed together on the sofa in the living room were learning the new Protestant, colonial-liberal sentiments of early twentieth-century northern Europe: they should feel compassion for Zulu girls whom they were told were so capable when young and then turned into ineffective mothers, they should help atone for the past wrongs of European slavers by wanting to help, they should be grateful they were not born Muslim, they—as girls—should be treated well, and they lived in "Christian Europe," a continent given form through its contrast with "dark" Africa. In these combined sentiments, the Protestant and imperialist and feminist aspects cannot be picked apart. Together they presented to the young Norwegian girls a new sense of feminist responsibility: "What will you do?" (Dons 1920a, 6).

In this context, I think Dons's incorporation of stories of helpless "heathen" and Muslim women in her text was not "antifeminist" but rather a core part of her feminism. In certain sites, though not all, her feminism matches what the historian Susan Thorne has termed "missionary imperial feminism"; Thorne (1999, 60) argues that in this feminism, the emancipatory aspirations of white Protestant women in the North Atlantic world were braided together with the "female Other," at home and abroad, who was stereotyped as unfree. Similarly, mission feminists in Norway were able to combine their new ideas about gender relations with their loyalty to male-led Christian institutions in part through concentrating on the discursive, affective presence of this "other" woman, in particular in the colonies.[19] I suggest that rather than the "other," it is more accurate here to say the "third," because the imagined woman in the colonies was placed in a triangular relationship: the figure of "the Zulu woman" or "the Muhammedan woman" in Africa disrupted the relation between Christian women and men in Norway. Such third figures—the imagined religious women figures around the world—served as fictionalized depictions that nevertheless were meant to be experienced as quite real. The figures stood at a distance, helping to show the perceived harms of both non-Christian religions and gender inequality, without directly addressing gender inequality in Norway itself. The figures also helped to make urgent two related questions: Who is responsible for this? And who will respond? In *Africa is Waiting*, then, Dons's Protestant-feminist project is enacted in the stereotyped third figure—the young Zulu woman "sold" into marriage, the mistreated Muslim girl-bride in North Africa—who could so effectively teach Norwegian girls piled into a rural living room the new affects of Protestant feminism, laminated as they were with both contemporary liberalism and colonialism.

A WOMEN'S BOOK

I imagine a group of young women friends in their teens in Norway in the late 1920s. Perhaps they live in a small town, and one or two of them are toying with the idea of moving to attend a teachers' college or nursing school. Perhaps they first became intrigued by the expansion of overseas mission through a local children's group and later through meetings held by NMS's traveling male preachers showing lantern slides from Madagascar or China. Maybe one of them found the intrigue significant enough to ask her father to buy one of the books the preachers displayed—a small book about women and mission, authored by Henny Dons. Now she invites her friends to read the book with her in a mission study circle.

This is the second text I will examine: *Den kristne kvinne og hedningemisjonen: En historisk oversikt* (*The Christian Woman and the Heathen Mission:*

A Historical Overview) (Dons 1925a). The forty-six-page book was published in 1925 by a Norwegian Christian publishing house, Lutherstiftelsens Forlag. Dons explained in the foreword that she wrote this book to mark the twenty-fifth anniversary of the education of female missionaries in Norway, since the Ladies' Committee was formed in Kristiania in 1900 and began arranging ad hoc courses for a couple of young women every two years. Dons, who chaired the Ladies' Committee from 1910 until it was dissolved when NMS's Mission School for Women was formally established in 1920, said she wished to write the history of women and mission for contemporary young people (1925a, 3).[20] To facilitate the use of the book, she included a two-page study guide in the back, and she suggested it could be used in a Young Women's Christian Association group or in a "study circle" (*studiekrets*). A study circle referred to a small, self-organized group of youth who gathered to study different aspects of Protestant mission, and Dons supported such groups through being a member of the Mission Study Council of Norway, the committee that organized the popular Mission Summer Schools and helped publish mission literature.

My imagined study circle of young women friends take to heart Dons's guidelines: five to ten members is sufficient, and they ought to meet four times to go through the book. They can read a section beforehand, then gather to talk about it so as to gain "greater insight and deeper understanding" before praying together (Dons 1925a, 46). The friends pass the book from one to another until everyone has read the introduction, and then they meet to talk about its themes: Jesus gathered "women too" as "his messengers," and he is the one who "released woman from the spirit of helplessness that had weighed on her from generation to generation" (1925a, 5–6).[21] Perhaps the young women discuss what it means that their contemporaries among "Jews and heathens" still have this spirit of helplessness, according to Dons, whereas they, as Christian women, are "happy and free" (1925a, 6). They may talk about how women have great influence in homes, and in turn on the next generation, and how Christianity cannot make inroads in a society unless women are reached in their homes. Therefore, "Christ is calling women" to "help their sisters to claim their right," and this is "the same right" as men—"the right to salvation and service" (1925a, 7).

At their next meeting, they start at the beginning of Protestant mission history, which Dons locates around 1800 with the wave of new evangelical mission organizations in Europe and North America. The young women learn that some women formed all-women's mission societies in England and the United States. However, Dons does not mention the British Empire.

In fact, she does the opposite here of what she did in her children's book, where she discussed Britain's role in abolishing the slave trade and ruling colonial territories but did not mention British women engaged in mission.

The study circle then turns to the history of women's roles in the mission movement in Norway, and they work through the mass of information methodically. Dons spends a long time on the history of the mission women's groups in the latter half of the nineteenth century, and the young women read a description of one of the first women's groups, gathered together by pastor's wife Gustava Kielland when she invited some of her friends to bring their crafts and join her in the parsonage for a workday each month. They also read a description of the women's groups started by bishop's wife Henriette Gislesen, which all prayed the same written prayer at each meeting—"Mrs. Bishop Gislesen's Mission Prayer." The young women consider the fact that NMS's mission ship *Elieser*—the sailing vessel that carried missionaries between Norway and Southern Africa from the 1860s to the 1890s—had been purchased with donations gathered by the female teacher Louise Olsen in Bergen. They learn how the movement of mission women's groups spread across Norway and became NMS's main source of income, and they answer the question: "What is it about the women's groups that have turned them in particular into such great blessing?" (Dons 1925a, 46).

At their final meeting, they work to understand how the Mission School for Women was established through the logistical work of the Ladies' Committee, while the committee's chair, Bolette Gjør, provided information about the cause in NMS women's magazine. They turn to the final item in Dons's study guide: "To examine the particular demands that the mission work today makes of women at home and out there" (1925a, 46). They marvel at the centrality of the missionary wife, who usually spends most of her time on "these small things that a woman knows to take care of, because so much in the course of daily life is made up simply of these small things," yet in doing so she is showing her "heathen" sisters their "human worth" (1925a, 34). They might try to remember the many names and the wealth of information Dons provides about contemporary Norwegian female missionaries, or perhaps they note these women's roles as teachers and nurses and in women's work, and answer the questions: "Which education should young women seek if they wish to become missionaries? Which character traits are necessary?" (1925a, 46).

They end by studying the numbers Dons discusses on the last few pages: two hundred, four hundred, and four hundred million. Dons says that at the time of writing there were around two hundred Norwegian female missionaries and missionary wives in "the heathen mission." Moreover, she says, there were around four hundred female missionaries among the many participants at the World Missionary Conference in New York in 1900, which gathered mission leaders from Europe and North America; "Who could have foreseen such a possibility in 1800?" This conference shows "the peculiar development" in women's life over the past century, Dons tells her readers. Finally, Dons says, there are more than four hundred million "heathen" and "Muhammedan" women "in the deepest darkness" (1925a, 42–43). I imagine the young women studying what these numbers mean for them: two hundred Norwegian women in "the mission field," four hundred women at a mission conference, four hundred million "heathen" and "Muhammedan" women in the world.[22] Perhaps they wonder about their own connection to these numbers as they consider the question that concludes the book: "What is the response of Christian women to this call?" (1925a, 44).

PRODUCING PROTESTANT-FEMINIST SUBJECTIVITIES

If we think of Christian language through an infrastructural lens, as Handman (2017, 2018, 2019) suggests, we see how Dons used writing to produce certain circulations. Her writings circulated through audiences—various mission groups—that used similar texts in similar ways to produce something as part of a circuit. As the texts and the audiences came together, we might say they operated in what Britt Halvorson (2018) has called "conversionary sites"—that is, spaces that connect dispersed communities through the circulation of objects and values but transform both the objects and values as they pass through. The sites act as "busy moral crossroads" (Halvorson 2018, 4).

Dons's book *The Christian Woman and the Heathen Mission* was meant to be used and converted into something, such as knowledge, then engagement and donations, then women's missionary education and women as missionaries, and eventually Christian conversions of women around the world. In this sense, it was similar to Dons's children's book, *Africa is Waiting*, which was also a text meant not just to be read but also to be turned into something: children's learning, interest in the mission, and future donations and actions to benefit the mission. The written texts created connections between places and people—between the two hundred, the four hundred, and the four hundred million. The young friends in my imagined study circle could use Dons's book to work out their place in this circuit. They could locate themselves in a women's world, which was presented to them as having importance: it was a world made up of two hundred important Christian women missionaries and four hundred million non-Christian women whom it was important to reach.

But I wonder about the points that seem to be breaks in the infrastructure, breaks in the circuit between Dons's children's book and her women's book. In particular, there are breaks in the production of gendered subjects. Dons urges the young women in the study circle to learn about British women's mission societies, but not the British Empire. She wants the girls in the children's group to do the opposite: to learn about the British Empire, but not women's mission societies. She makes the little girls vividly imagine the third figure of the Zulu mother or Muslim girl-bride, but not the names or actions of Norwegian women. On the other hand, in the study book for young women she thinks it important to paint a detailed picture of Norwegian women's actions in relation to a number: four hundred million women who need to be reached around the world. In both cases, she is working to produce Protestant feminist subjects, but the way in which this subject is gendered is inconsistent—as if under construction, with different aspects being torn down and erected at different angles.

There are also breaks in the production of racialized subjects. Dons's writing is one of the areas in which her racialized subjectivity—her lived, embodied conceptualization of being white—emerges most clearly. She enacted white womanhood through writing. However, this too did not result in a stable identity category—"a white Protestant woman"—but rather a series of distributed operations that differ across sites. Dons's children's book indicates that whiteness is tied to light, the opposite of dark. The lightness is in turn tied to Europe, but the Europe that emerges is primarily one constituted by men—by their abolition and imperialism, their atonement and knowledge—rather than by women. In Dons's women's book, on the other hand, she indicates that whiteness is tied, for example, to a list of names of Norwegian women missionaries, as juxtaposed with the large number of "heathen" and "Muhammedan" women. In this book, Dons also wishes to make explicit a recent change in whiteness, namely the possibility that has opened up for white women to work in missions or to attend conferences alongside white men. Her different enactment of whiteness in the two books is an example of how whiteness was enacted unevenly across her texts, but also how experiences of white subjectivity can shift.

In this broken-up infrastructure, Dons's Protestant writing was a technology that operated to produce readers or listeners as certain people with certain relations, though the exact characteristics of these people and relations were harder to pin down as they shifted from one text to another. As an author, then, it appears Dons was both affected by and sought to affect changes in gendered and racialized subjects as she worked on her project of Protestant feminism, but the enactment of her project spanned various sites that were only partially connected.[23]

AN UNPUBLISHED MANUSCRIPT

I imagine the women around the large oak dining table preparing to take notes during Henny Dons's lecture in the residential schoolhouse of NMS's Mission School for Women.[24] Dons is in her early sixties and has taught this material many times before; she has been responsible for the class on mission history at the school during the 1920s and 1930s, from her midforties until now, one hour per week.[25] She has used her lecture notes as the basis for a book manuscript she is teaching from this term—a stack of typed pages lying in front of her on the table.

We know about Dons's typewritten book manuscript on mission history because she saved it, with a title page that says, in her handwriting, *Misjonshistorie, utarbeidet av frk. Henny Dons* (*Mission History, Written out by Miss Henny Dons*), and then someone else saved it, eventually making it part of the archival collection of the Mission School for Women. The manuscript is based on her two sets of typed lecture notes for her class on mission history, which have also been saved in the same archive.[26] A note has been made on the front page of one of these sets of lectures, saying that it was used for many years by teachers after Dons.[27] Similarly, in the typewritten book manuscript, several pages have been annotated with handwritten notes by someone other than Dons, suggesting that someone else used her manuscript to teach mission history after Dons retired.

The draft manuscript consists of a stack of 107 pages altogether. It begins with seventy-nine typed pages with sections not yet placed in order (though the intended order is given in the table of contents) and continues with another twenty-eight typed pages at the end containing various additions probably meant to be incorporated into the main text. There is no date on the title page, but it seems likely that this is the manuscript Dons mentioned in a letter to NMS in 1936, in which she said she had completed a book manuscript on mission history to be titled *Evangeliets vei til folkene* (*The Gospel's Way to the Peoples*).[28] The title is a slight revision of the title she gave one set of her lecture notes: "God's Way to the Peoples."[29] She said in her letter to NMS that she had asked the Christian press Lutherstiftelsen if they would publish it; they had published her earlier book *The Christian Woman and the Heathen Mission* as well as her Bible studies on women in the Bible and for youth (Dons 1925a, 1928, 1933). However, they were not interested. She therefore turned to NMS, which had published her books for the children's groups and a pamphlet on women and mission (Dons 1919, 1920a, 1920b, 1922, 1923a, 1923b), to ask if they would publish it. She explained why she thought there was a need for such a book. I do not have NMS's reply; all I know is that NMS did not publish the book.

The large communal house where Dons still lived with other women in Oslo, at Pilestredet 83, was not far from the Mission School for Women at Colletts Gate 33. Dons may have walked the ten minutes to teach her weekly lesson, through the park and down the old streets of Wilhelms Gate and Louises Gate until she arrived at the three-story residential schoolhouse on the corner across from another park. There were usually around ten young women enrolled in each two-year cohort at the school.[30] Their life at the school was strictly regulated and formed another all-women's community. Two or three students shared each bedroom. They ate all meals together, took lessons together around the dining table, did their homework in the afternoon, and enjoyed each other's company in the living room after dinner. They took turns helping with dinner, dishes, and laundry. They were not allowed to go out without permission.[31] As they readied themselves for Dons's lesson, they were likely wearing the dresses or long skirts and blouses we see in pictures from the school, with their long hair pinned back.[32] If it was cold and windy outside, perhaps they had adjusted the central heating, a modern invention installed just a few years earlier, following the recent novelties of an electric refrigerator in the kitchen and running water in the bathroom.[33] I imagine them taking their seats and placing their composition notebooks on the dining table as Dons took out her typed pages. Since her unpublished book manuscript was based on her lecture notes and was used to teach this class after her retirement, it is likely she herself used it to teach the class in the late 1930s.

What does she wish to teach the women students as they all sit down around the dining table? Dons begins the term by addressing early and medieval Christian mission. She is primarily concerned to provide historical data—a sequence of men, places, and events. But she intersperses brief evaluations to communicate a larger argument about what she thinks mission ought to be. For example, when outlining the sequence of political and at times violent events that led to the Christianization of Norway in the tenth and eleventh centuries, she concludes that we see "quite a mixed picture when we look at Norway as a mission field," and she terms these events "a mission of the sword."[34] She is sharply critical of the Crusades, because "one cannot imagine a mission method that is less Christian," and "conquest and mission went hand in hand" when conquered people were baptized by force, she instructs the students.[35] She is also critical of the Christianization of Latin America during the early modern period, because she argues that mission was at times used as a rationalization for political conquest, and much of this mission too was carried out by force, which led, in her view, to a "superficial" Christianity. However, she speaks favorably of those Catholic missionaries "who defended the natives against the European colonists" to prevent violence.[36]

In her next lesson, she moves on to the Reformation, and I wonder whether any of her students noticed that her portrayal of "conquest" now shifts from negative to positive. The Reformation, she argues, provided a vision of "faith that achieves victory over the world," and through the pietistic movement (which was closely associated with the evangelical revivals in Scandinavia) this vision became "an active conquering force."[37] She proposes that the "breakthrough of the thought of mission [*misjonstanken*]" occurred around 1800 with the evangelical "mission revivals" and their resulting mission organizations. Perhaps she and her students discuss how she saw mission history as the history of a long Catholic lead-up to a remarkable Protestant evangelical breakthrough that marked the beginning of "Christianity's greatest time of conquest."[38] She is sharply critical of the transatlantic slave trade, instructing the young women that this is "the darkest shade on the 'Christianity' of the white race."[39] On the same page, she discusses the rise of the British Empire in favorable terms. She repeats this view in a later discussion of Southern Africa, telling her students that the British Empire's rule over the area has allowed mission work to progress.[40]

Long sections of her lessons and manuscript are then devoted to a historical overview of Protestant mission from around 1800 until the early 1900s. The tone is mostly descriptive, and I imagine Dons lecturing in detail on events, organizations, places, and a series of men. She focuses on the mission in India, Africa, Madagascar, and China. In each section, she outlines Protestant mission activities in general as well as the contributions of Norwegian mission organizations and male staff. The overall picture she paints is one of exciting growth over the past hundred years, which she and her contemporaries are in the midst of experiencing.

In her lecture notes and manuscript, two thousand years of Christian mission history is presented as a history of men. She does not seek to demonstrate the role of women in mission, and only mentions women in passing, such as when mentioning the plight, as she saw it, of women in India.[41] She does not mention the mission women's groups in Norway nor the long series of women missionaries to whom she devoted so many pages in the book discussed above, *The Christian Woman and the Heathen Mission*. Her lecture notes indicate that she sometimes, though not always, added a supplemental lecture at the end of the term titled "Women's mission work" or "The women and the mission."[42] Having spent the course presenting two thousand years of mission history largely without speaking about women, she would speak about them on the last day. In her book manuscript, however, even this final lecture on "the women and the mission" has been removed.

PRODUCING PROTESTANT-FEMINIST SIGNIFICANCE

As with her previous mission histories, Dons's manuscript too can be seen as part of an infrastructural circuit. Dons, and teachers after her who continued to use her lecture notes and unpublished manuscript to teach mission history at the Mission School for Women, converted the text into women's knowledge, which was in turn meant to be converted into conversions—in Zululand, Natal, Madagascar, India, and China. It was also meant to be converted into the elevation of Norwegian women within NMS in Norway. But again I have paused at the apparent breaks in the circuit. Why teach mission history to women students in the Mission School for Women with almost no mention of women? In this manuscript, Dons dwells neither on the third figure of "the heathen woman" or "Muhammedan woman," nor on the figure of the female missionary or the Norwegian women who supported the mission through prayer and donations. Why spend a term presenting and discussing a long sequence of men? She had written material readily available, from *The Christian Woman and the Heathen Mission* as well as other texts, that addressed the contributions of the mission women's groups in Norway, the history of women's mission societies, the names of female missionaries and descriptions of their roles. But she chose not to use it. How to understand, from her perspective, her ethical project here?

As I contemplated this puzzle, the first option I considered was that she took on the limitations of the genre in which she was writing. It is possible she was finding her way as a woman author in this male-dominated genre of mission history and knew only the way that had been staked out ahead of her. Within this genre, one might write about women in a separate book, for a separate audience. But if one was recounting the main mission history, selecting the most important people and events, one would not select women or their actions. The central historical events were all male. This option says something about the genre. However, it does not seem plausible to me that Dons unthinkingly took on this limitation, since she argues strongly in other contexts for the pivotal role played by women in this history.

I therefore considered another possible explanation: perhaps she strategically chose to exclude women from her manuscript to ensure it would not be rejected. She may have been protecting herself and her work as a woman author entering a published, public forum. However, this option does not seem plausible either, because she also excluded women in her lecture notes. When sitting around a dining table with a small group of women mission students, it does not seem likely that she needed to strategically keep women absent to avoid rejection.

A third possible explanation, then, and one that seems most likely to me, is that her scene of writing is difficult for me to understand because her ethical project was enacted differently across different sites. Dons's written texts and their circulation formed the concrete infrastructure for her ethical project, but each text and its interactions were only partially connected to the others. At the site of the Mission School for Women in Oslo in the 1930s, Dons—a woman teacher of mission history—was sitting at a table with young women studying to become missionaries. She was teaching on a topic, mission history, that had been taught to men in the Mission School (for men) in Stavanger for almost a century, since the 1840s. Perhaps Dons's ethical enactment in this site, in the relatively new Mission School for Women, was simply to be a woman who was writing and teaching mission history to young women in the same way men were writing and teaching mission history to young men in Stavanger. In other words, perhaps she simply wished to participate in the genre on equal terms. If so, then *women* was a word she could not use frequently or freely in this project site. She could neither elaborate on the third figure of the "heathen" woman nor place her audience in relation to a historical line of Norwegian women who had been central to supporting the mission. If she had done so, she would no longer have been engaging on equal terms, nor would she have taught her women students how to engage on equal terms. Perhaps, in her view, speaking and writing about women in this instance would have undermined their importance.

Dons's Protestant feminism was expressed here simply in the stack of typewritten pages lying in front of her on the table: a mission history about men (not women), written by a woman and taught to women, in the same way that this same history about men (not women) had been written by men and taught to men. Dons was producing the significance of women by remaining silent about them.

MAPPING: PROTESTANT WRITING AS PARTIALLY CONNECTED INFRASTRUCTURE

Wittgenstein's student and friend Rush Rhees (1970, 45) once observed that to understand Wittgenstein's approach to language, we must understand that when we are looking at language, we are looking at "lives in which there is language." When I am looking at Dons's writing in the genre of mission history, I am looking at lives in which there is language—in this case, the life of Dons as well as the lives of women and girls as these lives intersected with particular mission history texts. Her texts circulated through these lives in different material-discursive interactions: at a writing desk, in girls' groups in living rooms, in books for sale, around the dining table at the Mission School for Women, in a letter to NMS asking if they would publish a manuscript, in stacks of papers saved by women. Her acts of writing, the printed books and typed pages, their circulations and interactions all helped to form the concrete infrastructure for her project of Protestant feminism in Norway. Her writing also had long-term ripple effects on lives elsewhere, such as the lives of Africans who lived in and against the northern European stereotypes of "Africans" that Dons helped to build. Dons's writing encompassed not just her words on the page but also this circulation of figures, meetings and money, sentiments and subjectivities and significance. Her writing operated in lives both near and far.

How can we understand this instance of Protestant writing? I have argued that Dons's writing constituted the productive but partially connected infrastructure for her ethical project of Protestant feminism, showing us that this project itself lived in the world as a partially connected project, distributed across texts and sites and enacted slightly differently from one instance to the next. In short, in Dons's writing we can trace how her Protestant feminism was spelled out and "spread" out in protean fashion (Mol 2002, 50). Rather than attempting to classify her written texts according to a hierarchical structure of ethical values, we can instead follow her ethical project and trace its internal multiplicity across these writing sites. In her children's book, the project was entangled with colonialism and the third figure, such as "the heathen woman" or "Muhammedan woman." In her women's book, it was expressed in numbers that connected Christian and non-Christian women in a women's world: two hundred Norwegian women missionaries, four hundred million non-Christian women. In her unpublished manuscript, which she used to teach women mission students, I think the project was expressed in a desire to participate equally on men's terms in the genre; the project was embodied in her, a woman, and the stack of typed pages that lay on the oak dining table in front of her as she lectured to the women students. Different enactments of Protestantism and feminism appear and disappear across the pages of her written texts and along the circuits they traveled, as do different enactments of womanhood and whiteness, liberalism and imperialism. There are breaks in this infrastructure. The third figure, the two hundred and four hundred million, the stack of typed pages: they hang together, but also pull apart.

How does this help us understand ethical projects? In her study of atherosclerosis, Mol observes that the different sites in which the disease is apparent in and around the hospital are not usually enacted together. One way of reading Mol's book is to say that she, in distinction from the people she studies, aims to hold these sites open at the same time (e.g., 2002, 160–166). As Mol puts it, this allows us to "open up differences" (2002, viii). Her phrasing is reminiscent of Wittgenstein's remark to Maurice O'Connor Drury: "Hegel seems to me to be always wanting to say that things which look different are really the same. Whereas my interest is in shewing [sic] that things which look the same are really different" (Drury 1981, 171). And this is how I have tried to map an ethical project in this chapter: by looking at what happens in detail across sites, by holding the sites open alongside each other, to "open up differences." Dons and her colleagues might close one site when they move to another. She might discuss the Empire in one space and then close that space when she describes the mission women's groups in another space. She might tell a horrifying story about a Muslim girl-bride in one text but close this text when she presents a dry list of male missionary names in a different one. Here I have tried to hold these open at the same time to examine more carefully the breaks in the infrastructure of Dons's ethical project. This helps us see that the relations within this project were partial connections, informing each other but also drawing apart, and thus materializing in the world as a multiple project.

AFTERWARD

In 1943, four years after Henny Dons retired from her position as NMS's children's secretary, the organization published a centennial mission history. It was edited by John Nome, a well-known professor of mission history at NMS's Mission School (for men) in Stavanger. Despite this historical work being published so shortly after Dons's retirement, and despite its large scope (it encompassed five volumes), Nome chose to include only three short sentences about Dons. In these three sentences, he mentioned briefly that she had chaired the Ladies' Committee, served as NMS's children's secretary, and authored mission books for children (Nome 1943b, 123, 155). The male history writer had already closed off mention of her published work on the mission as a women's world, her teaching of mission history to young women over several decades, or even her unpublished manuscript on mission history. It is tempting to conclude that Nome wrote Dons out of his history, just as she had written women out of her own unpublished history. But I think it is more realistic to conclude that both Dons and Nome's written texts show how difficult it is to rethink women-word operations in life and the spread-out, partially connected, ethical projects they constitute.

04
READING

Around 1953, Henny Dons was sitting at her desk in the large, communal house at Pilestredet 83, where she still lived with a handful of other Lutheran women in Oslo. She was in her late seventies, her long white hair gathered together in a bun, writing out notes by hand in a lined notebook for the next talk she would give to a Christian women's group. She probably had her Bible open on the table, turned to the first pages of Genesis with its account of the creation of the world and the first humans. Perhaps Dons remembered how this account of Adam and Eve had threatened to hinder her from having the right to vote in the Norwegian Mission Society (NMS) half a century earlier, in 1904. Or perhaps she recalled that she had published a Bible study for young women in the 1920s saying Eve introduced temptation to Adam and this was "deeply humbling for us women" (1928, 9). Now, in the 1950s, Dons wrote out a line in cursive that contradicted her previous reading. A little while later, facing a room filled with women, she spoke the line out loud, expressing what she now understood to be prophesied in the Garden of Eden: "Through the man, Satan would be able to attack the woman."[1]

This chapter is about Dons's reading and rereading of the account of Adam and Eve in Genesis, chapters 1–3, over the course of her life, while she remained loyal to her pietistic Lutheran mission tradition in Norway. In particular, I explore how reading the Bible shaped her as a Protestant feminist subject. Drawing on Ludwig Wittgenstein's ([1953] 2009, §1) observation that we "operate" with words, I am interested in how reading was configured as an operation in Dons's life and what was produced by this operation. I use the term "her reading," then, to refer to her approach to reading the Bible (for example, her tendency to identify with the character of Eve) as well as the effects of her reading in life. Several anthropologists have drawn our attention to different ways Christians read the Bible (e.g., Bielo 2009b; Cannell 2006; Engelke 2007; Haynes 2020; Irvine 2010; Keller

2005; Kirsch 2011). Together with Britt Halvorson, I have sought to extend this conversation by observing that many of these studies on Christian reading often implicitly posit an androgynous reader, and we have suggested that other reading operations come to light if we include the gendered body of the Christian reader in our analyses (Halvorson and Hovland 2021). Here I wish to explore further the relationship between religious reading and the religious feminist subject.

I will begin by situating Dons's biblical reading in relation to the process of gaining women's voting rights, a common focus for the so-called first wave of the feminist movement in the regions around the North Atlantic at the turn of the twentieth century. However, although Dons was part of the first wave, this chapter also contributes to the exploration of how women who use religion to form their feminism may not fit neatly within the feminist "waves." As Dawn Llewellyn (2015, 4) has argued, the waves have a "secular temperament," because Western feminist theory today often presents the progression of the waves as "a secular narrative" of progress disconnected from religion. At times, this narrative may be based on the tacit assumptions that the secular and the religious are opposed and that "a feminist" is a secularly oriented subject who has managed to shed the conservative dogmatism of religion. This self-liberating feminist subject does not read or subject herself to patriarchal biblical texts. However, Dons presents us with a different type of feminist subject. Therefore, while I will discuss her feminism in relation to the first-wave issue of voting rights, I will also situate her in relation to her religious tradition and its cosmic imaginary. As Hillary Kaell (2020b) has suggested, Christian women in the nineteenth- and early twentieth-century North Atlantic world did not just operate in relation to a regional history but also a global one, which for them included "other" figures and more-than-human presences. As I explore Dons's reading and rereading of Eve, I will configure her ethical project of Protestant feminism in relation to local institutional concerns about voting as well as a cast of global characters and more-than-human forces. Thinking about religious feminisms in this way is thus also a contribution to thinking critically—and creatively—about the feminist waves and how feminist histories are formed (e.g., Hewitt 2012), including how we describe the feminist subject today.

At this point, readers may object that the secular, self-liberating feminist subject has already been thoroughly critiqued, most prominently by Saba Mahmood (2005). Mahmood studied women actively engaged in the Islamic revival in Egypt. She argues that the feminist project of these women does not center on a sense of "freedom" or even "resistance" to patriarchal religious traditions; they do not match the humanist, secular subject posited by modern liberal feminisms. Instead, drawing on poststructuralist virtue ethics, Mahmood suggests that these Muslim women are best understood as self-cultivating subjects within a patriarchally marked religious space—"subjects" in the double sense, as a subject who acts and is subjected simultaneously, an ongoing process of double-edged "subjectivation" (e.g., Butler 1993; Foucault 1978). As subjects, they seek to enact virtues, such as piety. We might say that, in Mahmood's view, these women skillfully inhabit their patriarchally assigned place in the tradition's discourse, using it for their own self-cultivation, and in so doing they present an alternative vision of "human flourishing" (Mahmood 2005, xxiv).

My understanding of modern religious feminisms has been deeply shaped by Mahmood and the many ethnographic studies that have developed similar arguments about religious women's self-making practices, such as R. Marie Griffith's (1997) work on the "power of submission" among evangelical women in the United States who meet to pray together, or Kate Dugan's (2017) description of the "flourishing" of young Catholic women on American college campuses who similarly choose to embrace their submissive role as women and to adopt gendered prayer practices (see also Fader 2009; Jouili 2011; Zwissler 2018). However, in this chapter I will go beyond Mahmood's and others' focus on religious women's self-cultivation within the theoretical frame of a poststructuralist virtue ethics. As Amira Mittermaier (2012, 247) has argued in her study of Sufi Muslims in Egypt, religious practitioners work with a more distributed agency than that tied to the self, as practitioners also see themselves as working with agency that stems from more-than-human actors such as God, and she suggests we might move "beyond the trope of self-cultivation" when studying religion in the world.[2]

Building on these lines of thought, which take us beyond both the self-liberating secular feminist subject of the waves and the self-cultivating religious feminist subject of poststructuralist virtue ethics, I want to instead place the religious feminist subject in the conversation on new materialism. Feminist new materialism urges us to pay attention to the impact of the material and to rethink the question of what, for example, the natural and the real are in relation to a woman (Alaimo and Hekman 2008). This is a further development of the poststructuralist view of the subject as an effect of discourse, but with a shift in emphasis toward a more realist attention to the organic, technological, and linguistic components that meet in a circuit that then continuously becomes, for example, "a woman."

Here I will engage one scholar in this conversation, Karen Barad, and their view of how bodies are constituted as "material-discursive phenomena" (2008, 141). Barad outlines this view in contrast with that of Judith Butler. Butler draws on the poststructuralist tradition to argue that a woman is constituted through "performativity," defined as iterative citationality: Butler (1993, 15) sees the matter, or materialization, of women's bodies as "a kind of citationality . . . the citing of power." Barad (2008, 146), on the other hand, argues that we should not understand performativity "as iterative citationality . . . but rather as iterative intra-activity." I suggest here that we can use Barad's vision of an intra-active, material-discursive body to think about a Protestant woman's language use. Barad (2008, 137–138) would not agree, arguing that discursive practices do not entail actual words but instead make words possible through materially reconfiguring the world. I am therefore retooling Barad's thought to draw discourse into my interpretation in a stronger sense, to incorporate actual words and human interactions and operations with those words.

What was happening as Dons was reading words about Eve over the course of her life? I argue that this case of Protestant reading shows us a material-discursive subject, Dons, constituted through a series of iterated intra-actions. While Dons in her Norwegian-Lutheran world in the early twentieth century stood far apart from current feminist theory in most respects, I have been intrigued by a curious overlap between her and the current conversation on feminist new materialism. Dons demonstrated a similar understanding of a woman as someone being continuously pieced together of materiality and language, of human and more-than-human entities, amid "the weightiness of the world" (Barad 2008, 144), and as someone who could not cultivate an ethical self on her own but instead had to work on ethical values generated by and distributed among multiple entities. I therefore follow Dons's readings and rereadings of Eve as an example of a religious feminist who engaged devotional reading as part of the process of being "a woman" as a distributed entity. It seems to me that Dons was reading about the creation of women, and was herself being a woman, as iteration: in her reading she was continuously "being created woman" by something else.

The Protestant feminist subject that emerges here might be called a series of woman-word operations in which a body and words operated together as a collective ethical agent. I suggest this ethical stance is not fully captured by the frame of self-cultivation; the feminist subject in this case could instead be seen as an intra-active material-discursive circuit. The lens of feminist new materialism thus moves us beyond virtue ethics toward project ethics, drawing our attention to a project not primarily anchored in the self but rather anchored in a material-discursive subject—or circuit—produced through ongoing intra-activity. From this angle, the figure of Dons reading the Bible emerges as a multiple subject—that is, a subject who is both composite and changeable. Ultimately, rather than concluding that women who willingly submit to patriarchal religious discourses have "power" or are "flourishing," I attend here to the contradictory effects of their forming and being formed as these types of ethical subjects.

This chapter describes three moments of reading Eve in Dons's life: first, Lutheran men reading Eve in 1904 when they were deciding whether women could vote; second, Dons reading Eve in her published Bible study in 1928; and third, Dons's handwritten notes on Eve for one of her talks to Christian women's groups around 1953. Between these three scenes, I have inserted brief interludes discussing Dons's approach to reading the Bible: reading as receiving, reading as arranging and dwelling, and reading as iterating. In the conclusion, I return to the process of being made a subject, or "being created woman," in Dons's ethical project of Protestant feminism.

NORWEGIAN-LUTHERAN MEN READING EVE IN 1904: CAN WOMEN VOTE?

In 1903 and 1904, men in NMS debated whether women could vote in their organization. The bulk of the official organization consisted of the grassroots network of local, mixed-gender mission groups across the country. (The organization did not formally include the mission women's groups, which had only women members.) Each mixed-gender mission group voted every three years on which delegates they would send to the NMS general assembly, and although both women and men attended the mixed-gender groups, only men were allowed to vote in these elections and to be elected.[3]

In 1903, the question of whether women should also be allowed to vote in the mixed-gender mission groups, and to be elected by them, was put forward for discussion in the organization. The NMS board asked each regional NMS assembly to debate the matter. In the assembly held for the eastern region around Kristiania, Henny Dons, then a young schoolteacher, attended the meeting on behalf of NMS's women's magazine *Mission Reading for Women's Groups* at the request of the magazine's editor, Bolette Gjør. Dons afterward reported to the magazine's readers that the men who opposed women's vote had said it would go against God's word, in particular two biblical verses they took to be authored by Paul: "But I suffer not a woman to teach, nor to usurp authority over the man, but to be in silence" in 1 Timothy 2:12, and "Let your women keep silence in the churches" in 1 Corinthians 14:34. These epistles both refer to the creation story in Genesis as justification, arguing that God created the man first and the woman second: "For Adam was first formed, then Eve. And Adam was not deceived, but the woman" (1 Timothy 2:13–14); "For the man is not of the woman: but the woman of the man. Neither was the man created for the woman; but the woman for the man" (1 Corinthians 11:8–9). Dons commended their argument that God's word must be the definitive guide. But, she wrote approvingly, many male delegates at the meeting had clarified "that Paul in these verses never thought or spoke about the administration of mission societies"; instead, when he said women must be "silent," he was referring to "women's behavior in public church services."[4] Though she did not report it afterward, during the meeting itself she stood up, asked to speak, and reminded the gathering that in other places, dissatisfied women had simply formed their own mission societies.[5]

Following the regional assembly debates, the NMS governing board sent out a proposal to the whole organization.[6] I imagine the thirty-year-old Dons receiving the thirty-five-page document with its closely spaced Gothic lettering and poring over it. The nine men on the board stated that, on the one hand, there were several arguments in favor of women's vote and electability, including the extent of women's grassroots involvement and their contributions to the organization. On the other hand, there was "only one single objection" that had any significance, but "if justified, it would be *decisive*." The objection was that Paul required women "*to be silent in the assembly*" in 1 Corinthians 14:34–35 and 1 Timothy 2:12, and he did so on the basis of "certain *foundational relations in the origins of humankind*."[7] They spelled out these foundational relations: "the man was created first" and "the woman was the first to sin." The order of creation (Adam first, Eve second) formed the backdrop for the rest of their discussion. They argued that the woman cannot "guide" a group, cannot act as "the head" in marriage, cannot have "authority" or "preach God's word" in a congregation, and cannot "teach others." These are all roles that indicate primacy; thus, they are roles for men. A woman should instead be a "listener" and "receive" teaching in a church setting.[8] Implicit in their reasoning was the observation that the secondary creation of Eve was a position of being in relation to something else, of being an iteration. And this position of being an iteration had concrete implications for women's language use: they should not "preach" words, but "receive" them.

However, the men on the governing board still thought women could participate in administrative settings such as mission committees, where participants did not teach or preach God's word but instead carried out a "*practical* action" as "a *service* for the Lord."[9] They recognized the objection that women on committees would have "authority" if they participated in drawing up organizational rules. However, the board countered that this was not the kind of authority that Paul forbade women from exercising. They stated that the Greek word Paul used to describe women's forbidden authority, *authentein*, could be translated as a woman "acting independently and autonomously (autocratically) in relation to the man." Acting independently was a position of primacy, of a "master" or "superior." But mission women who voted or ran for election were not taking on a "master" role, the board reasoned; instead they were "*cooperating* with men."[10] Thus, it was also "most decent" that men "give" women the opportunity to exercise this specific influence of voting "*without* [women] having demanded it." Indeed, they added approvingly, "mission women" would "surely be the last to demand their rights."[11]

Against the backdrop of this reading of Paul's reading of Adam and Eve, the board proposed that women should receive the right to vote in NMS as well as electability to mission group committees and as delegates to the regional assemblies and the general assembly; they suggested that electability to the regional committees might come later. (Only one board member added a dissenting opinion, saying that women should not be electable at all because of "the relations that God established in his Word and in nature itself.")[12] With regard to women joining them on the governing board, the nine men on the board said that though there was no "theoretical" objection to this, there was a "practical" hindrance, namely that the board met once or even twice a week, and women "according to the nature of the matter might have to be absent for months" because of "family circumstances."[13] Therefore, they did not recommend that women should be electable to the board. The board's proposal was debated by the male delegates at the NMS general assembly in 1904 for two days. There was some vocal opposition, but many more spoke in support, and in the end the proposal was passed with a large majority among the Lutheran men.[14]

NMS's voting decision of 1904 was made surprisingly early; it occurred almost a decade before women achieved universal enfranchisement in Norway's elections in 1913. The progressive women's magazine *Nylænde* (*New*

Frontiers) stated in an editorial at the time that the decision by "such a conservative meeting" to grant women the right to vote would surely serve as "the most effective forerunner" for universal suffrage in every "out-of-the-way place."[15] Since NMS had an extensive grassroots network of four thousand to five thousand local groups across the country, the gender politics within this religious civil society organization had widespread ripple effects in both urban and rural areas.[16] Scholars have later described the voting decision in detail (Norseth 2007, 300–336; Nyhagen Predelli 2003, 133–169; Skeie and Norseth 2003). They argue thoughtfully for the political and civil importance of this moment in women's history as part of the broader democratization process in Norway, of which women's enfranchisement was a core component (though we might note that the image of the Norwegian political "citizen" as male still lingered for several decades afterward; Blom 2012).

However, the current scholarly assessment of the relative importance of NMS's voting decision does not seem to have been shared by Dons and her mission-feminist peers. As I have studied the mission feminists, I have been struck by the fact that although some of them, such as Gjør and Dons, advocated for women's vote in NMS in 1903–1904, they do not seem to have viewed this advocacy—or even the right to vote—as central to their work. For example, when Gjør wrote to NMS Secretary Lars Dahle in 1908 to try to persuade him that "it is God who speaks to us" through the women's movement, she also mentioned as an aside that some Christian women in Denmark were requesting women's right to vote, but commented: "For me this side of the matter is not as significant."[17] Similarly, when Dons wrote her book about women in the mission movement in Norway, she did not describe the 1904 voting decision as important. In fact, she hardly described it at all; the careful reader would only know about it because Dons mentioned it in a single sentence, tucked away in passing in the middle of a paragraph, in a section about the Mission School for Women (1925a, 31). Dons's book does not provide any further commentary about women's voting. To feminists in the North Atlantic world today, this downplaying of women's enfranchisement may seem strange, and it does not fit well with our typical conceptualization of Western first-wave feminism as centrally focused on women's political rights. But precisely this tension may help us ask further questions not only about the wave metaphor but also about how feminisms have been formed. The mission feminists in Norway, while contributing to the process of Scandinavian democratization, themselves chose instead to pay greater attention to a different contested terrain.

For Dons and her peers, Christianity functioned in some ways as what Brendan Jamal Thornton (2019) calls "a gender project," in the sense that being "a Christian" was at the same time about being "a woman" or being "a man." Or, as William Garriott and Kevin Lewis O'Neill (2008, 394) put it, Christian groups may perceive the question of who is a "real" Christian as equivalent to asking who is a "real" man or a "real" woman. Thus, Christianity can sometimes bring "gender distress," as has happened, for example, for Pentecostal men in the Caribbean (Thornton 2018). Among the Lutherans in Norway, however, the gender project of Christianity played out somewhat differently. The masculinity of Protestant men in the NMS tradition tied understandings of Lutheranism, leadership, and manhood closely together (Tjelle 2013) and does not appear to have been significantly threatened by the prospect of women voting. Most of the men seem to have agreed that women's right to vote did not change what it was to be "a woman" or what this meant in relation to being "a man." The tepid response of the mission feminists confirms this interpretation. The reading of Eve that took place in NMS in 1904 had been a limited gender project, asserting certain formal rights for women within the Christian organization, but it had not been a gender project in the more complex sense of asking how a Christian "woman" was created or what she could be.

As we continue to rethink the feminist waves, we might consider that the right to vote was in itself peripheral to the gender project of some first-wave feminists, such as Dons. To her and her peers, rethinking—or redoing—the act of biblical reading was far more important. In particular, they regarded the question of how to read Eve—that is, how to read the creation of woman—as foundational.

READING AS RECEIVING

So far, I have considered men reading the Bible in NMS. But how did women read? Women's reading had at times been an activity that NMS sought to limit quite strictly. In the 1860s, the organization's magazine explained that women should not "work in the word," mentioning in particular that women must not gather to read in their mission women's groups.[18] We might guess that the comment was especially aimed at a specific type of reading—namely, women reading the Bible together without a man.

However, by the early twentieth century this perception had changed within NMS. In 1920, Dons and nine young women could sit around the dining room table of the residential schoolhouse of NMS's Mission School for Women as Dons taught a class called "Methodical Bible Study."[19] Dons informed the young women in the first lesson of their two goals: "To learn to know the Bible. To learn to use the Bible."[20] She told them to practice by using Paul's first letter to the Thessalonians as an example. They sat around the table and read the whole letter, first silently to themselves, then aloud. As homework, they had to find out who wrote it, when, where, to whom, and why.[21] In the next lesson, they went over the main content of each of the five chapters.[22] After this, they spent most of the remainder of the term reading one verse together at a time and asking for each one: "What can we learn from this verse?"[23] For instance, when Paul praises the Thessalonians, the students could learn: "Criticism kills, praise builds."[24] They looked up related biblical verses when relevant. Dons spent an especially long time on the mention of "boldness" in 1 Thessalonians 2:2, noting in her lesson plan thirty-three related biblical passages that came up in the class discussion of this term:

> Hebrews 10:19, Hebrews 4:15–16, Hebrews 10:22, John 1:9, Mark 4:40, Mark 6:50, Hebrews 12:1–29, Hebrews 10:35, Matthew 10:32, Luke 11:9, John 14:13, Matthew 15, 2 Kings 19:14, Hebrews 2:17, Matthew 4:1, Isaiah 43:25, Psalm 32:5, 2 Samuel 12:13, Proverbs 28:13, 1 John 1:9, Psalm 37:14–17, Psalm 32:7, Acts 12:5, Acts 4:24, 2 Corinthians 8:9, Matthew 28:20, Mark 6:50, Psalm 50:15, 1 Peter 5:7, Psalm 37:5, Romans 10:9, Mark 8:38, Revelation 21:8.[25]

In her notebook, she recorded some keywords next to many of these verses and interspersed the points made in the class discussion.

Half a century after the statement in NMS's magazine that women must not gather to read without men, Dons was able to do just that. Moreover, in her reading of the Bible with this group of young women, they formed new series of verses. They "worked in the word," as the 1860s phrase put it, by making their own connections. And the connections implicitly returned to the women themselves: creating a long series of biblical verses on the theme of "boldness," for example, seems to have been shaped by, and perhaps shaped, their own sense of acting boldly.

Another space in which Dons worked in the word was when she joined other female teachers for the monthly meetings of the Female Teachers' Mission Association. According to the meeting minutes, she often gave talks at the meetings about biblical verses. For example, in 1921 she gave a talk at a meeting in which she read two Bible verses that had "given her Christmas joy," Luke 15:21 and John 1:13, and said that "if we live under" these verses, "we will *receive* blessing and *become* a blessing."[26] These themes of giving and receiving, and of placing oneself in a spatial configuration with verses (such as "under" a verse), are echoed in many of her other comments. When the female teachers said goodbye to departing female missionaries, the minutes record that Dons "gave" them Bible verses, such as Matthew 10:8 or 1 Corinthians 8:9, by reading these verses out loud to them.[27] More often, Dons perceived Bible verses that took on particular meaning for her to be "given" by God, as when she wrote to the NMS general secretary in 1924 that she had "received" Isaiah 42:16 and was passing it on to him as a New Year's greeting.[28] Similarly, when she recounted how she and four other teachers had founded the Female Teachers' Mission Association, she said they began "under the promise in Isaiah 60:22" and "received boldness" from 1 Corinthians 1:27–29, which "was the word on which we started."[29]

When Dons and her peers were reading the Bible, then, they perceived themselves to be interacting directly with God, being "given" words from God. In this context, there was a certain agency in "receiving," as it connected the women's bodies directly to God's authority, placing them "under" God's word or "on" God's word. Through biblical reading they created (or, in their view, God created) an intimate and important mingling of God's authoritative words and women's thoughts and bodies, within a larger religious context in which they were materially marked—by virtue of their bodies coded *female*—as being second, an iteration. We see here how the material and the discursive interacted, or rather intra-acted, within these religious feminist subjects.[30]

In Dons's view, this relation of receiving was not passive. In a talk she gave to NMS's female traveling secretaries, the women who traveled around to speak to NMS groups, she explained how they should read the Bible when they were preparing to give a devotional talk. Although she advised them not to overinterpret—"It is an old and known truth that 'God's word interprets [*tolker*] itself'" (1945, 12)—they should still put in considerable time and effort. "Use a notebook," Dons told them, as well as a dictionary of biblical terms and a concordance in which they could look up groups of biblical verses based on a topic (1945, 13). They also needed to set aside sufficient time: "One must study the material properly, work with God's word under prayer, use secondary literature, look up references, write down the thoughts one has" (1945, 14). Dons encouraged them to give Bible-study participants some biblical passages to read beforehand so they could ask each participant in the meeting to share what God had "given them" during their preparatory reading (1945, 14). The act of relating to the words of the Bible, then, involved being "given" words, but this went hand in hand with reading, rereading, preparing, studying, praying, writing, thinking, and trusting that reading would have effects.

Overall, Dons's willingness to "receive" words still largely fit within the view put forward by the NMS governing board in 1904 that women should not take on roles of primacy but should rather take on secondary, receptive roles. However, when she connected God's words and women's bodies, placing women in certain relations with God, or when she created relations among biblical words in series, fostering boldness in women, she also pushed the boundaries of what the relation of "receiving" could be.

This attention to receiving and relating marked Dons's approach to reading the Bible when she published the book *Bibelens kvinner* (*Women of the Bible*) in 1928, in her midfifties. At this time, she was employed by NMS as their children's secretary, and the book was written to be used as part of a Bible-study program for youth in the Young Women's/Men's Christian Association in Norway. One of the many women figures she discussed in the book was Eve.

HENNY DONS READING EVE IN 1928: "WHAT IS DEEPLY HUMBLING FOR US WOMEN"

The young women who gathered in groups to discuss Dons's book would start their Bible study by attending to the two moments in Genesis when woman was created. First, "male and female" are created at the end of the prose poem about the seven days of creation in Genesis 1. Under the heading "Created in God's image," Dons wrote: "On the Bible's first page we read about the woman's elevated origin. 'And God created the human in his image, in God's image he created it, male and female he created them'" (1928, 7).[31] Perhaps she was implicitly in dialogue here with Paul, who says man, not woman, "is the image and glory of God" (1 Corinthians 11:7). However, she did not highlight her difference with Paul explicitly, instead simply moving on to the second moment dealing with woman's creation. This occurs in the narrative about the Garden of Eden in Genesis 2, after the creation of Adam, when God sees that Adam needs a helper. God causes Adam to fall asleep, takes something from his side, and makes a woman. Dons says: "In addition God said this about the woman: 'I will create a helper for him [Adam] who is like him.' This shows even more clearly that God from the dawn of creation has given the woman a position of equal prominence to the man" (1928, 7). Again, she seems to be in implicit dialogue with Paul, who says woman was created *from* man and *for* man (1 Corinthians 11:8–9)—a different understanding of what it means to be a "helper." Again, however, Dons did not flag this difference between her and Paul, but instead simply asserted that the woman's "helper" role indicated "equal prominence."

Dons then turned to what she thought of as "the fall" in Genesis 3—that is, "sin" entering the world.[32] As has been common in Christian readings of the creation account, she located this "fall" in the moment in which the woman took the forbidden fruit in Eden, ate it, and gave some to the man. In her commentary, Dons emphasized that the woman and man both sinned, and moreover that all humans sin. She commented: "The third chapter in Genesis is a ... depiction of sin through all generations and in each person's life. The fall is mine and yours" (1928, 8). But, she continued, the responsibility can be laid more on Eve than on Adam: "What is deeply humbling for us women is that the temptation comes to the man through the woman. And this is repeated through all of humanity's history every day" (1928, 9). Unlike her earlier implicit disagreement with Paul's readings, here she tacitly agrees with the argument in 1 Timothy 2:14 that Eve was deceived, not Adam, and that this has consequences for all women. From her perspective, Eve and all women afterward, including Dons herself, are responsible in some way for temptation "com[ing] to the man," and this pattern is "repeated ... every day."

The creation account in Genesis concludes with God pronouncing three judgments, the consequences of Eve's and Adam's actions. Dons dwelled on the judgment over the woman, who was punished with great pain in childbirth and told that her desire would be for her husband, who would rule over her. Dons commented that, as a result, woman became "a tool ... for the sake of the reproduction of generations" (1928, 65). The judgment, Dons argued, "included an impoverishment of the character of the original woman, and this impoverishment is inherited by all of humanity's women," as woman was "placed under the authority of the man, ... given a slave spirit, whose desire does not reach higher than to please the man. But this is not how the woman was created" (1928, 9). In other words, Dons drew a distinction between what she saw as the woman's original character, created "in God's image" as the man's important "helper," versus what she saw as woman's post-judgment "impoverished" character. Drawing into her argument the figure of the "slave," Dons argued that God's judgment transformed the woman's prominent role as "helper" to one resembling a "slave" who wanted only to please the man. In Dons's reading, then, Eve—and all women after her—were here placed under the rule of men, and while "the condition of slavery is the woman's punishment" (1928, 9), this state of affairs is also a more general "curse over humanity" (1928, 16).

The judgment over the snake was also of interest to Dons. In this curse, God says the woman's human descendants will strike snakes on the head, and snakes will strike humans at the heel. Dons did not read this literally as a description of humans and snakes having the ability to kill each other. Rather, she followed the history of Christian interpretation and suggested that the woman's offspring was Jesus and the snake was Satan. She commented that this curse was actually a "promise" from God, namely the promise that the woman's offspring, Jesus, would crush the snake, Satan. This action would, in Dons's view, lead to "salvation" for humanity (1928, 10). This was significant to her because it meant that Eve not only brought sin into the world but also, through her offspring, the promise of salvation. As Dons put it: "In this way the woman was allowed to be the bearer of the promise" (1928, 11). While she still portrayed life under the curse more negatively for women than men, Dons introduced some nuance into this picture by attaching a promise to the woman.

The creation account in Genesis ends with God expelling the humans from the garden. For Dons, however, the overarching story did not end there. She wrote: "One day the woman was found" who would fulfill the promise (1928, 29). This woman was Mary, mother of Jesus, about whom the angel said, "Blessed are you among women" (1928, 30). Dons argued that in the moment Mary gave birth to Jesus, "the curse over women is transformed through Jesus Christ into blessing" (1928, 30), mirroring God's original blessing over the male and female humans he created. In her view, the coming of Jesus changed the existential state of women. Dons now drew into her argument the stock figures of "the heathens" and "the Jews," as well as quoting Paul explicitly: "Against the saying of the heathens that 'a man's life is worth more than a thousand women's,' and a fairly similar perception among Jews at the time of Jesus, Christianity places its saying: There is no difference . . . 'Here is neither Jew nor Greek, here is neither slave nor free, here is neither man nor woman, for you are all one in Christ Jesus' . . . Galatians 3:27–28" (1928, 65). She also drew in the stereotyped figure of "the Muhammedan" (or the Muslim), arguing that the cursed state of woman being dominated by man could still be observed in certain areas of the world: "Out in the big heathen and Muhammedan world the woman still sits in the deepest denigration and the thickest darkness" (1928, 103). But, in her view, whenever women became Christian they were set "free" by Jesus, and "this freedom is our holy right as women of the new covenant" (1928, 103). We see, then, how her reading was formed by, and formed, a cast of more-than-human characters and human stock figures distributed throughout history and around the world in her cosmic imaginary—the woman, the man, Satan, Jesus, the slave, the Jew, the "heathen," the "Muhammedan," the Christian.

When Dons argued that Christian women were "free," and that Christian men and women were "one," this seems to have meant to her that there was no difference in status. But she did not think it meant having the same tasks: "In the life and work of the congregation there is a deep need for the natural gift that God has given the woman—motherliness. This is what is simultaneously strong and mild in the female nature, which gives her the ability to carry on, keep vigil and wait, suffer and sacrifice" (1928, 97). Just as she perceived women to receive words from God, then, she also perceived them to receive effects in and on their bodies, such as the "gift" of making their bodies and dispositions "motherly." Since, like most of the middle-class female teachers in her circles, Dons herself was not married and did not have any children, we can assume she was referring to "motherliness" in a figurative sense rather than a literal one, echoing one of the maternal feminist arguments of her time that the ability to mother (broadly understood) ought to confer social status on women.[33] But she saw a development in woman's motherly role: first Adam and Eve were told to multiply and this was "good"; then woman became a childbearing "tool" under the curse; after Jesus, however, woman can beneficially use a natural, God-given gift of motherliness, which, Dons argued, filled an important need in the Christian social world.

A little later in her Bible study, Dons observed, "Even today we are working on these questions about the position of the Christian woman" (1928, 68), commenting that the reason the questions had not yet been resolved was because "it is difficult for the man to voluntarily give up the power he has had over the woman since the fall. And it has not been easy for the woman to start using the entire grace that is at her disposal" (1928, 67). Both men and women, in her view, might still relate to each other in the hierarchical way introduced by God's judgment, rather than accept that they were now "set on an equal footing" (1928, 67).

READING AS ARRANGING AND DWELLING

Let me return to the question of how Henny Dons read the Bible as a Protestant woman and how this helps us describe her as a Protestant feminist subject. Anthropological studies that address the phenomenon of biblical reading have often conceptualized reading as a cognitive act, such as when Susan Harding (2000) asked how the reading and use of biblical language among fundamentalist Protestants in the United States bolstered their sense of belief. However, more recent work has instead analyzed the sometimes surprising relations between Bible reading and materiality, as in Matthew Engelke's (2007, 2013) study of the Friday Apostolics in Zimbabwe, who desire to engage with the word of God "live and direct" without using physical Bibles, or his study of Bible Society staff in England, who attempt to capture the Bible in publicity materials. Anthropologists have explored the multilayered social interactions that occur when Christians read the Bible collectively, as in Eva Keller's (2005) fieldwork among studious Seventh-Day Adventists in Madagascar or James Bielo's (2009b) ethnography of Protestant Bible groups in the United States (see also Bielo 2009a). Most recently, Bielo (2022) has examined the tendency of Christians, including evangelical Protestants in the United States, to "materialize" the Bible so they can physically walk around in it—for example, in biblical gardens, models of Jerusalem, or a replica of Noah's ark—and Naomi Haynes (2020, 59) has described Pentecostals in Zambia as "identifying with" biblical characters and "inserting themselves into" these characters' stories as templates for their own lives. This insertion transforms the reader; for example, when a Pentecostal bishop reads about the biblical figure Ezekiel, "Bishop Ndhlovu becomes Ezekiel" (Haynes 2020, 60). In these examples, Bible readers form social and material arrangements between themselves and biblical words, or arrange this relation in different ways to live with and in it, just as Dons did.

A different version of arranging the reader-word relation can be found in what Andreas Bandak has called "seriation" (2015, 51). Bandak has discussed Christian "series" using the example of a sermon given by an Eastern Catholic priest in Syria. In the sermon, the priest presented a series of exemplary historical figures, moving from one to the next. Bandak argues, quoting Wittgenstein, that the challenge to the listener was to catch the "drift" of the series (2015, 59; Wittgenstein [1953] 2009, §210)—that is, to understand how this series could function as an example for, and be continued in, the listener's own life. In this sense, "the example is not finished" (Bandak 2015, 57).[34] Dons too produced series—in her case, of Bible verses. The groups and strings of Bible verses she assembled had the effect of relating biblical words to each other in new ways, making new sequences among words as well as among figures: "Jewish" men and "heathen" men, then Jesus; the "Muhammedan" woman, then the "Christian" woman; Eve, then Mary, then Dons. As she reorganized relations between biblical words, she could also reorganize relations between gendered bodies, imagined human figures around the world, and more-than-human forces.

In the 1950s, Dons wrote a reflective piece that gives further clues to how her biblical reading was a type of arranging of relations so she could live in them. In a chapter on "What life has taught me," she stated on the first page: "God himself meets us in the Bible" (1952, 11). She elaborated: "*Every day. We need to receive a word from God every day*" (1952, 12). To read—that is, to "meet" God and to "receive" a word—required, in her view, "both time and work" (1952, 11). She encouraged her readers not only to follow "a plan" when reading the Bible and to gain an overview, but also to find particular short passages they could "dwell in [*bo i*]." She explained that "dwelling in" biblical words meant "one can read them over and over again for a longer period of time" and that she had, for example, dwelled in Psalm 23 (1952, 13). Some years later, in 1960 when Dons was in her mideighties, she returned to the term in a letter to her friend Ida Herstad: "I have dwelled for a long time in this word from Lamentations [3:23]."[35] The word she had "dwelled in" this time was a brief sentence on God's "compassions": "They are new every morning: great is thy faithfulness."

This concrete image of "dwelling in" words from God during particular periods is connected to Dons's view of what it meant to be a human. For example, in a talk she gave in the late 1940s, she paused at the question of how to conceptualize human beings, and as before, she emphasized that humans have bodies: "In the Bible there is no division between soul and body. Humans do not just *have* bodies, we *are* bodies, we are a body-soul unity. Salvation encompasses both soul and body." Moreover, she said, this body-soul unity that is a human is made "to exist for others." In her talk, she used this observation to argue that women were needed as paid deaconesses or social workers in congregations, resonating with her earlier argument that women (not men) receive the maternal gift.[36] In other words, Dons thought of both women and men as "body-soul unities," but the bodies of women and men were materially marked and different, in her view. Thus, from Dons's perspective, a woman reading the Bible was a reader with a materially different body in her body-soul unity than a male reader. When a woman reader "dwelled in" Bible verses, Dons thought this could have different effects on her body-soul, such as helping her receive and enact what she, as a woman, needed to receive and enact.

It seems to me that the woman-word configuration that emerges in Dons's reading is not fully captured by the frame of self-cultivation but instead is better described as a distributed circuit. Dons did not see herself as a subject made primarily by herself but rather by forces and figures that shaped her. For example, because of the material resemblance between Eve's body and her own—namely the "femaleness" of these bodies—Dons knows she must humble herself; in this case, Eve's body is making up hers. Some of these series, then, such as the one that led from Eve to Dons, could not be materially escaped, in Dons's view, but had to be received and lived in. In Dons's experience, she lived as a religious feminist subject in series that were received, arranged, and dwelled in.

HENNY DONS READING EVE AROUND 1953: "WOMAN'S PLACE"

Let me return to the imagined scenario with which I opened this chapter: Dons sitting at her desk, in her late seventies, remembering her previous readings of Eve as she prepared a talk. The notes she wrote for this talk show that she had continued to reread the creation account over the roughly twenty-five years since she published her Bible study in 1928. We would not know about her rereading of Eve if she had not saved this notebook (along with a stack of other notebooks) containing her handwritten notes for talks she continued to give to Christian groups. The notebook is likely from the early 1950s, perhaps 1953.[37] As I have contemplated her rereading of Eve, I have wondered whether it was set against the backdrop of her experiences in NMS during her last decade of employment as the organization's children's secretary, up until her retirement in 1939. During this time, she faced a series of rejections from the organization's male leadership. Although it is difficult to tell from the formal correspondence in the archive, she does not seem to have been given straightforward explanations for these rejections.

The first rejection came in 1929. In 1928, Dons traveled by steamship to visit South Africa, and especially the mission station Eshowe, where she had thought she would work when she was young.[38] She was away for almost a year, and during this time Pastor Otto Emil Birkeli, a teacher at the Mission School in Stavanger, took over her job as editor of NMS's *Children's Magazine* (*Barnebladet*). When Dons returned, she wrote to him to ask which issue she should start preparing.[39] However, she received a reply instead from Carl Fredrik Bjertnes, the acting general secretary, informing her that the NMS board had decided Pastor Birkeli would be taking over the editorship of the *Children's Magazine* permanently.

Dons was clearly taken aback by this news. She sent the general secretary a letter that she asked him to put before the NMS board, which explained that the editorship of the *Children's Magazine* was one of her most important tasks as NMS's children's secretary, since it allowed her to support the leaders of the children's groups through the material she published. It also functioned as a means of communication, because both leaders and children sent letters to her in response to the magazine.[40] The general secretary sent her a reply the same day he received her letter. His reply has not been saved, but he seems to have reiterated the board's decision. He had previously indicated it might cause difficulties that she lived in Oslo while the printing press was in Stavanger (though, as Dons pointed out, this had not caused difficulties before). He had also said Pastor Birkeli needed some more work to do. Now he added that the *Children's Magazine* had seen a reduction in subscribers under her editorship. Dons responded that it was the first time she had heard about this matter, and that it might be because three other Christian organizations were now distributing their own children's magazines (the Santal Mission, the China Mission, and the Sunday School Association).[41] A few days later, she was invited to Stavanger to discuss NMS's children's work with the board, the general secretary, and Pastor Birkeli.[42] She took a trip to do so in April 1929.[43] The archive does not reveal what happened at the meeting; what we know is that Dons continued as children's secretary while Pastor Birkeli remained editor of the *Children's Magazine*.[44]

Two years later, in 1931, three further rejections arrived. At the NMS consultation meeting (*rådsmøtet*) that year, which gathered all the central decision-makers of the organization, one of the items on the agenda was the children's work. However, Dons was not invited to attend. She wrote to the NMS general secretary Einar Amdahl to express her surprise, adding: "Now it almost feels as if I have been excluded from [*satt utenfor*] this work."[45] The same year, the NMS leadership at the organization's head office in Stavanger decided that Dons would no longer report directly to them, but would instead report to a lower-level steering committee for the children's work in Oslo.[46] This effectively removed her from the organization's central administration. Finally, one of the work areas she had been overseeing, the NMS Home Crafts Circle, was queried.

Dons had established the NMS Home Crafts Circle (Det Norske Misjonsselskaps Husflidsring) in 1918. It was a network of women who volunteered to lead NMS children's groups and wished to receive ideas for crafts; it was also open to other women who wanted to use some of their spare time on crafts to donate to mission sales for NMS.[47] When Dons was given an assistant, Anna Michelsen, their work with the Home Crafts Circle complemented the courses on craftwork Michelsen provided for NMS children's group leaders.[48] By September 1920, Dons reported that her new assistant, Julie Ellingsen, who took over from Michelsen that year, had sent out three hundred membership cards to members of the Home Crafts Circle.[49] From their perspective, the children and the crafts were closely connected, as Dons wrote to General Secretary Amdahl in 1931: "We have viewed the two branches as two parts of the same work—NMS's children's work."[50] The NMS board apparently saw the matter differently, because, although Dons does not acknowledge it explicitly in her official response, it seems she was asked to stop reporting on the Home Crafts Circle in her work as children's secretary.[51] As with her loss of the editorship of the children's magazine, the loss of overseeing the Home Crafts Circle also meant she was removed from a means of communicating with a network of Christian women across Norway.

In December 1931, Dons wrote to Amdahl in Stavanger: "There are several things that have made my and Miss Ellingsen's work heavy." She said this had been due partly to illness and partly to "the difficulties that have gathered around our work."[52] Dons remained in her post as children's secretary until she reached the age of 65 in 1939, when she retired, while Amdahl continued as general secretary until 1957.

In retirement, Dons remained vigorously involved with her all-women's community in the Female Teachers' Mission Association. However, she likely registered the loss of vigor in the women's movement in postwar Norway in the late 1940s and early 1950s (echoing a similar trend in the United States and England), as the earlier strands of maternal feminism from the first wave were firmly reduced to the argument that woman's place was in the home. (The second wave was still far off, developing in the United States in the 1960s but not taking hold in Norway until the 1970s; Hagemann 2004).

It was against this background that Dons recorded, in cursive handwriting on the lined pages of her notebook, her reworked thoughts on Eve around 1953, titling her exegesis "Woman's place in the Kingdom of God."[53] She again started with the creation of "male and female" and emphasized that the first humans were both created in God's image, blessed, and told to multiply. However, this time she did not mention the woman's beneficial role as "helper," as she had done before. Instead, she used new terms for the relation between the woman and the man, saying they were created for "community and cooperation with God and each other."[54]

She then reconsidered the "fall."[55] In her earlier reading in 1928, Dons had stated that both Adam and Eve sinned but Eve sinned first. In her notes in the 1950s, she shifted her attention. Instead of focusing on Eve's action of eating the forbidden fruit and giving it to Adam, she focused instead on the responses that the humans gave when God confronted them afterward. The woman responded that the snake tricked her and she ate of the fruit. Dons commented: "The woman immediately admits and confesses her sin to God. But at the same time she accuses the Snake as the seducer. She told the whole truth without excuse, and thereby she broke with the sin."[56] In Dons's view, the woman's statement was a confession of how she acted against God's will, and thus she "places herself completely under God's power."[57] Dons suggested that Eve's orientation toward God might be called belief, concluding: "The woman is the first to believe in God . . . therefore Eve can be called mother of all those who believe . . . just as Abraham is called 'father of those who believe.'"[58] Dons was in dialogue here with Galatians 3:29, where Paul refers to Christian believers as children of God and descendants of Abraham. Dons's rereading argued that Christian believers were not just Abraham's children but also, before him, Eve's children, tracing their lineage back to her original moment of belief in Eden. Again, Dons was arranging biblical verses and figures in new series.

Dons viewed the man's response to God differently. When God confronted him, Adam responded that the woman, whom God gave him, gave him the fruit, and he ate. Dons observed, "The man excuses himself and blames both God and the woman, but he does not mention the Snake."[59] In Dons's view, Adam blamed God (because God gave him Eve) and Eve (because she gave him the fruit) but not the snake, who, in Dons's symbolic reading, was Satan and thus the true responsible party. Adam's blaming God instead of the snake was a wrong assignment of blame, Dons argued. Recall that in Dons's earlier reading in 1928, she agreed with the claim in 1 Timothy

2:14 that Eve was the one who was deceived, not Adam. By contrast, in her reading in the 1950s she dwelled on the difference between the two humans' responses to God and concluded that the woman confessed and demonstrated belief in God while the man misplaced blame and excused himself. Dons elaborated that the man implicitly "placed himself on Satan's side by not accusing him as the seducer," contrary to the woman's clear accusation against the snake.[60] Here it seems that Dons replaced one hierarchy (Eve was more fully deceived than Adam, so she is more sinful) with another (Eve confessed more fully than Adam, so she is more faithful). From Dons's perspective, this replacement, or rereading, allowed her to move away from the experience of finding the creation account "deeply humbling for us women," as she had put it in 1928.

Dons further speculated that when Eve responded that the snake tricked her, she made a bitter enemy of the snake. In Dons's view the snake was Satan, and so the woman "made Satan . . . her enemy and opponent for all of time."[61] Dons saw this enmity theme confirmed in God's pronouncement that there would be enmity between the snake's offspring and the woman's offspring. Ever since this moment in Eden, Dons suggested, there has been an ongoing battle of Eve versus the snake—that is, women versus Satan. Just as in her reading in 1928, she again found a "promise" hidden in the curse of the snake: "The woman's offspring shall crush the head of the Snake," which she read as a foretelling of Jesus crushing sin or Satan.[62] She added, "Satan [the snake] is himself present and hears the Lord pronounce these words about the woman's elevated destiny."[63] The curse ends with the statement that the snake's offspring will strike the woman's offspring, and this sentiment was folded into Dons's further elaboration: "From this moment Satan will do everything in his power to hinder the woman from fulfilling her elevated destiny. He will do everything to oppress her and fight against her."[64]

Dons then commented on God's judgment of the woman. Contrary to her earlier reading, she now suggested that when God pronounced that woman would be ruled by man, this was a foretelling of the method Satan would use to fight against the woman: "It was a small step for Satan to use as his tool *the man* who was closest to the woman . . . Through the man, Satan would be able to attack the woman in the most sensitive area. She must be cowed and made into nothing. She must be treated in such a way that her *faith in God* and her elevated calling and dignity will die in her . . . Therefore the woman had as her opponents both her husband and Satan."[65]

Recall that in 1928, Dons thought God's pronouncement that men would have authority over women was part of God's punishment of women. However, in her rereading in the early 1950s, she instead thought this pronouncement was God's foretelling of how Satan would continue to attack women. In Dons's view in the 1950s, then, when men rule over women, Satan advances in his long-standing battle against Eve. Similarly, although in 1928 she argued that when the woman handed the fruit to the man she acted as Satan's tool to make the man sin (that is, to destroy the man), Dons now refused this reading, saying, "To portray the woman as a tool that Satan uses to destroy the man is a completely heathen thought."[66] We see here that she briefly draws in the stock figure of the "heathen," again as a foil for its perceived opposite, the "Christian." She argued that the Christian way of thinking was to recognize that when the man rules over the woman, *he* is the one who is Satan's "tool," destroying the woman. Again, she seems to replace one hierarchy with another in her rereading: while she had previously agreed that the woman acted as Satan's tool, she now argued the man was Satan's tool instead. She was familiar with the Church Father Tertullian's (1869, 304) view that each woman was "an Eve" and his statement to women that has echoed down through the ages: "*You* are the devil's gateway."[67] Perhaps, given the strength of this Christian reading of Eve, Dons may have seen no other way out of this position than to situate the man as the devil's gateway instead.

What did life under "grace" look like in her rereading in the 1950s? It was more complicated. In 1928, she reasoned that woman brought sin into the world and God punished her by causing her to be dominated by the man, but when Jesus conquered sin, the effect of God's judgment ceased so that women should no longer be ruled by men. In her rereading around 1953, on the other hand, she argued that the reason for men's domination of women was different. It was not God's punishment. Instead, it was part of the historic battle between women and Satan, in which Satan used men to dominate women. Even after Jesus, Dons argued, this battle continued, so men still ruled over women. The picture is nuanced, though, because Dons also affirmed, using the words of Paul: "In Christ woman as man is '*a new creation*' (2 Corinthians 5:17)."[68] In other words, her final picture this time had more layers than in her 1928 reading. After Jesus, women and men were new creations, or created again, but at the same time the battle between Eve and Satan was still ongoing. This view was perhaps more realistic in its assessment of the difficulties Dons still faced in attempting to address gender relations in her own Christian circles.

READING AS ITERATING

Dons demonstrated a tendency to read and reread Eve, and this in turn effected a repeated rereading of herself as woman. A repeated use of Bible verses is common in Christian communities, as verses are constantly connected to new contexts and reread (Tomlinson 2010, 2014). Matt Tomlinson (2014, 166) argues that this action of repetition is "not quite change and not quite continuity, but rather an ongoing act of transformative reengagement." In Dons's reading and rereading of Eve, she seemed to approach both reading about being a woman, and being a woman, as iteration. She not only read iteratively, she also noticed the iterations inherent in the creation of Eve: Eve was created by someone else, after someone else. And women after Eve came out of a series of generations of women, iterations of Eve. When Dons in her late seventies raised a question about one aspect of these iterations, namely the positioning of Adam first and Eve second, she did so not by questioning whether there needed to be a first-second order, but by asking whether the order should be inverted so that Eve was first (to believe) and Adam second. In her repetition of this series, she was creating something new as well as maintaining the same first-second structure. Thus, while she approached her reading about the creation of woman—and the experience of being created woman—as iteration, this does not mean that reading generated either an obvious change or, on the other hand, a straightforward continuity. Rather, her iterated rereading, as a core part of her Protestant feminist subjectivity, produced ongoing, transformative reengagements.

MAPPING: PROTESTANT READING AS MATERIAL-DISCURSIVE INTRA-ACTIONS

For Dons, her female body was created, and this was a creation of "woman." Moreover, this creation was an iteration of another creation, that of the first woman, Eve, who again was a created iteration of the first human, Adam. Dons elaborated the position of "being created woman" as an iteration, or as something received from someone else. In her attention to the multiple entities involved, there is a curious overlap between her religious feminism a century ago and today's conversation on feminist new materialism.

How might we map her Protestant reading? I have argued that this instance of Protestant reading takes the form of a series of iterated intra-actions that constitute Dons as an iterated, material-discursive subject. In other words, Dons's repeated rereadings can be illuminated if we retool Barad's argument that performativity (such as, in this case, performing a gendered body) is a process of iterative intra-activity, given the many bodily and linguistic forms Dons was working with, in, and on. The intra-activity of some of these forms—God, biblical words, bodies—constantly iterated the creation of her as a woman as she "received" words from God in her reading and "gave" words to others, and was "on," "under," and "in" words. This resonates with Barad's (2008, 141) view of bodies as "material-discursive phenomena," though, unlike Barad, I include here the importance of words. For Dons, this intra-activity was both something she "received" and something that moved far beyond her control, as non-self actors determined who and how she was as a woman: God creating her, Jesus changing her status, Satan working through her to destroy the man or through the man to attack her. She was also connected to other human figures in history and around the world, being formed by her ancestor Eve's belief, by the angel's blessing on Mary, and by her view of various foil figures: "heathen" women, "the slave," "the Jews," or "the Muhammedan world." Dons, as a Protestant reading woman, emerges as not only a material-discursive subject but also a multiple one.

I have suggested that against this background the concept of ethical self-cultivation, or the broader theoretical framework of virtue ethics, does not fully capture the religious feminist subject that was "being created woman" and that emerged through Dons's readings of Eve. Rather, Dons was concerned with a more distributed and iterative formation of "woman" by and among multiple material and discursive entities, intra-acting in a circuit. We might say that her readings show us a series of woman-word operations in which words and body together operated as a distributed, collective ethical subject. This ethical analysis is more akin to the Wittgensteinian perception of Veena Das (2015, 57) when she suggests that our ethical concepts grow within particular forms of life, which is also "what gives them life" and allows us to extend them. From this perspective, an ethical project is an iterative process. There was a certain multiplicity, then, to Dons as an ethical subject and to her ethical project of Protestant feminism. She was not primarily focused on cultivating herself. Instead, hers was a more composite project, working through, with, and in several entities (that existed within, around, before, and beyond her) and changing over time.

AFTERWARD

Although Henny Dons was part of the feminist first wave in northern Europe, her readings of Eve give us a glimpse into the complex questions that remained unresolved after women gained the vote. Dons's encounter with men's reading of Eve and her own enfranchisement in NMS in 1904 seem to have had limited impact on her view of the lived, gendered body, though they formed the starting point for her iterated readings over the course of her life. She continued to grapple with Eve, placing herself as a woman reader not just in a regional history of advocating for "secular" rights but also, and more importantly to her, in an imagined global geography of "Christians" and "heathens," in a history spanning from Eve through Mary to herself, as well as in a created cosmos attacked by Satan and sustained by God. From Dons's perspective, the world and life that emerged through her continued rereadings, elaborations, and applications was not just the Garden of Eden or the first place in the world, but also the entire world or cosmos itself, including "woman's place" within these spaces. Working in this space, she iteratively engaged and reengaged questions about what a woman was in the cosmos and why and how (or even whether) she was secondary, producing Christianity repeatedly as "a gender project" (Thornton 2019). In this way, she wove together language, subjectivity, and ethics in her Protestant life in language.

However, though she was employed by NMS and shared her changing readings of Eve in talks to other Christian women, the organization itself does not seem to have been directly affected by her or other women's discussions of the Bible in the 1930s, 1940s, and 1950s. This is another puzzling difficulty that Dons presents to us today: How can we account for the ease with which she was sidelined by the leadership of NMS in the 1930s, when she was still so widely known? I have had to rethink what it meant to be a first-wave feminist through this lens. While Dons achieved prominence through innovation—becoming the first woman to be employed in NMS's central administration, speaking widely in public, being willing to reread the Bible—this did not remove the precarity of her authority as a woman. In the first wave, prominence and precarity came hand in hand.

The balancing act of a first-wave feminist also came with contradictory consequences. The NMS governing board's statement in 1904 that women ought to "receive" words had been based on the "foundational relations" they saw between Adam and Eve at the original moment of creation: man was created first, woman second. Their injunction on women's ordained leadership held sway in the organization until 1990, when the general assembly voted that NMS could hire women as pastors. Perhaps this long delay was also partly the outcome of Dons's emphasis on reading as "receiving" and "being created" in relation to others; her stance matched the view of the men on the NMS governing board that women ought to "receive" words. In this way, Dons's ethical project of Protestant feminism, and her use of reading as part of this feminism, had contradictory effects in the world.

CONCLUSION

A Material-Discursive, Multiple Protestantism

In May 1964, Henny Dons is about to turn ninety years old. The Christian newspaper *Vårt Land* has sent a journalist to interview her on this occasion, and the journalist follows the white-haired Dons as she moves quickly up the stairs to her room at Fossheim, a home for retired missionaries in Oslo.[1] Dons has been living there for the past three years. She and the journalist settle into chairs in her sunny room, next to a desk piled high with stacks of mail, and talk about what Dons spends her days on now. Dons shares that she can speak, read, and write as before, but she cannot hear as well and needs to use a hearing aid. She conducts an extensive correspondence, especially with missionaries abroad and female teachers in Norway; in the past year, she sent six hundred letters. She keeps up with several mission periodicals. She has some pain in one knee, but she still travels and can move around well. She recently attended two large meetings in Trondheim and Kristiansand to mark the fifty-year anniversaries of the local chapters of the Female Teachers' Mission Association.

Dons reaches over to her desk to show the journalist a small, pressed flower posy that came in one of the many letters she has received for her birthday. The journalist reports that this one is "from Africa." Dons places the posy back in a small glass and picks up another item received from Africa, a photograph of staff and students at the Bible school of the Norwegian Mission Society (NMS) in Eshowe, Zululand. The journalist adds an explanatory note for the reader: Eshowe was where Dons thought her path would lead in 1903, six decades earlier, but instead her path led to the sanatorium and then to a life in Norway. The journalist notes that Dons speaks eagerly and smiles as she answers questions; Dons, for her part, clarifies that she is not drawn to the term "hobbies" and prefers instead to say that all elderly people should "work." She impresses upon the journalist that if a "heading" is needed for her work over the past six or seven decades, then it should be the sentence from Ephesians 2:10: "For we are his workmanship, created in Christ Jesus unto good works, which God hath before ordained that we should walk in them."

I study this scene that Dons, about to turn ninety, has constructed for the journalist and the newspapers' readers. She has filled it with the importance of using words. But she moves easily between several elements with which she populates the scene—elements that are not just linguistic but also material, technological, human, and more-than-human: stacks of mail, a network of women teachers, a pressed posy, a photograph, "Africa," mission periodicals, a hearing aid, women's meetings, a biblical sentence, God. And she is at pains to emphasize that in her view, the outcome of this collection of elements is not, strictly speaking, hers, but rather God's work. Dons's framing captures one of my underlying themes in this book: there are both great distances and curious overlaps between my Wittgensteinian-inflected material-feminist analysis and her own perspective on her life in language.

This book has been a story about what happened when a Protestant woman used words. For Dons, I believe that story was about working as a created, embodied, collective subject—working in, with, and through various objects, entities, beings, and spaces, and being worked through by them in different ways, again and again. And for me, as an anthropologist in the archive, that story is about moving away from the prevailing scholarly image of a singular Protestant self who revolves around interiority and separation from materiality, and instead moving toward mappings of Dons's material-discursive, multiple life in language, including its slightly changing configurations from one instance to the next, making it possible to engage more carefully with her own story.

The main argument of this book has been that when we look at this Protestant woman using words, we see a Protestant life in language—that is, a series of woman-word operations weaving together language, subjectivity, and ethics in her life—characterized by being both material-discursive and multiple. The chapters have formed a fragmentary linguistic biography, a series of glimpses into Dons's language use that yield, in Wittgenstein's terms, "sketches of landscapes" arranged side by side ([1953] 2009, 3e–4e). As we look across these sketches, we see that Dons's life in language was part and parcel of her embodied life, composed in collective, changeable arrangements. As I have followed it across the preceding chapters, it has shown its shape-shifting possibilities as it was enacted in slightly different instantiations across sites: the woman-word operation of listening generated a responsive relation to their world; Dons's speaking body formed the composite site of a thrown-together voice; her writing constituted the productive but partially connected infrastructure for a protean ethical project; her reading was carried out in a series of iterated intra-actions that constituted an iterated, material-discursive subject. This was her life in language. It was not a singular life, though neither was it plural lives; it was "more than one, and less than many" (Mol 2002, 82). It was a material-discursive, multiple Protestant life in language.

Henny Dons died at Fossheim, the retired missionaries' home in Oslo, in June 1966, at ninety-two years old.

WOMEN AND WORDS

In the introduction, I mentioned that one of the voices that has continuously surfaced for me as I have worked with the archival materials from Dons is the voice of Luce Irigaray, asking: Do women have a place in language? Can they produce value? "No possible place," she observes; in the Western discursive canon, the father holds "the monopoly on value" ([1977] 1985, 68, 73). And in many ways, it is not difficult to draw a connecting line between the problem of women using words that Dons worked with a century ago in northern Europe and the same problem in today's Western contexts, including patterns of language use in our academic spaces—in classrooms and meetings, on reading lists, in conference halls, and in the endnotes—not to mention the many other places of our everyday interactions. It might be easy to jump from such observations about gendered language use to a general picture of Western patriarchal relations.

But in this book, I have attempted to find a different point of orientation than the patriarchal relations that are often the focal point of feminist theory. I have not wanted the book, at its core, to be about relations of power. I have not used the words *patriarchy* or *power* except in the opening discussion of chapter 4, where I drew brief outlines of the self-liberating feminist subject (who preoccupies secular feminism) and the self-cultivating feminist subject (who preoccupies scholars investigating religious feminisms). Both the self-liberating and the self-cultivating feminist subject can only exist within patriarchy, which she either resists or embraces. That is her purpose. But is that all there is? While feminist questions about women, religion, and language have often been framed within patriarchal relations, in this book I have instead aimed to contribute to the feminist new materialist shift away from a focus on "female" or "feminine" as "other" and toward a feminist theory that considers lived subjecthood and then, for example, "simply poses the question what a *woman* can do" (Dolphijn and van der Tuin 2012, 33).

This is not to say that we should stop discussing how we might define patriarchal relations nor to downplay that crosscutting affinities among women's language use in the modern West can be grouped together to help build such definitions. But here I attend to how other relations are also enacted in these lives in language—for example, in a woman's life in language in early twentieth-century Protestant northern Europe. If we think of this life as a form of life that is both assembled and distributed, collective and shape-shifting, it becomes apparent that aspects of it are easier to study if we do not place it under the panoptic gaze of the patriarchy. This shift in focus, from power to life, has formed the backdrop for my interest in mapping Dons's Protestant life in language as a complex form of life in itself.

This shift can help us move beyond a poststructuralist virtue ethics that focuses on self-cultivation when we describe women in historically patriarchal religious traditions, such as Protestantism. While Dons's ethical engagements through language can be mapped in many ways, I think they are illuminated more fully through the lens of project ethics than the lens of virtue ethics. Her language use took place within her ethical project of Protestant feminism, and this project was made up of both imaginative and material resources, forming a partially connected web of discursive, physical, technological, human, and more-than-human elements and forces. She enacted it in slightly different forms across different sites, and the project reached far beyond her in the world. This has helped me think about her use of ethics in life as being about much more than an idealistic orientation revolving around an interior, sincere self. I hope to have shown that if we retool the conversation on feminist new materialism to incorporate words, then this conversation can indeed offer conceptual resources to map the many elements involved in gendered lives in language, such as the life in language of a composite Protestant feminist subject with an ethical project.

One of my underlying themes in this book has been difficulty. We run into difficulties in feminist conversations too, such as the difficulty of conceptualizing how feminist histories have been formed around the North

Atlantic, as these histories have closely intertwined seeming opposites, such as the liberal and the conservative, the democratic and the imperial, the religious and the secular. It is difficult to give up a coherent story of feminism. It is also difficult to give up a singular feminist subject who demonstrates simply resistance and freedom (in a secular mode) or simply virtue and flourishing (in a religious mode). And then there is the difficulty of giving up coherence when examining women's use of words—the difficulty of giving up the sense either that women have no place in language or, conversely, that promoting women's voice has solely beneficial effects, however those are defined. It is difficult to continuously return to the acknowledgment that women's life in language is composite in itself and that, though this is easier to see in retrospect, it has contradictory effects in the world—creative, conforming, destructive, and enlivening. Yet this is a description that I think provides a more adequate engagement with the situation. Wittgenstein suggested that another way of saying "Now I understand" is to say "Now I know how to go on" ([1953] 2009, §154), and I think we can go on by exploring a feminist use of language that makes space for such difficulty.

PROTESTANT MODERNS

I began this book with the inauguration of the Mission School for Women one cold evening in October 1920 in Kristiania (soon renamed Oslo). That evening, Henny Dons spoke to a small crowd in the living room of the three-story schoolhouse. She was one of the first Lutheran women in Norway to arrange for herself to speak to a mixed-gender audience in a formal, Protestant space—this time, at the new school owned and managed by NMS. As the first school year got under way, things seemed to go smoothly with both lessons and living arrangements; in fact, the schoolhouse itself soon became a gathering place for mission-supporting Lutheran women in the capital. However, while Dons was helping to establish the Mission School for Women in Kristiania, a few women also continued to apply to NMS's Mission School (for men) in Stavanger on the west coast. Their applications continued to be denied for the next decades. I do not know what Dons thought about this. I have not found any statement in her documents that would indicate she thought the Mission School (for men) in Stavanger should open its doors to women, perhaps because she felt strongly that having one's own physical place—an all-women's residential schoolhouse with a living room, a dining room, and bedrooms—provided the necessary material environment for Protestant women to try out their new embodied use of words.

In 1972, however, the tide turned. The second feminist wave was just starting to make itself felt in Norway, and when two young women again applied to the Mission School (for men) in Stavanger, the men on the teachers' council recommended they be admitted. The council added a condition: unlike the male students, the women would not be ordained as pastors at the end of their theological studies. The decision was approved by the NMS governing board (Mosevoll 1992, 217). Following this policy change, women students at the Mission School for Women in Oslo began requesting to be transferred to the Mission School in Stavanger through the 1970s. It became challenging to secure teachers for the Mission School for Women, and the schoolmistress began contemplating retirement. NMS's governing board established a committee to consider possible options. The committee's final recommendation was to close the Mission School for Women, and their recommendation was presented for a vote at the NMS general assembly in 1978. However, the assembly's vote was negative; apparently, many of the representatives who had come together from mission groups across Norway, including from many women's groups, did not approve of the recommendation. The Mission School for Women remained open. By 1980, the school had no students (Mosevoll 1992, 216).

We have come far from the festive inauguration night in October 1920. Just over half a century later, the school's living room now stood empty as part of a large three-story schoolhouse without students or teachers, and with a mistress who was about to retire. The school's fate was finally decided after a second attempt at a vote at the next NMS general assembly in 1981. This time, the governing board's recommendation to "transfer the education of female missionaries" from Oslo to Stavanger was approved by the assembly (Mosevoll 1992, 217). The Mission School for Women was closed.

In the particular Protestant tradition of NMS, language and materiality and their relations play a significant role. In this tradition it has been important, for example, to pay attention to where exactly women use words. Which buildings are they in? Which rooms? Which city? Which other bodies do they sit next to? The relations between women's use of words, their bodies, and various spaces and places have been carefully noted, have had consequences, have prompted lively debate, and have shifted over time— even from one half-century to the next. Which picture of Protestantism does this leave us with?

The prevailing picture of Protestantism in the study of religion, including in my own subfield of the anthropology of religion, is one in which Protestants are assumed to be centrally preoccupied with belief at the expense of materiality. In this view, Protestants supposedly strive toward the (impossible) ideal of dematerialized language use, subjectivity, and ethics: a faith set apart from material forms. As noted in the introduction, this view has given rise to such shorthands in our scholarly conversations as "the Protestant bias," "the Protestant ethic," or "the Protestant language ideology," indicating a scholarly picture of Protestantism as a tradition that, at its core, desires dematerialization. This dematerialization drive is also viewed as the defining impact of Protestantism on Western modernity and modern persons; in this view, modern selves are all a little Protestant in their mentalistic interiority, in their separation of belief from body, in their struggles against the base confines of material existence, and in their thoroughly disenchanted world. However, as I have written and rewritten a book with a Protestant woman using words at its center, I have come to doubt the reach of this view.

I still agree with the argument that Protestantism has played a significant role in shaping modern Western life, but I now disagree that this shaping influence is primarily the ripple effects of an assumed Protestant desire for dematerialization. The lens of dematerialization has especially precluded closer analysis of gendered embodiment (and other embodiments) in our conversations. This has led to a mismatch between scholarly analyses of Protestant language use and the concerns of Protestant communities themselves, in which it has been unthinkable, over the past five hundred years, to consider language use without also noticing gendered embodiment. The scholarly focus on dematerialization has also nudged us toward a strong focus on an assumed singular ethical subject. Dons can instead help show how Protestants strive for life composed of linguistic and material parts in shifting arrangements, shaped by collections of figures and forces beyond the self and in turn shaping the world through protean ethical projects. Protestant life, as glimpsed through the example of Dons's life, is composite. This is a Protestant story that assembles bodily and linguistic elements, social technologies and spiritual forces, global spaces and intimate places, in changing configurations.

Perhaps it is easier to see that Protestants desire to use words in ways that are life-embedded and embodied when we are studying a woman, given the closer associations between women and materiality in Western modernity. One possible conclusion would be that Protestants of different genders use language differently because some (especially, many women) are forced to remain cognizant of their material bodies while others (especially, some men) have the option of ignoring theirs. This captures some of Dons's experience. However, I do not believe this conclusion takes us very far because it simply repaints the edges of the picture, suggesting that differently gendered people take on different linguistic roles but the central motif of Protestantism can still be analyzed in the same way. I think there is more to Dons's example. Placing a Protestant woman at the center of our analysis can help us rethink Protestantism itself.

While my study does not provide grounds for sweeping conclusions about the impacts of Protestantism on modernity, I suggest we start by revising our questions: instead of asking about individual sincerity in modernity, we might ask about body-word operations; instead of asking about the interiority of selves, we might ask about internal multiplicity. Dons wished to connect her body and her words, and her life in language was constituted through this material-discursive intra-action, which shows up in a variety of flexible configurations. There are affinities between this material-discursive range of Protestant language use and the range of combinations of linguistic and material elements we see in modern lives. Dons was also caught up in and contributed to some of the ethical megaprojects of Western modernity, including feminism, liberalism, and imperialism. There are affinities between her adaptive multiplicity—a multiple subject with a multiple project—and the multiplicity required to continuously enact these centuries-long, spread-out, protean projects that have to such an extent come to mark modern life.

When Henny Dons stood up to speak to a small crowd in the living room of the three-story schoolhouse one cold evening in October 1920 to mark the opening of the Mission School for Women, she was not enacting a desire to separate her words from her body, her ethical project from her material surroundings. She was not enacting an impossible Protestant language ideology aimed at dematerialization. Instead, she was experimenting with a new way of combining words and bodies because her Protestant life in language made this possible: she could combine and recombine material and discursive elements again and again, and the configurations could be enacted differently from one instance to the next. The configurations shifted from one site to another within her own life in language, and they continued to change in the tradition after her. If Protestant language use has been difficult for scholars to describe, perhaps it is because this life in language continues to make possible more options. Far from having presented an impossibility to the modern world, then, Protestantism has done the opposite, presenting moderns with proliferating linguistic possibilities—experiments with the many potential combinations of language and materiality, with the many potential connections of assembled subjects and protean projects. That is, Protestantism has presented us with the proliferating possibilities of a life in language that is marked, more than most, by material-discursive multiplicity.

ACKNOWLEDGMENTS

This project has taken shape in the midst of so many moments of interaction and conversation over the years. I feel incredibly fortunate to be among such kind colleagues in the anthropology of religion who ask interesting questions, give thoughtful feedback, take time to talk at conferences, and even occasionally email me Wittgenstein quotes. In particular, I want to thank Andreas Bandak, Jon Bialecki, James Bielo, Fadeke Castor, Simon Coleman, Girish Daswani, Kate Dugan, Omri Elisha, Matthew Engelke, Britt Halvorson, Courtney Handman, Jessica Hardin, Naomi Haynes, Eric Hoenes del Pinal, Brian Howell, Hillary Kaell, Omar Kasmani, Fred Klaits, Ashley Lebner, Marc Loustau, Maya Mayblin, Vlad Naumescu, Elayne Oliphant, Elizabeth Pérez, Devaka Premawardhana, Bruno Reinhardt, Joel Robbins, Anna Strhan, Brendan Jamal Thornton, Matt Tomlinson, Joe Webster, Leanne Williams Green, and Laurel Zwissler.

The archival research was made possible by the expert help of the archivists and other staff who support the Mission and Diakonia Archives in Stavanger, especially Nils Kristian Høimyr and Bjørg Bergøy Johansen. Many scholars based in Stavanger or passing through have been willing to share in my enthusiasm over the archival sources; special thanks here to Tomas Sundnes Drønen, Torstein Jørgensen, Kristin Norseth, Karina Hestad Skeie, and Kristin Fjelde Tjelle for the excitement of our exchanges at an early stage of this project.

I am also grateful to my colleagues at the University of Georgia for a long series of lunches, coffees, and hallway conversations as I kept writing. I have particularly discussed this project with Liz Browne, Robert Foster, Derrick Lemons, Jodie Lyon, Kendall Marchman, Rumya Putcha, and Nanette Spina, and many more have offered friendly encouragement along the way. A warm thanks to Patricia Richards for her support. Jamie Kreiner's reflections on the writing process twice moved the project forward, and Jennifer Palmer and Cassia Roth generously invited me into their Gender and History workshop.

When the manuscript was nearing completion, Laura Portwood-Stacer taught me a better way of writing a book proposal. Katie Lofton and John Lardas Modern went far beyond the call of duty when they provided insightful comments that led to significant revisions. And I have appreciated the friendliness and efficiency of Kyle Wagner, Kristin Rawlings, and the whole team at the University of Chicago Press as they have guided me through the publishing process.

This book would not be what it is if it were not for Wayne, who has read multiple drafts, discussed numerous interpretations of the life of Henny Dons, and always made sure I have time to write. Our two daughters, Sophia and Simone, are truly wonderful just the way they are, and it makes me very happy to look forward to many more conversations with them in the future.

The book includes material that has been previously published: a shorter version of chapter 1 appeared as "An Ethics of Response: Protestant Christians' Relation to God and Elsewheres," *Religion and Society* 11, 120–132, in 2020, and a shorter version of chapter 4 appeared as "The Religious Feminist Subject as Material-Discursive Circuit: A Christian Woman Reads and Re-Reads Eve," *Religion and Gender* 14(1–2), 153–172, in 2024.

NOTES

INTRODUCTION

1. See, for example, the photograph of Dons with students from the Mission School for Women in Nome (1943b, 151, see also 148).
2. Archive of the Mission School for Women (Misjonsskolen for Kvinner Arkiv, hereafter MFK), Bok nr. 2: "Protokol, Damekomiteen," Damekomiteens protokoll 1906–1920, Forstanderskapets protokoll 1920–1938 (hereafter Book 2), "Missionsskolens indvielse," October 1, 1920; and Bok nr. 6: "Hjemmet for kvindelige missionselever, Kvindelig missionsskole," 1912–1919 (hereafter Book 6), "50 års jubileum for Misjonsskolen for Kvinner," not dated, but the date June 14, 1950, is mentioned in the text. The MFK archival collection is held in the Mission and Diakonia Archives, housed at VID Specialized University, Stavanger. Archival sources used in the book are in Norwegian, and translations are my own, unless otherwise noted.
3. MFK, Box 23-3, Olden to Dons, June 22, 1912 (in which Olden cites a letter from Dahle to him).
4. MFK, Box 23-3, Olden to Dons, June 22, 1912 (in which Olden cites a letter from Dahle to him).
5. MFK, Book 2, Dahle to Gjør, December 22, 1908.
6. MFK, Book 2, Meeting of the Ladies' Committee, November 24, 1919; Book 6, "Grunnregler og plan for Det Norske Misjonsselskaps misjonsskole for kvinner."
7. MFK, Book 2, "Timefordelingstabell: Første år," 1920, and meeting of the Management Committee, June 17, 1930.
8. Several Norwegian scholars have created a conversation around the "mission feminists" and the associated "mission women's movement" in Norway as well as Norwegian women missionaries overseas; see especially Mikaelsson (2002, 2003), Norseth (2002, 2007), Nyhagen Predelli (2003), Skeie (2005, 2015a, 2015b), Skeie and Norseth (2003), and Tjelle (1990, 1999, 2002). Some of this work mentions Dons alongside other women leaders, and two longer discussions of Dons's life and contributions can be found in Norseth (2007, 422–440) and Mikaelsson (2002).
9. *Norsk Missions-Tidende* 1867, 25. Copies of *Norsk Missions-Tidende* (hereafter *NMt*) can be found in the Mission and Diakonia Archives, Stavanger. The spelling of the

magazine's name changed to *Norsk Missionstidende* in 1883 and to *Norsk Misjonstidende* in 1929.

10. Ethnographic studies of Christianity have rarely used a biographical lens, but there is much to be gained from using nontraditional "biographies" to illuminate the material, social worlds of Christianity, as shown, for example, by Bandak (2022) and Klassen (2018).
11. I am inspired here by Lisa Lowe (2015), who urges us to read the liberal and colonial archives together.
12. See also Das (2015, 58n2). Though "lives in language" is a focal point of Moi's (2017) reading in particular, Wittgenstein did not, as far as I know, use this exact phrase himself.
13. In Dons's circles, both 1 Corinthians and 1 Timothy were believed to be written by Paul. I use the King James Version in this book, as it is close to the Norwegian Bible translations published by Bibelselskapet (the Norwegian Bible Society) in 1904 and 1930, which Dons and her peers used during the first decades of the twentieth century.
14. Though there is also discussion within anthropology about the desirability or even possibility of comparing cases across settings (e.g., Strathern [1991] 2004).
15. Though for an innovative use of many archives to think anthropologically about the case of Christian "materializations" of the Bible, see Bielo (2022).
16. For discussions of a "Protestant bias" in the study of religion, which have especially been articulated in the conversation on material religion, see, for example, Meyer (2010), Meyer et al. (2010), and Vásquez (2011).
17. The concepts I discuss in the introduction are positioned in (and against) current conversations about language, subjectivity, and ethics in the anthropology of religion, linguistic anthropology, and the anthropology of morality and ethics. For those readers who are interested, I will use the endnotes to explain, even if briefly, why and how I am using certain theoretical concepts from these conversations rather than others. Let me begin with the concept of "language ideology" and a comment on why I have chosen not to use it.

    One of the first linguistic anthropologists to use "language ideology" as a theoretical concept was Judith Irvine, who defined it as "the cultural (or subcultural) system of ideas about social and linguistic relationships, together with their loading of moral and political interests" (1989, 255; see also, e.g., Blommaert 1999; Irvine and Gal 2000; Schieffelin, Woolard, and Kroskrity 1998). Just over a decade later, Alessandro Duranti (2003) suggested that language ideology could be thought of as the most recent paradigm of linguistic anthropology. Another decade later, Laura Ahearn (2012, 21) described language ideologies as a "fast-growing, exciting area" and a key term for linguistic anthropology. However, despite its ubiquity, I am hesitant to use the concept, because the way it has been tied to the theoretical underpinnings of (Marxist and post-Marxist) political economy makes it difficult to disentangle from certain understandings of ideas, power, and identity.

    First, while I agree it is interesting to pay attention to people's ideas about language use in different situations, subsuming these into the concept of "an ideology" (rather than "ideas about language use") can quickly imply that it is possible for the scholar to uncover a coherent, abstracted *system* of ideas driving people's language use, and that people's variation in language use can only be explained by positing that there must be two or more language ideologies present and in conflict. As will be evident by my turning to Wittgenstein in this book, I find it more plausible that the meanings people tie to language use can only be found in instances of use, and that scholars can at best describe a crisscrossing web of family resemblances among them that will remain somewhat incoherent and open to change in any particular instance (as I will explore later).

Second, the concept of ideology is difficult to disentangle from a Marxist understanding of power as an entity that a group "has" (or does not have), which may easily push us toward describing an ideology as either "powerful" or "not powerful." It seems to me the nuances of the relationship between language and power are more fully captured within the more recent poststructuralist framework that moves toward describing how the microphysics of power shape our actions at all scales (e.g., Butler 1993; Foucault 1978). (In this book, however, as I will discuss later, I will not engage with poststructuralism but instead with feminist new materialism and the provocative question it has raised for me of what might be obscured by a centering of power.)

Finally, the concept of ideology typically focuses researchers' attention on the question of which group uses which ideologies, thus tying ideology closely to a question not just of group power but also of group identity. Here too it seems to me that this quickly leads us to thinking of identity as an entity or a set of fairly stable characteristics that a group "has" or "is." Again, I think the nuances of social subjectivities and relations are captured more fully by later theoretical frameworks; while I am especially drawn to feminist new materialism, I also engage below with postintersectional feminist theory.

18. Some of the most influential versions of the idea of a "Protestant language ideology" or "Protestant semiotic ideology" have been presented with different emphases by Webb Keane, Matthew Engelke, and Birgit Meyer. Keane proposes that Protestants aim to distinguish between humans, words, and things by setting agentive humans "apart" from "material forms" (2007, 289), and this (attempted) purification produces Protestant subjects who are "Christian moderns." Engelke suggests that Protestantism brings with it an emphasis on words, especially the divine Word, "as a kind of immaterial presence" (2007, 21). And Meyer argues that Protestantism has an iconoclastic tendency that "dismisses form" (2011, 30) or demonstrates "misgivings about the use of material forms" to mediate divine presence (2010, 748).

Their conceptualizations have gained widespread use; Joel Robbins (2012, 15) has suggested that "the notion of language ideology has been one of the most successful theoretical product launches within anthropology as a whole," and he singles out its importance for the extensive conversation it has prompted in the anthropology of Protestantism. In this conversation, the language ideology of Protestant/Pentecostal communities is assumed to differ from Catholic/Orthodox ones, usually suggesting that a Catholic/Orthodox ideology ties signs more tightly to materiality (e.g., Robbins 2012). Much of the anthropological conversation on Protestant language use has thus moved toward consensus, and already in 2011 Jon Bialecki and Eric Hoenes del Pinal were able to sum up some "remarkably regularized" features as follows: Protestants have "a marked predilection for sincerity, interiority, intimacy, intentionality, and immediacy as an ethics of speech" as well as "a discomfort with . . . the social, material and

19. Dons was appointed acting mistress (*forstanderinde*) of the school during its first academic year of 1920–1921, and she seems to have lived at the school at Colletts Gate 33 during this time; see MFK, Book 2, "Husorden for Missionsskolen for Kvinder," September 21, 1920; and Archive of the Norwegian Mission Society (Det Norske Misjonsselskap Arkiv, hereafter NMS), Hjemme 1920–1970, Gen-sek 90, Inn-brev-hjem 1920, Box 428-4, Dons to Nilssen, June 25, 1920, and Dons to Nilssen, December 11, 1920. The NMS archival collection is housed in the Mission and Diakonia Archives, Stavanger. When referencing this collection, I have used the following shortened forms: "Hjemme" for *Hjemmearkiv*, "Gen-sek" for *Generalsekretariatet*, and "Inn-brev-hjem" for *Innkomne brev hjemlandet*.

20. I focus here on some concerns of the "later Wittgenstein" in his posthumously published *Philosophical Investigations*, especially as these are elaborated in ordinary language philosophy (e.g., Cavell 1999; Laugier 2013). My understanding of the ordinary-language reading of Wittgenstein is deeply indebted to Moi (2017), though I depart from her when I extend Wittgenstein into new materialism, a move she regards as incompatible with Wittgenstein's spirit (2017, 13–14). I have also benefited from Das's discussion of the later Wittgenstein. Das does not align herself with ordinary language philosophy (2015, 58n2), instead referring to her reading as a type of "ordinary realism" (2020, 197); more broadly, she has embraced the label "ordinary ethics" (2015, 2020).

21. Wittgenstein scholars commonly cite his works using standard abbreviations (e.g., PI for the *Philosophical Investigations*), but for the sake of clarity, I have retained author-date citations.

22. Other anthropologists who have picked up Wittgenstein's "form of life" have elaborated it in different and interesting ways; see especially Asad (2020; Martin 2014) and Myhre (2018a, 2018b). They both work to understand language as embedded in material life. In this sense, they share the impetus of recent work in linguistic anthropology to analyze language and materiality together, though linguistic anthropologists have largely drawn on Peirce rather than Wittgenstein to do so (see, e.g., the discussions of lineage in Keane and Silverstein 2017; Shankar and Cavanaugh 2017). C. S. Peirce, an American linguist at the turn of the twentieth century, was interested in the work of "signs"—that is, something that represents something else to somebody—including not just words but also, for example, things, colors, or sounds. Something becomes a sign as soon as it stands in a triangular relationship with an object and an interpretant, and Peirce (e.g., 1991) thought we might distinguish between different types of triangular sign relations. Even at a cursory glance, it is easy to see that "language" was quite different for Peirce and Wittgenstein: while Peirce lived in a world of signs, Wittgenstein lived with language as a form of life. In this book, I therefore use "language" in Wittgenstein's sense—as forms of life and live operations in the world—rather than in Peirce's sense, as types of signs.

23. This raises the related question of whether and how to cite Wittgenstein in feminist scholarship, such as in this book; I have discussed this question in Hovland (2024).

24. Feminist new materialism is usually grouped under the umbrella term "new materialism," which has been used in the humanities and social sciences since the late 1990s to cover such diverse approaches as actor-network theory (ANT), affect theory, object-oriented ontology, posthumanism, and more. A recurring thread across these approaches is the question of how matter matters. There is also a common interest in rethinking binaries that surround matter, such as person versus thing, subject versus object, alive versus inert, or language versus materiality, and to instead think in terms of various types of collectivities, networks, or assemblages. Several scholars have sought to trace the contours of feminist new materialism; I have especially appreciated Alaimo and Hekman (2008), Coole and Frost (2010), and Dolphijn and van der Tuin (2012). In this book, my thinking is particularly informed by the lineage of Donna Haraway, Marilyn Strathern, and Annemarie Mol. Strathern and Mol do not usually use the label "feminist new materialism," but I am drawing them into this field because of their close engagement with Haraway and their interest in rethinking wholes, parts, and relations. Gad and Jensen (2010) have suggested that Strathern and Mol's work can be described as "post-ANT," since they are interested, as is ANT, in the relations among collections of forms (e.g., Latour 1993), though they go beyond ANT in their greater emphasis on the multiplicity of a form and in thinking of forms themselves as composed of relations. I have also found Sonia Hazard's (2013) overview of new materialism and religious studies helpful. For good examples of new materialist analyses of religion, see Bialecki (2014), Chambon (2020), and Tremlett (2021), and for an interesting comparison, see Hardin's (2023) discussion of Oceanic epistemologies.

25. The material feminist scholar Susan Hekman (2008, 98) sees a more straightforward fit between Wittgenstein and new materialism, given Wittgenstein's emphasis on language as an activity carried out "*in* the world," inextricable from a form of life. I agree with this point but also think that Wittgenstein himself would have experienced a fundamental mismatch between his thought and new materialism's posthumanist orientation, because he usually—though not always—posits a bounded, humanist self (such as in his discussion of general human inclinations; [1967] 2018, 40).

26. My summary of "discourse" and "discursive" here is roughly equivalent to Wittgenstein's "language-games"—that is, our variable ways of carrying out social operations with language in shared "practices," or "language and the activities into which it is woven" in specific interactions ([1953] 2009, §7). Wittgentein's examples include presenting, storytelling, acting, singing, guessing, joking, problem-solving, translating, requesting, thanking, cursing, greeting, and praying ([1953] 2009, §23). In other words, I am neither adopting the new materialist sense of discourse, as exemplified by Barad, nor am I adopting the earlier poststructuralist use of discourse, as exemplified especially in Butler's Foucauldian analysis (e.g., Butler 1993; Foucault 1978), in which (in a grossly abbreviated form) we—our selves, our materialization, our reality—are largely effects of and within the limits of what we can think, say, feel, and be (our discourse).

27. Although the notion of multiplicity is widespread in feminist new materialism, the term "multiple" is not. While Mol (2002, 84) gravitates toward the term "multiple" rather than "pluralism," Strathern ([1991] 2004, 25–26) prefers to use the term "plurality" to convey the personified form in which "integration and fragmentation coalesce," rather than the

terms "composite" or "multiplicity," which she understands as aggregations of "ones" or individuals (and thus, in her view, inaccurate). Haraway ([1985] 1990, 191) does not elaborate on any of these terms, instead describing "cyborgs" who are "hybrids" and "chimeras." Other models of multiplicity have emerged within linguistic anthropology, directed more toward language use than toward subjects, such as Mikhail Bakhtin's (1981) notion of "heteroglossia," which illuminates the constant interaction of multiple voices and genres, or Erving Goffman's (1981) work on the multiple participant roles involved in speaking. In my assessment, these models can usefully push against the singularity implied in the language ideology model, but they still tend to linger on aggregations of "ones," in Strathern's term, and thus do not move fully into the composite and changeable types of multiplicity evoked in new materialism. However, for studies that draw out the helpful complexity of Bakhtin in relation to Christianity, see Hoenes del Pinal (2022) on Catholic language use in Guatemala, and Harkness (2014) on Presbyterian singing in South Korea. Loustau (2022, 207–227) similarly presents an interesting discussion of polyvocality in the Catholic Rosary, and Naumescu (2019) shows the plural actors and histories involved in a ritual speech act among Syrian Orthodox Christians in India.

28. Mol's line "more than one, and less than many" (2002, 82) is an adaptation of Strathern's line "one is too few but two are too many" ([1991] 2004, 36), which in turn is taken from Haraway ([1985] 1990, 219).

29. One of the most famous examples of this type of multiple subject is Haraway's ([1985] 1990) "cyborg," a posthumanist woman subject who is a social circuit of connections, part animal/human organism and part machine, part physical and part fictional. This image overlaps to some extent with Strathern's (1988, 13) later analysis of the Melanesian "dividual," a person who is divisible rather than indivisible, produced as a "plural and composite site" out of relationships. A few anthropologists of Christianity have taken up such complexity when describing Protestant/Pentecostal subjects by conceptualizing them, for example, as "dividuals" (Mosko 2010), "unstable" selves (Bialecki 2011), or persons who are "situational" and have "intrinsic mobility" (Premawardhana 2018, 18). However, the anthropological conversation on the whole still conceptualizes Protestant subjects as individuated, singular selves.

30. I am using the term "ethical" for this aspect of Dons's life in language to capture her engagement with ethical value, which I define as something that emerges as collectively important, even if contested, with its importance being located in the relations between subject and world (Hovland 2022); for an overview of the anthropological discussion on definitions of ethics, see Mattingly and Throop (2018). Wittgenstein did not write much explicitly about ethics, though there are fragmented notes in *Culture and Value* ([1977] 1998), and he has sometimes been used as a precursor to Aristotelian, first-person virtue ethics (e.g., MacIntyre 1985). However, I have used his thought in this book to build a different overall ethical analysis. In the same way that I am interested in the Wittgensteinian question of language use in life (and how a Protestant woman operated with words across different instances), I am also interested in ethics use in life (and how this Protestant woman operated with ethics across different instances).

31. The term "project" has not been used much in the anthropology of ethics, except in

strands of first-person virtue ethics where it is tied to the reflection and aspiration involved in individual projects of self-cultivation (e.g., Laidlaw 2014). I am not using "project" in this exact sense here but rather in a new materialist sense that seeks to take human aspiration into account without centering it. Thus, my analysis lies closer to Keane's sketch of "human projects," which he suggests are constituted in the midst of the interrelated conditions of (undetermined) affordances alongside (determined) physical causes and effects, conditions of possibility as well as constraint (Keane and Silverstein 2017, 33–34; see also Keane 2016). To avoid confusion, I should point out that I am also not using "project" as it has been developed in European existential phenomenology or in the practice theory of American anthropology, which again have centered desires and aspirations; for a good overview and critique, see Droney (2024). However, I agree with Damien Droney's (2024, 165) observation that when these understandings are transformed through the lens of science and technology studies, they can helpfully illuminate how projects need not be tied to individual subjects but instead can create subjects and make worlds discoverable. For example, we might say that Strathern's work shows how the ethical project of the gift creates dividuals or that Mol's work shows how the ethical project of healing atherosclerosis creates the multiple body. In the case of Dons, as I explore here, the ethical project of Protestant feminism created her as a material-discursive circuit subject.

32. It seems to me that the anthropological conversation on ethics and morality is currently clustered around three overlapping groupings (Hovland 2022): first, neo-Kantian deontological ethics, which emphasizes moral codes or value structures; second, Aristotelian or first-person virtue ethics, which pays attention to people's experiences, responsibility, and agency as they go about their daily lives, deliberate over their actions, and strive toward moral good (I place both phenomenology and ordinary ethics as loosely related to this grouping); and third, poststructuralist virtue ethics, which examines how subjects are formed as effects of a Foucauldian play of power and discourse (for a helpful discussion of the distinction between first-person and poststructuralist virtue ethics, see Mattingly 2012). While some anthropological work on Protestant/Pentecostal ethics has drawn on the first grouping, namely deontological ethics, by suggesting that Christian actions aim to realize ethical values from a hierarchical value structure (for a thoughtful example, see Robbins 2013), most anthropological analyses have tended to fall into either first-person or poststructuralist virtue ethics—or a combination—through an emphasis on how Christians cultivate, for example, sentiments, commitments, or selves (for thoughtful examples here, see Daswani 2015; Elisha 2011; Klaits 2010). My lens of project ethics, in which I think of ethical projects as constituted in material-discursive, protean configurations that are both enacted by subjects and produce subjects, is shaped to some extent by poststructuralism. However, I wish to move beyond poststructuralist virtue ethics (and thus beyond the third grouping above) and into the field of new materialism in my emphasis on the open-ended, internal multiplicity of both subjects and projects.

33. Wittgenstein uses the term *übersichtliche Darstellung*, often translated "surveyable representation," to refer to the result he wishes to gain from his crisscross description ([1953] 2009, §122). However, I have reservations about his tying of this term to "seeing" and

"clarity." While I have learned much from the discussions of his particular use of "clarity" (and his crisscross method in general) by Drury (1973, ix-xiv) and Diamond (2004), I have chosen to use the alternative term "mapping" in this book to indicate more strongly my own role in making and remaking possible maps and their provisional character.

34. In addition to canonical work on the relation between Western modernity and Protestantism (e.g., Mauss [1938] 1985; Weber [1905] 2002), a recent and widely read contribution is Keane's (2007) *Christian Moderns*. Keane argues that the Protestant missionary encounter and developing Protestant tradition in Sumba, Indonesia, throw into sharp relief the Protestant ideal of dematerialization that runs through or in parallel to the moral narratives of modernity, such as the modern desires, in Keane's view, for emancipation, purification, interior authority, self-mastery, and human agency free from encumbering, inert materiality. A different version of this argument has been put forward by Bialecki, Haynes, and Robbins (2008), who point out that Protestantism/Pentecostalism is sometimes portrayed as modern and sometimes as antimodern, though they suggest the underlying cause of these portrayals is the same, namely the Protestant/Pentecostal insistence on a dematerialized, individualized relationship to transcendence.

35. I might add that, while I concentrate on the material-discursive enactment of Protestantism and not Catholicism in this book, I agree with Elayne Oliphant's (2021) argument, presented in her careful readings of art and the Catholic secular in Paris, that Catholicism has developed a different but equally intriguing relation to secular modernity.

CHAPTER ONE

1. Archive of the Female Teachers' Mission Association (Lærerinnenes Misjonsforbund Arkiv, hereafter LMF), Dons: "LMF Minnebok," 1–4; LMF, "Til norske lærerinder," November 20, 1902. The LMF archival collection is held in the Mission and Diakonia Archives, Stavanger. Dons later said they had invited thirty (LMF 1927, 5–6; cf. Tjelle 2002, 68, 84n4). The spelling of the organization's name changed from Lærerindernes Missionsforbund (or alternately Lærerindernes Missions-Forbund) to Lærerinnernes Misjonsforbund in 1923 and to Lærerinnenes Misjonsforbund in 1928.
2. NMS, Hjemme 1842–1919, Gen-sek 90, Inn-brev-hjem 1901–1902, Box 111-7, Gjør to Dahle, January 3, 1902.
3. Tjelle (2002, 73), who cites the first minute book of the Kristiania/Oslo LMF group (LMF Protokoll 1902–1911, September 20, 1902). For further discussions of LMF, see Mikaelsson (2002), Norseth (2002), and Skeie and Jalagin (2017).
4. LMF, Dons: "LMF Minnebok," 4.
5. The attention to affect, bodies, and materiality has allowed anthropologists to ask new questions about religious communities, such as how to describe Christians' sense of "belonging" in a group (Dilger, Kasmani, and Mattes 2018) or how to trace the unfolding intensities of a Pentecostal talk (Bialecki 2015).

6. For a thoughtful defense of the concept of mediation, see Meyer (2020, paragraphs 13–17). For recent critiques of the concept by anthropologists working from different theoretical angles, see Lebner (2021), Reinhardt (2020), and VanderMeulen (2021).
7. Robbins (2020, 128–151) has suggested that agency and "passivity" intertwine in Lutheran theology, which forms the theological backdrop for the women's listening practices, even though the women themselves do not explicitly use this phrasing in their meeting minutes. On the many ways theology might be used to illuminate anthropological questions, see Lemons (2018).
8. For a study that extends Mittermaier's work in another interesting direction in the anthropology of Christianity, see Scherz (2017), who especially elaborates on "divine agents."
9. The phrase "come over and help us" is a reference to Paul's vision of the man in Macedonia (Acts 16). For an exploration of the painting's connections to similar images and its evolving meanings in NMS, see Gullestad (2007, 69–88).
10. For fuller discussions of the socioreligious context of the establishment of NMS in 1842, see Jørgensen (1990, 63–93), Mikaelsson (2003, 37–94), and Nome (1943a). The Norwegian word for mission groups, *missionsforeninger* (today *misjonsforeninger*), was usually capitalized in the 1840s, following the Norwegian convention of capitalizing common nouns at the time. However, this convention gradually fell out of use in the decades before and after the turn of the twentieth century, and for the sake of consistency, I render most Norwegian common nouns without capitalization.
11. The spelling of the organization's name changed from Det Norske Missionsselskab to Det Norske Missionsselskap in 1917 and to Det Norske Misjonsselskap in 1929.
12. *Missionslæsning for Kvindeforeninger* 1892, 52–53. *Missionslæsning for Kvindeforeninger* (hereafter *MfK*) was NMS's women's magazine, and copies can be found in the Mission and Diakonia Archives, Stavanger.
13. Tjelle (1999, 176) provides details of other early women's mission groups formed in the towns of Trondheim in 1826, Christiania (later Kristiania) in 1839, and Drammen in 1841.
14. Kielland ([1882] 1996), quoted in Dons (1925a, 12–13).
15. Kielland ([1882] 1996), quoted in Dons (1925a, 15).
16. *NMt* 1903, 180; see also Tjelle (1999, 175–176).
17. See, for example, *MfK* 1887, 61, though this may have been somewhat flexible in practice; Tjelle (1990, 31–32) documents that one large group in Stavanger decided to hold their monthly meetings on Monday afternoons instead.
18. The population of Norway, as surveyed in 1900, was just over 2.2 million, with 1,064 women recorded for every 1,000 men (Thorsnæs 2022, 2023).
19. I have come across only one archival reference to a mission group established by working-class women in Kristiania; they met at a different time, Sundays instead of Mondays, likely to accommodate their work shifts (*MfK* 1889, 78).
20. *MfK* 1905, 2. The author's name is not given, but the piece is certainly authored by the editor, Bolette Gjør. Also cited by Dons (1925a, 22).
21. *MfK* 1905, 3; also cited by Dons (1925a, 23).
22. *NMt* 1867, 25; see also 1866, 257. Tjelle (1990, 167–172) provides a good discussion of

the statements, noting that in practice the mission women's groups became more than merely "work groups," and it was impossible for NMS to fully monitor this development.
23. *MfK* 1905, 4; see also Ebbell (1946, 120).
24. See especially 1 Corinthians 14:34–35; 1 Timothy 2:9–13; and 1 Peter 3:1, 4.
25. Their regular meeting time seems to have been 5:30 p.m. on the last Saturday of each month; see, for example, *Misjonshilsen* 1929, 55. *Missionshilsen* (hereafter *Mh*) was the magazine of the Female Teachers' Mission Association, and copies can be found in the Mission and Diakonia Archives, Stavanger. The spelling of the magazine's name changed to *Misjonshilsen* in 1923.
26. The minutes do not usually record the number of attendees. However, the Kristiania LMF minutes report thirty, sixty, and thirty attendees at the "Christmas meetings" in 1912, 1914, and 1916 (LMF, Referatbøker, Oslo LMF 1911–1929, minutes for December 26, 1912; January 3, 1914; December 30, 1916). Assuming that the Christmas meetings were slightly more popular, I estimate that regular monthly meetings may usually have been attended by twenty to forty women. The number of attendees at the "annual feast" each October ranged from 100 to 110 in 1913, 1916, and 1917 (LMF, Referatbøker, Oslo LMF 1911–1929, minutes for October 27, 1913; October 28, 1916; October 27, 1917).
27. The minutes of the Kristiania LMF group do not specify when Dons stepped down as their local "chairman," but it was sometime between 1927 and 1930; see LMF, Referatbøker, Oslo LMF 1911–1929, minutes for October 29, 1927; October 24, 1928; October 26, 1929; and Oslo LMF 1929–1946, minutes for October 26, 1930.
28. See, for example, the location given ("Fagerborg menighetshus") in LMF, Referatbøker, Oslo LMF 1911–1929, minutes for May 25, 1918. Once the Mission School for Women was opened at Colletts Gate 33 in 1920, the group seems to have met there (e.g., *Mh* 1929, 55).
29. On the establishment of the NMS Home Crafts Circle (Det Norske Missionsselskaps Husflidsring) in 1918, see NMS, Hjemme 1842–1919, Gen-sek 90, Inn-brev-hjem 1919, Box 127-2, Dons: "Arbeidsoversigt for 1918," sent with letter from Dons to the NMS board, January 13, 1919. Dons and the Ladies' Committee also arranged for crafts to be part of future female missionaries' training (see NMS, Hjemme 1842–1919, Gen-sek 90, Inn-brev-hjem 1909–1910, Box 118-4, Dons to the NMS board, August 23, 1910, and Dons to Dahle, September 12, 1910).
30. *MfK* 1923, 54.
31. NMS, Hjemme 1920–1970, Gen-sek 90, Inn-brev-hjem 1925–1926, Box 436-6, Dons to Amdahl, September 13, 1926; Inn-brev-hjem 1928–1929, Box 440-5, Dons: "Arbeidsoversikt for 1928," January 23, 1929.
32. MFK, Box 72-1, Notebook by Rachel Lange, entry for April 29, 1920. Bolette Gjør made a similar comment about the groups; see MFK, Book 2, Gjør to Dahle, April 21, 1907.
33. LMF, Referatbøker, Oslo LMF 1911–1929, minutes for March 31, 1913.
34. In Norwegian: *der ute*, also spelled *derute* or *derude*; see, for example, LMF, Referatbøker, Oslo LMF 1911–1929, minutes for October 28, 1916; September 22, 1917; May 25, 1918; August 5, 1920; December 28, 1921; April 25, 1925.
35. LMF, Referatbøker, Oslo LMF 1911–1929, minutes for May 25, 1918.
36. LMF, Referatbøker, Oslo LMF 1911–1929, minutes for June 22, 1912.

37. See, for example, LMF, Referatbøker, Oslo LMF 1911–1929, minutes for December 26, 1912; October 28, 1916; October 27, 1917.
38. LMF, Referatbøker, Oslo LMF 1911–1929, minutes for October 28, 1916; the minutes note that the statement was prompted by Revelation 1:5–6.
39. In Norwegian: *vakkert, herlig, deilig, vidunderlig, nydelig, fredelig, rikt, stemningsfullt, hyggelig, koselig, festlig* (LMF, Referatbøker, Oslo LMF 1911–1929).
40. LMF, Referatbøker, Oslo LMF 1911–1929, minutes for May 25, 1918.
41. LMF, Referatbøker, Oslo LMF 1911–1929, minutes for October 29, 1927.
42. See discussions in Mikaelsson (2002, 2003, 267–279), Norseth (2007, 16–23), Nyhagen Predelli (2003, 247–256), Skeie (2005, 2015b), and Tjelle (2002).
43. MFK, Box 72-3, three typed pages with the heading "Kvinnens liv og tjeneste i menigheten: Svar til sogneprest Erling Ruud," inserted after the typed lecture notes on mission history, dated March 1947, unsigned but certainly written by Dons based on the biographical details given. Since the three-page text has been given a formal heading, it seems likely Dons submitted it to *Vårt Land* as a response to Pastor Erling Ruud.
44. See, for example, Strathern (1988, [1991] 2004). My understanding of Strathern's work on relations has been shaped significantly by Ashley Lebner (2017).

CHAPTER TWO

1. *Mh* 1911, 41.
2. *Mh* 1911, 44.
3. Of the four Protestant language practices examined in this book (listening, speaking, writing, reading), anthropologists have developed the most long-standing and elaborate conversation around Protestant speaking. One of the earliest contributions was made by Bauman's (1983, 5) historical study of Quaker speech, in which he drew on the ethnography of speaking to understand how Quaker speech functioned in the midst of "ideology, social relations, groups, and institutions." Since then, as noted in the introduction, an extensive anthropological conversation has developed around the notion of a "Protestant language ideology" in the anthropology of religion (alongside the extensive conversation on "language ideologies" in linguistic anthropology). For some of the most theoretically sophisticated conceptualizations of a "Protestant language ideology," see Engelke (2007), Keane (2007), and Meyer (2010, 2011).
4. Though some anthropologists have included descriptions of gendered language practices in Protestant communities, especially Bielo (2009b, 60–63), Handman (2017), Kaell (2020b), and Webster (2013, 101–123). Eriksen (2008) and Mayblin (2010) discuss speech practices as part of their studies of gender dynamics among, respectively, Pentecostals in Vanuatu and Catholics in Brazil.
5. As in classic contributions to (a liberal version of) difference feminism (e.g., Gilligan 1982) and intersectional feminism (e.g., Lugones and Spelman 1983). The conversation on voice in linguistic anthropology has branched more widely because it also encompasses more technical work on, for example, vocal quality (such as Harkness's 2014

study of song among Presbyterian Christians in South Korea). However, this work is also often understood in relation to individual or group identity and agency, or in relation to a language ideology that is in turn tied to expressions of such identity and agency. Similarly, within the anthropology of Christianity, Klaits (2010, 163–212) has offered a rich analysis of voice as influence and agency among Apostolic Christians in Botswana—though he adds a careful attention to intersubjectivity.

6. Massey does not use the label "feminist new materialism" for her work, but the approach she outlines in *For Space* (2005) resonates with new materialism's attention to materiality. This interest in space overlaps to some extent with the spatial turn in religious studies (for a good overview, see Knott 2010) and related work on place and space in the anthropology of Christianity (for a discussion, see Hovland 2016). However, Massey goes beyond these conversations in her analyses of the shifting collectivities that come together to form space and the unpredictability of mapping them.
7. *Mh* 1911, 27–28.
8. *Mh* 1911, 28.
9. *Mh* 1911, 27–28.
10. LMF, Dons: "LMF Minnebok," 54.
11. *Mh* 1911, 41.
12. *Mh* 1911, 42.
13. *Mh* 1911, 42.
14. *Mh* 1911, 42.
15. Though a few subversive practices have been documented of Norwegian women preaching in the Salvation Army and in some pietistic Haugean groups (Mikaelsson 2002, 114; Nyhagen Predelli 2003, 217; Seland 2021).
16. *Mh* 1911, 44.
17. *Mh* 1911, 44; see Galatians 5:13–15; 1 Peter 1:7.
18. *Mh* 1911, 28.
19. LMF, Dons: "LMF Minnebok," 53.
20. LMF, Dons: "LMF Minnebok," 53–54.
21. NMS, Hjemme 1842–1919, Gen-sek 90, Inn-brev-hjem 1901–1902, Box 111–7, Dons to the NMS board, January 10, 1902.
22. NMS, Hjemme 1842–1919, Gen-sek 90, Inn-brev-hjem 1901–1902, Box 111–7, Dons to the NMS board, January 10, 1902.
23. NMS, Hjemme 1842–1919, Gen-sek 90, Inn-brev-hjem 1901–1902, Box 111–7, Gjør to Dahle, January 3, 1902.
24. NMS, Hjemme 1842–1919, Gen-sek 90, Inn-brev-hjem 1901–1902, Box 111–7, Dons to the NMS board, January 10, 1902.
25. *MfK* 1901, 44; see also her fictionalized autobiography *Missionsbarnet* (Gjør 1892).
26. Lars Dahle, as leader of NMS, held the formal title of secretary at this point; in 1916 the title was changed to general secretary.
27. NMS, Hjemme 1842–1919, Gen-sek 90, Inn-brev-hjem 1901–1902, Box 111–7, Gjør to Dahle, January 3, 1902.
28. LMF, Dons: "LMF Minnebok," 6.

NOTES TO PAGES 65–66   153

29. NMS, Hjemme 1842–1919, Gen-sek 90, Inn-brev-hjem 1902–1903, Box 112-6, Dons to Hove, October 17, 1903.

30. In addition to the committees mentioned in the text, Mikaelsson (2002, 111) reports that Dons was a founding member of Norway's Christian Teachers' Association (Norges Kristelige Lærerforbund) in 1909 and served on its board, as well as being a member of the Norwegian Women's Christian Temperance Union (Hvite Bånd). Dons also joined the Female Mission Workers' Association (Kvindelige Missionsarbeidere, or KMA), a small, independent Norwegian women's mission organization that supported a couple of women missionaries in Armenia and in northern Norway; on KMA, see, for example, Dons (1925a, 41–42, 1925b), Norseth (2002), and LMF, "Kvinners innsats i norsk misjonshistorie," typed manuscript, unsigned but certainly authored by Dons, not dated (but written around 1945, referred to as the current year on page 13), 17–20.

31. When the Ladies' Committee secured a house in Kristiania for their women students, Dons joined the new Committee for the Home for Female Mission Students, moved into "the Home" (*Hjemmet*), and acted as its manager (*bestyrerinde*) from 1912 to 1919. On the Home for Female Mission Students, see, for example, MFK, Bok nr. 1B: "Damekomiteen, Utdannelse av kvindelige missionærer, Korrespondanse ved formanden," Henny Dons, 1910–1911 (hereafter Book 1B), Meeting of the Ladies' Committee, August 24, 1910; MFK, Book 2, Meeting of the Ladies' Committee, January 14, 1913; MFK, Box 23-3, Dons: "Oversigt over de første halvaars arbeide i missionshjemmet," April 20, 1913; MFK, Book 6, "Indstilling til LMFs 4de landsmøte," July 4–6, 1919. The Home was first located at Eugenies Gate 22, then moved to Pilestredet 83 in 1914 (Mikaelsson 2002, 117–118).

32. The Norwegian Women's National Council was a chapter of the International Council of Women, established in the United States in 1888 by Susan B. Anthony and May Wright Sewall. In Norway, the National Council comprised several women's organizations, including those for public health and hygiene (Norske Kvinders Sanitetsforening); social purity, especially regarding prostitution and trafficking (Centralstyret for de Norske Sædelighetsforeninger); temperance (Norske Kvinders Totalafholdsselskap); housewifery and homemaking (Hjemmenes Vel, later Norges Husmorforbund); and women's right to vote (Kvindestemmerettsforeningen). These organizations were all familiar to Gjør; see MFK, Book 2, Gjør to Dahle, December 30, 1908. On the other hand, the organized movement of working-class women was not directly represented in the National Council, as Arbeiderpartiets Kvindeforbund (the Norwegian Labor Party's Women's Federation)—established in 1901 and encompassing groups of "washer women," machine knitters, "matchgirls" (who worked in match factories), and others—did not join the upper- and middle-class National Council. For a detailed discussion of the National Council, see Tokheim (1975).

33. The first committee meeting for the Mission Workers' Circle (Misjonsarbeidernes Ring) was recorded in April 1907 in MFK, Book 2, Meeting of the Committee for the Mission Workers' Circle, April 1907. However, it seems Gjør formed the Circle earlier than this, because the Norwegian Women's National Council received an application for its membership in February 1907 (Tokheim 1975, 78–82). On the tensions surrounding the

Circle and its brief history, see the documents assembled in MFK, Book 2, as well as discussions in Mikaelsson (2002, 119–121), Norseth (2007, 138–141), Nyhagen Predelli (2003, 256–280), and Tjelle (1990, 187–204).

34. MFK, Book 2, Copy of letter from Dahle to Gjør, March 20, 1906.
35. I agree here with Tjelle's (1990, 196–197) and Tokheim's (1975, 78–82) assessments of the situation at the national meeting: it seems the situation mirrored debates about the women's movement among first-wave feminists around the North Atlantic more broadly.
36. The Circle needed a two-thirds majority of the vote to become a member. The result of the vote was thirty-seven in favor and twenty-four against; forty-one votes in favor would have constituted a two-thirds majority. See MFK, Book 2, Copy of Gjør's open letter in the magazine *Husmoderen* (*The Housewife*), no. 25: "Aabent brev til foreningerne og enkeltmedlemmerne i 'Missionsarbeidernes ring.'"
37. MFK, Book 2, Dahle to Gjør, December 22, 1908.
38. MFK, Book 2, Gjør to Dahle, December 30, 1908.
39. On the Mission Study Council, see, for example, NMS, Hjemme 1842–1919, Gen-sek 90, Inn-brev-hjem 1914–1915, Box 122–7, Dons to the NMS board, January 15, 1915. Dons remained a member until the Mission Study Council was disbanded in 1917.
40. Nyhagen Predelli (2003, 230), citing Theodor Olsen (Olsen's diary no. 5, 1896, printed version, NMS Archive); translation by Nyhagen Predelli, bracketed exclamation mark in original.
41. MFK, Book 2, Copy of letter from Dahle to Gjør, March 20, 1906.
42. *MfK* 1887, 95.
43. *MfK* 1887, 95–96.
44. *MfK* 1896, 78–79.
45. MFK, Book 2, MAR Cirkulære nr. 3: "Aarsberetning for Missionsarbeidernes Ring," Gjør, not dated but probably written in March or April 1908.
46. *MfK* 1887, 60.
47. *MfK* 1887, 61–62. The Norwegian word *ørkesløs* is unusual and Gjør likely used it to allude to 1 Timothy 5:13, where the same word occurs in the Norwegian Bible translation; in the King James Version, this verse says: "[the widows] learn to be idle ... tattlers also and busybodies, speaking things which they ought not."
48. *MfK* 1887, 61.
49. *MfK* 1914, 31.
50. MFK, Box 72–1, Notebook by Rachel Lange, entry for April 29, 1920.
51. *MfK* 1923, 52.
52. *MfK* 1892, 47–48.
53. *MfK* 1892, 47; 1893, 1.
54. *MfK* 1892, 48.
55. *MfK* 1904, 50.
56. *Vort Blad* 1912, 54, quoted in Norseth (2007, 435); Dons (1925a, 15).
57. *Mh* 1911, 44.
58. *Sambaandet* 1911, no. 45, 1. Thanks to Kristin Norseth for sharing this archival find with me.

59. *Nylænde* 1911, 249; see also Mikaelsson (2002, 114); Norseth (2007, 433).
60. NMS, Hjemme 1920–1970, Gen-sek 90, Inn-brev-hjem 1921–1922, Box 430-8, Dons: "Aarsmelding for 1921," January 10, 1922.
61. Her handwritten notes for talks can be found in MFK, Box 72-1, "Bibelstudium" by Dons; MFK, Box 72-4, "Vintreet og grenene: Bibeltimer i LMF" by Dons; MFK, Box 72-5, "Guds ord til kvinnen / Kvinnens stilling i menigheten" by Dons; MFK, Box 73-1, "Den Hellige Ånd / Sjelesorg for barn under evighetens sysnvinkel" by Dons; MFK, Box 73-2, "Bønnens skole" by Dons; MFK, Box 73-3, "Studier over frelsen i Kristus" by Dons. In addition, Dons has inserted her handwritten notes for a number of devotional talks between two typed stacks of her lecture notes on mission history (MFK, Box 72-3), and she also saved her handwritten notes for a lecture to the NMS national board meeting in 1949 (MFK, Box 73-4, "Misjonsarbeidets stilling, 1949, Ute og hjemme: Fra NMS' landsstyremøte" by Dons). The LMF archive has preserved a notebook containing her handwritten notes for a lecture on pastoral counseling among children and youth (LMF, "Sjelesorg blant barn og ungdom" by Dons, handwritten notebook, dated 1943 and 1949).
62. For an overview of this historical development, see Oftestad, Rasmussen, and Schumacher (2005, 249–250). The majority approach to biblical interpretation within NMS in the early 1900s seems to have been a conservative one that nevertheless did not view the Bible as inerrant and was open to using recent scholarship; see Dahle (1911).
63. NMS, Hjemme 1842–1919, Gen-sek 90, Inn-brev-hjem 1909–1910, Box 118-4, Dons to the NMS board, August 23, 1910; MFK, Box 23-2, Gundersen to Dons, August 24, 1910.
64. MFK, Book 1B, Dons to Gundersen, August 25, 1910.
65. MFK, Box 23-2, Gundersen to Dons, August 30, 1910.
66. MFK, Book 1B, Gundersen to Dons, received August 29, 1910, note added by Dons, August 29, 1910. Gundersen also inquired about her belief in Jesus's atoning death and the Trinity. For his explication of how these questions related to views of the Bible, see MFK, Box 23-2, Gundersen to Dons, September 22, 1910.
67. Some decades later, she again indicated this view, though indirectly, when she referred to the 1925 decision to allow women to preach: she explained that here "the church" had "shown" Paul's injunction against women speaking was not "a binding God's word for all time" (MFK, Box 72-3, three typed pages with the heading "Kvinnens liv og tjeneste i menigheten: Svar til sogneprest Erling Ruud," inserted after the typed lecture notes on mission history, dated March 1947, unsigned but certainly written by Dons based on the biographical details given).
68. Dons occasionally expressed a sentiment that came close, though at other times she chose to remain silent, and the archival material is elusive on this point. In 1910, Dons wrote to NMS Secretary Dahle that, although she defended women's right to preach, she was not trying to "prove" a woman could be an ordained pastor (NMS, Hjemme 1842–1919, Gen-sek 90, Inn-brev-hjem 1909–1910, Box 118-4, Dons to Dahle, October 17, 1910). However, the following year she signed a letter, in her capacity as a board member of the Norwegian Women's National Council, urging the Norwegian government to make it legal for women to be employed as ordained pastors in the state church (Mikaelsson 2002, 130n25). The Council decided to send a similar letter ten years later,

in 1921, but this time Dons declined to be part of the deputation, without explaining her reasons (Norseth 2007, 440). At this time she was employed by NMS. In 1938, while still employed by NMS, she published a short, unsigned note in *Misjonshilsen* (on page 20) that asked why women should not have "access to the positions of the church." This short note is discussed by Mikaelsson (2002, 114) who, although she has not found any direct statement by Dons on women's ordination, suggests that the unsigned note "more than indicated a standpoint." I am not so sure, because Dons's phrasing here, as always on the matter, seems intentionally open-ended. This was also the case after her retirement from NMS. In 1947, she wrote a response to a male pastor who had printed an opinion piece in the Christian newspaper *Vårt Land* stating that women could not be pastors; in her response, Dons argued forcefully for women's "calling" and "service" as wives, mothers, and teachers in the congregation, and she said these roles were akin to that of a pastor. However, she clearly phrased her response in such a way that it allowed her to avoid saying women should be ordained as pastors (MFK, Box 72-3, "Kvinnens liv og tjeneste i menigheten: Svar til sogneprest Erling Ruud").

CHAPTER THREE

1. See discussion of Dons's lecture notes later, and MFK, Box 73-5, "Misjonshistorie, utarbeidet av frk. Henny Dons" (hereafter "Misjonshistorie").
2. I have listed those published texts of which I am aware (excluding magazine articles) in the reference list. Dons published three books with the Christian press Lutherstiftelsen on women and mission, women in the Bible, and Bible studies for youth (Dons 1925a, 1928, 1933), as well as six books for use in the mission's children's work, mostly published by NMS (Dons 1915, 1919, 1920a, 1920b, 1922, 1923a). She saved an unpublished manuscript on women in Norwegian mission history that repeats and expands on some of the sections of her published book on the same topic (LMF, "Kvinners innsats i norsk misjonshistorie," typed manuscript, unsigned but certainly authored by Dons, not dated but written around 1945, which is referred to as the current year on page 13; cf. Dons 1925). She also wrote a book manuscript on mission history that remained unpublished, which I discuss in this chapter ("Misjonshistorie"). She published shorter pieces of 3–16 pages as chapters or pamphlets on women and mission and on youth and mission (Dons 1914, 1923b, 1925b, probably 1937, 1938; LMF 1927). After her retirement in 1939, she published the lectures she delivered at a course for NMS's female traveling secretaries (Dons 1945) and a chapter on "what life has taught me" (Dons 1952). She saved several notebooks containing typed and handwritten notes for her lectures at the Mission School for Women, talks presented at other courses, and numerous Bible studies given, for example, to meetings of the Female Teachers' Mission Association and at other Christian meetings, and these can be found in the archival collections of the Female Teachers' Mission Association (LMF, Dons: "Sjelesorg blant barn og ungdom") and the Mission School for Women (MFK, Box 72-1, 72-2, 72-3, 72-4, 72-5, 73-1, 73-2, 73-3, 73-4). She also saved a handwritten notebook of memories of her work in the Female

Teachers' Mission Association (LMF, Dons: "LMF Minnebok"). Her unpublished writings included her stream of official and unofficial correspondence, some of which has been kept, as well as her extensive personal letter-writing, especially after retirement, most of which has not been saved. In addition, she regularly wrote articles for periodicals throughout her working life and afterward, such as for NMS's magazine *Norsk Missiontidende*, NMS's women's magazine *Missionslæsning for Kvindeforeninger*, NMS's youth magazine *Kamp og Seier*, NMS's children's magazine *Barnebladet* (which Dons edited 1918–1928), the Female Teachers' Mission Association's magazine *Missionshilsen* (which Dons edited 1905–1913 and 1929–1947), the Young Women's Christian Association's magazine *Vort Blad* (which Dons edited 1906–1917), and the women's newspaper *Norges Kvinder*.

3. "Misjonshistorie"; for the dating and title, see subsequent discussion.
4. Handman's work presents an innovative engagement with (and also goes beyond) the infrastructural turn in anthropology and related fields, which has directed our attention to the operations of a wide variety of systems—from roads and sewers to telephones and social media. Some of the work on infrastructure falls under the new materialist umbrella, especially when drawing on actor-network theory or science and technology studies. For a good overview, see Larkin (2013).
5. For a different but interesting approach to combining infrastructure and ethics, see Benussi (2022).
6. As outlined in note 32 of the introduction, it seems to me that the anthropology of ethics and morality can currently be clustered into three broad, overlapping groupings (deontological ethics, first-person virtue ethics, and poststructuralist virtue ethics), and the work on value structures, especially by Robbins (2013), falls within the first grouping of deontological ethics.
7. NMS, Hjemme 1842–1919, Gen-sek 90, Inn-brev-hjem 1919, Box 127-2, Dons: "Arbeidsoversigt for 1918," sent with letter from Dons to the NMS board, January 13, 1919; Hjemme 1920–1970, Gen-sek 90, Inn-brev-hjem 1928–1929, Box 440-5, Dons: "Arbeidsoversikt for 1928," January 23, 1929.
8. MFK, Box 72-1, Notebook by Rachel Lange, entry for April 29, 1920.
9. NMS, Hjemme 1920–1970, Gen-sek 90, Inn-brev-hjem 1921–1922, Box 430-8, Dons: "Aarsmelding for 1921," January 10, 1922; Dons (1925a, 33).
10. NMS, Hjemme 1920–1970, Gen-sek 90, Inn-brev-hjem 1920, Box 428-4, Dons to Dahle: "Arbeidsoversigt 1919," January 13, 1920; Inn-brev-hjem 1920–1921, Box 429-4, Dons: "Arbeids-rapport for 1920 fra Henny Dons," January 11, 1921.
11. NMS, Hjemme 1920–1970, Gen-sek 90, Inn-brev-hjem 1920–1921, Box 429-4, Dons: "Arbeids-rapport for 1920 fra Henny Dons," January 11, 1921. The house at Pilestredet 83 had previously been rented as the Home for Female Mission Students while the Ladies' Committee ran its ad hoc courses for future female missionaries, before NMS's Mission School for Women was established in 1920 in the residential schoolhouse at Colletts Gate 33, purchased by NMS (MFK, Book 2, Meeting of the Ladies' Committee, November 24, 1919). NMS purchased Pilestredet 83 in 1922 (NMS, Hjemme 1920–1970, Gen-sek 90, Inn-brev-hjem 1921–1922, Box 430-8, Dons to Nilssen, May 13, 1922).

12. NMS, Hjemme 1920–1970, Gen-sek 90, Inn-brev-hjem 1921–1922, Box 430-8, Dons to Nilssen, January 13, 1922.
13. Brenna Moore (2021) has provided a beautiful analysis of how such friendship—in her case, among Catholic intellectuals from around 1920 to 1950—may contain many layers of connection, desire, or satisfaction that elude the rigid categories of heterosexuality versus homosexuality and instead point us toward a deeper understanding of the fullness of relationships.
14. See, for example, NMS, Hjemme 1920–1970, Gen-sek 90, Inn-brev-hjem 1920–1921, Box 429-4, Dons: "Arbeids-rapport for 1920 fra Henny Dons," January 11, 1921.
15. MFK, Box 72-1, Notebook by Rachel Lange, entry for April 29, 1920.
16. MFK, Box 72-2, "Henny Dons: Misjonshistorie & Bibeltimer og misjonsforedrag," 116.
17. She presented the argument in *Africa is Waiting* (Dons 1920a, 23–24) before her trip and in her unpublished manuscript on mission history ("Misjonshistorie," 39), probably completed around 1936, after her trip.
18. A few decades later, the issue of colonialism surfaced on the internal agenda of NMS again, as the 1940s and 1950s brought the bureaucratic unraveling of the British Empire, political decolonization, and discussions within NMS around the practical logistics and degree of self-rule in the so-called mission churches in Southern Africa (though the process was slow and ambiguous, as documented by Bakke 2012). However, by the 1940s, Dons had retired from NMS, and the archive does not reveal whether she participated in these discussions.
19. Gayatri Chakravorty Spivak (1985) has argued that the same phenomenon can be applied more broadly and that famous women's books such as *Jane Eyre* by Charlotte Brontë, a classic in the Anglophone feminist canon, in fact shows how north European women's subjectivity was made in imperial mode on the basis of the other "native" woman. For a thoughtful response, see Jolly (1993).
20. On the Ladies' Committee, see MFK, Bok nr. 1: "Protokol for Komiteen til Uddannelse af kvindelige Missionære," 1900–1905 (hereafter Book 1); Book 1B; and Book 2.
21. See also, for example, Dons (1923b, 1928).
22. This collection of numbers, including a very large one, is reminiscent of Kaell's (2020a, 3, 51–70) description of the effects of numbers in Christian child sponsorship literature: the combination of large numbers alongside the story of one person creates a sense of "immensity" alongside the "intimate."
23. Here I build on a postintersectional approach to the processes of whiteness and womanhood that emerge in Dons's writing. Postintersectional theory goes beyond intersectional feminism, which examined the effect of intersecting identity categories. In its most pared-down form, an intersectional lens on Dons as a white woman would start from the premise: "White women have been penalized by their gender but privileged by their race" (Collins 2000, 246). This insight did much to upend conversations in feminist theory in its time, but more recently, feminist theorists have wished to move beyond this depiction of stable, separate identity categories. Along with Suzanne Bost (2008, 341), they might express their frustration that discussions of gender/race/class/sex/etc. reify the categories themselves and "often protect their boundaries by *not* analyzing their interiors" (see also Nash 2018). Here I adapt postintersectional thought (and extend

NOTES TO PAGES 95-98   159

it into feminist new materialism) to ask whether we can gain more insight into processes of racializing gendered subjects if we shift away from thinking in terms of stable identities—"a white woman"—toward thinking in terms of embodied operations—such as experiencing, conceptualizing, or using "being white"—that are partially connected across sites.

24. The school held classes in the dining room and received the large oak dining table as a gift in 1930 (MFK, Book 2, Meeting of the Management Committee, June 17, 1930). It was not until 1949 that one of the rooms in the house was turned into a classroom with a desk and chair for each student; that was "a great day," a woman later recorded in an anonymous note, important enough to be saved (MFK, Book 6, two loose sheets added at the end: "Misj. sk. f. kv.," not dated, but the back of one sheet contains a program from 1978).

25. NMS, Hjemme 1920–1970, Gen-sek 90, Inn-brev-hjem 1929–1930, Box 441–5, Dons: "Arbeidsoversikt for 1929," January 21, 1930; and Inn-brev-hjem 1935–1936, Box 447–3, Dons to Kopreitan, October 31, 1936.

26. Her lecture notes have been saved in MFK, Box 72–2, "Henny Dons: Misjonshistorie & Bibeltimer og misjonsforedrag," and Box 72–3, "Henny Dons: Misjonshistorie," while her unpublished manuscript ("Misjonshistorie") is in MFK, Box 73–5.

27. Handwritten note on the title page of "Henny Dons: Misjonshistorie & Bibeltimer og misjonsforedrag" in MFK, Box 72–2.

28. NMS, Hjemme 1920–1970, Gen-sek 90, Inn-brev-hjem 1935–1936, Box 447–3, Dons to Kopreitan, October 31, 1936.

29. The title of the lecture notes can be found on the first typed page of "Henny Dons: Misjonshistorie & Bibeltimer og misjonsforedrag" in MFK, Box 72–2.

30. See, for example, Nome (1943b, 155) and the statement by Johanne Høeg, director of the school, in 1945 that "well over one hundred young women" had graduated from the school since its establishment in 1920 (Sæverås 1986, 109).

31. The daily timetable and rules can be found in MFK, Book 2, "Husorden for Missionsskolen for Kvinder," September 21, 1920, and June 23, 1928. See also the recollections by a former student in Sæverås (1986, 106–108).

32. See, for example, the photographs in Nome (1943b, 151) and Sæverås (1986, 107).

33. MFK, Book 2, Meetings of the Management Committee, November 9, 1925; June 7, 1933; June 27, 1933; September 14, 1933.

34. "Misjonshistorie," 71.

35. "Misjonshistorie," 75.

36. "Misjonshistorie," 79.

37. "Misjonshistorie," 7–8.

38. "Misjonshistorie," 8–12.

39. "Misjonshistorie," 11.

40. "Misjonshistorie," 39, 42.

41. "Misjonshistorie," 17, 24, 63–66. In her first set of lecture notes, she included an overview of the "Zenana mission" among women in India and the work of an Indian woman convert to Christianity, Pandita Ramabai, for the education of women (MFK, Box 72–2, 27–41). In her second set of lectures, this section was retained in the lesson on India

but shortened to one page (MFK, Box 72-3, 24); in her book manuscript it took up four pages ("Misjonshistorie," 63-66).

42. The lecture on women and mission was not part of her course overview for 1943-1944 (MFK, Box 72-3, typed course overview on page 4), but it was added at the end of her course overview for 1944-1945 (MFK, Box 72-3, handwritten course overview for 1944-1945, inserted after the handwritten Bible lessons). Her notes for the lecture on women and mission can be found toward the end of each of her two sets of lecture notes (MFK, Box 72-2, section titled "Kvinnenes misjonsarbeide"; and MFK, Box 72-3, section titled "Kvinnene og misjonen").

CHAPTER FOUR

1. MFK, Box 72-5, Notebook titled "Guds ord til kvinnen / Kvinnens stilling i menigheten" by Dons, section titled "Kvinnens plass i Guds rike," 6.
2. Mittermaier (2011, 2012) engages especially with the prominent work on self-cultivation in the anthropology of Islam (e.g., Hirschkind 2006; Mahmood 2005). A few other scholars have also pushed back against the trope of religion as self-cultivation, including Mayblin (2017) and Schielke (2009); and see Robbins's (2020, 128-151) interesting elaboration on Lutheran "passivity" as a contrast to self-cultivation.
3. However, for instances of women voting in NMS mixed-gender mission groups earlier, even though it was "illegal," see Nyhagen Predelli (2003, 148-149).
4. *MfK* 1903, 57-58.
5. As recorded in the minutes from the meeting, printed in NMS's magazine (*NMt* 1903, 2-3).
6. The thirty-five-page proposal was distributed as a pamphlet printed in 1904 by NMS's press in Stavanger (Det Norske Missionsselskabs Bogtrykkeri), titled *Cirkulære til Generalforsamlingen i Bergen 1904* (hereafter *Cirkulære*). It was also printed in *NMt* 1903, 175-182, and 1904, 244-267.
7. *Cirkulære*, 18-19.
8. *Cirkulære*, 19-20.
9. *Cirkulære*, 7.
10. *Cirkulære*, 22-23.
11. *Cirkulære*, 16.
12. *Cirkulære*, 28.
13. *Cirkulære*, 26.
14. Reports of the discussion are given in *MfK* 1904, 51-54; and *NMt* 1904, 344-351, 363-369.
15. *Nylænde* 1904, 226, quoted in Nyhagen Predelli (2003, 165), her translation.
16. At the turn of the twentieth century, NMS counted just over nine hundred mixed-gender "mission groups" and three thousand to four thousand "mission women's groups" (*Cirkulære*, 8-9).
17. MFK, Book 2, Gjør to Dahle, December 30, 1908.
18. *NMt* 1867, 25.

19. MFK, Box 72-1, Notebook titled "Bibelstudium" by Dons, section titled "Metodisk bibelstudium," 1920 (hereafter "Bibelstudium").
20. "Bibelstudium," 1.
21. "Bibelstudium," 15.
22. "Bibelstudium," 19–20.
23. "Bibelstudium," 20–32.
24. "Bibelstudium," 21.
25. "Bibelstudium," 24–25; in Dons's notes, some passages are recorded more than once as they were repeated during the discussion.
26. LMF, Referatbøker, Oslo LMF 1911–1929, minutes for January 6, 1921.
27. LMF, Referatbøker, Oslo LMF 1911–1929, minutes for January 3, 1914; September 25, 1915.
28. NMS, Hjemme 1920–1970, Gen-sek 90, Inn-brev-hjem 1923–1924, Box 433-4, Dons to Amdahl, January 3, 1924.
29. LMF, Referatbøker, Oslo LMF 1911–1929, minutes for May 26, 1917; and Oslo LMF 1929–1946, minutes for November 5, 1932. On being "given" verses, see also, for example, LMF (1927, 6); LMF, Referatbøker, Oslo LMF 1929–1946, minutes for October 26, 1930, and November 5, 1932; LMF, Landsmøtet 1937, Dons to LMF group leaders, May 4, 1937. On women going "under" words or words being "over" women, see also, for example, LMF, Referatbøker, Oslo LMF 1911–1929, minutes for August 26, 1916; and Oslo LMF 1929–1946, minutes for October 26, 1930.
30. Their description of reading as receiving is reminiscent of Simon Coleman's (1996, 112) discussion of Pentecostals in Sweden who internalize words from sermons or from the Bible in a manner perceived as "eating," and who do so repeatedly to "'get filled' with the Word"; on Protestants "eating" Christian words, see also Strhan (2015, 123–124) and Webster (2013, 75–100).
31. As noted, I use the King James Version (KJV) Bible translation throughout the book as it is close to the 1904 and 1930 Bible translations by the Norwegian Bible Society that Dons and her peers used. However, when translating biblical quotes directly from Dons's text, as here, I render the Norwegian phrasing as carefully as possible, and these biblical quotes therefore differ slightly from the KJV.
32. Dons (1928, 5) noted that she had drawn on the book *Kvinden: Fri eller træl* (*The Woman: Free or Slave*) by Maria Høyer (1925). Høyer was a Danish woman who had worked as a missionary wife among Muslims in South Arabia for two decades, and in her book she emphasized the imagery of captivity versus liberation.
33. The maternal feminist argument was especially articulated, for example, by the leader of the prominent Norwegian women's organization Hjemmenes Vel (Welfare in the Home), Marie Michelet (see, e.g., Michelet 1946), but the argument was also used more widely in the women's movement in Norway at the time, including by women advocating for legal rights and the vote (Blom 1990). On Dons's view of motherliness, see also her published essay on "Women's task and work in the mission" (1923b, 4). In addition, as Nyhagen Predelli (2003, 95–132) shows, Dons and her peers were influenced by maternal feminist arguments made in the broader North Atlantic context, especially regarding how to export Western domesticity to British and French colonial territories (and to Christian missions within these territories).

34. For a similar example, see Bielo's (2009b, 65) description of an American Bible study group generating a chain of Bible verses.
35. LMF, Henny Dons correspondence, Dons to Herstad, September 29, 1960.
36. MFK, Box 72-1, Notebook titled "Bibelstudium" by Dons, section titled "Kvinnens innsats i menigheten," 138–139, not dated but written in January or February 1948.
37. MFK, Box 72-5, Notebook titled "Guds ord til kvinnen / Kvinnens stilling i menigheten" by Dons, section titled "Kvinnens plass i Guds rike." The notebook contains handwritten notes for talks, including some loose sheets with added notes, and a short undated itinerary of four groups Dons spoke to in Kristiansand. While the notebook is not dated, Mikaelsson (2002, 123) suggests it might be from sometime around 1949 because Dons expresses similar views in a letter written in that year (Mikaelsson cites Dons's letter to Marie [Monsen], August 27, 1949, LMF Archive). I agree that this dating seems roughly correct; here I suggest it was probably written in the early 1950s because Dons says of the times that there has been "high inflation . . . expenses have tripled in the past few years" and there is "unrest" across all of Africa as Africans struggle for their right to also have "the white man's rights" (in the section titled "Hvor står vi?," 38–39). These two pieces of information seem to match the sharp rise in the consumer price index in Norway in the first years of the 1950s as well as the unrest leading up to the wave of political decolonization from the mid-1950s onward in certain African countries. I therefore suggest Dons likely wrote these notes around 1953. Another set of Dons's handwritten notes for a talk on Adam and Eve has also been preserved in MFK, Box 73-3, Notebook titled "Studier over frelsen i Kristus" by Dons, section titled "Bibeltimer om Bibelens kvinner / 'Skapt i Guds billed': Eva," 10–19, March 10, 1944. I will not discuss this talk here because it contains some of the same interpretations as Dons's 1928 reading while also hinting at new elements that seem to lead up to her later reading in the early 1950s.
38. Descriptions of her trip to South Africa can be found in *Mh* 1928, 2, 16, 19–21, 26–27, 34–39, 50–56, 66, 72–73, 78–79, 92; 1929, 4; LMF, Dons: "LMF Minnebok," 53–54; and Dons (1952, 34–35).
39. NMS, Hjemme 1920–1970, Gen-sek 90, Inn-brev-hjem 1928–1929, Box 440-5, Dons to Bjertnes, January 3, 1929.
40. NMS, Hjemme 1920–1970, Gen-sek 90, Inn-brev-hjem 1928–1929, Box 440-5, Dons to the NMS board, January 14, 1929.
41. NMS, Hjemme 1920–1970, Gen-sek 90, Inn-brev-hjem 1928–1929, Box 440-5, Dons to Bjertnes, January 19, 1929.
42. NMS, Hjemme 1920–1970, Gen-sek 90, Inn-brev-hjem 1928–1929, Box 440-5, Dons to Bjertnes, January 28, 1929.
43. NMS, Hjemme 1920–1970, Gen-sek 90, Inn-brev-hjem 1928–1929, Box 440-5, Dons to Bjertnes, April 13, 1929.
44. As so often, Dons fell back on the all-women's Female Teachers' Mission Association and decided to take over as editor of this organization's magazine *Misjonshilsen* in 1929 when the previous editor left for India (*Mh* 1929, 46). Dons remained the magazine's editor until 1947.
45. NMS, Hjemme 1920–1970, Gen-sek 90, Inn-brev-hjem 1930–1931, Box 442-4, Dons to Amdahl, November 7, 1931. Dons and Amdahl had corresponded about the consulta-

tion meeting previously; five years earlier, Dons had written to Amdahl to ask why the consultation meeting consisted only of men (NMS, Hjemme 1920-1970, Gen-sek 90, Inn-brev-hjem 1925-1926, Box 436-6, Dons to Amdahl, November 22, 1926). It is possible that her later appeal in 1931 had some effect, because a few years later when the children's work was again put on the agenda of the consultation meeting, Dons was invited, though her assigned role was to introduce a discussion on how the children's work could be "strengthened" (NMS, Hjemme 1920-1970, Gen-sek 90, Inn-brev-hjem 1936-1938, Box 448-2, Dons to Amdahl, October 30, 1937).

46. NMS, Hjemme 1920-1970, Gen-sek 90, Inn-brev-hjem 1930-1931, Box 442-4, Dons to Amdahl, December 16, 1931.
47. NMS, Hjemme 1842-1919, Gen-sek 90, Inn-brev-hjem 1919, Box 127-2, Dons: "Arbeidsoversigt for 1918," sent with letter from Dons to the NMS board, January 13, 1919. In 1919, Dons wrote a report on the Home Crafts Circle, stating its contributions to NMS's children's work, that was published in NMS's magazine (*NMt* 1920, 124-125).
48. For example, NMS, Hjemme 1920-1970, Gen-sek 90, Inn-brev-hjem 1920, Box 428-4, Dons to Dahle: "Arbeidsoversigt 1919," January 13, 1920.
49. NMS, Hjemme 1920-1970, Gen-sek 90, Inn-brev-hjem 1920, Box 428-4, Dons to Nilssen, September 3, 1920; see also Inn-brev-hjem 1920-1921, Box 429-4, Dons to Nilssen, February 21, 1921.
50. NMS, Hjemme 1920-1970, Gen-sek 90, Inn-brev-hjem 1930-1931, Box 442-4, Dons to Amdahl, December 16, 1931.
51. NMS, Hjemme 1920-1970, Gen-sek 90, Inn-brev-hjem 1930-1931, Box 442-4, Dons to Amdahl, December 16, 1931.
52. NMS, Hjemme 1920-1970, Gen-sek 90, Inn-brev-hjem 1930-1931, Box 442-4, Dons to Amdahl, December 16, 1931. Dons may be referring to her illness in 1929, when she was hospitalized for a month with pernicious anemia (LMF, Dons: "LMS Minnebok," 55). In 1934, she was again hospitalized for a month (NMS, Hjemme 1920-1970, Gen-sek 90, Inn-brev-hjem 1933-1934, Box 445-5, Dons to Amdahl, March 26, 1934).
53. MFK, Box 72-5, Notebook titled "Guds ord til kvinnen / Kvinnens stilling i menigheten" by Dons, section titled "Kvinnens plass i Guds rike," hereafter "Kvinnens plass."
54. "Kvinnens plass," 1.
55. In her reconsideration of Eve, Dons mentioned ("Kvinnens plass," 5) that she had drawn on the book *God's Word to Women* by Katharine Bushnell (1921). Bushnell was an American woman who had been a missionary in China and a first-wave feminist activist for temperance and social purity (that is, against prostitution and trafficking) in the United States. Unlike Høyer, the woman author Dons had drawn on previously, Bushnell offered a more thoroughgoing reevaluation of Eve. However, Dons was quite selective in what she took from Bushnell; she primarily used Bushnell's interpretation of Adam and Eve's responses in the garden and elaborated this interpretation further. This interpretation of their responses was unusual, and I have not come across anyone else using it at the time. Dons discarded many of Bushnell's other (also unusual) suggestions, for example that God told Eve the reason for her future subjugation was that she would turn away from God to her husband, and that Eve made the wrong choice precisely by following Adam out of Eden when he (not she) was expelled.

56. "Kvinnens plass," 2.
57. "Kvinnens plass," 3.
58. "Kvinnens plass," 3–4.
59. "Kvinnens plass," 2.
60. "Kvinnens plass," 5.
61. "Kvinnens plass," 2.
62. "Kvinnens plass," 3.
63. "Kvinnens plass," 5.
64. "Kvinnens plass," 5.
65. "Kvinnens plass," 5–6.
66. "Kvinnens plass," 3.
67. Dons likely encountered this view in several ways, including through Bushnell (1921).
68. "Kvinnens plass," 6.

CONCLUSION

1. *Vårt Land*, May 22, 1964, "Hun sender 'gode ord' over hele jorda."

REFERENCES

Abram, Simone. 2017. "Contradiction in Contemporary Political Life: Meeting Bureaucracy in Norwegian Municipal Government." *Journal of the Royal Anthropological Institute* 23(S1), 27–44.
Agerholt, Anna Caspari. 1937. *Den norske kvinnebevegelses historie*. Oslo: Gyldendal.
Ahearn, Laura. 2012. *Living Language: An Introduction to Linguistic Anthropology*. Oxford: Wiley-Blackwell.
Alaimo, Stacy, and Susan Hekman. 2008. "Introduction: Emerging Models of Materiality in Feminist Theory." In *Material Feminisms*, edited by Stacy Alaimo and Susan Hekman, 1–19. Bloomington: Indiana University Press.
Arroyo, Analisa, Alesia Woszidlo, and Anastacia Janovec. 2020. "Voice as a Mediator of Mothers' and Daughters' Feminist Attitudes and Psychological Outcomes: An Application of Silencing the Self Theory and Social Cognitive Theory of Gender Development and Differentiation." *Communication Monographs* 87(4), 506–526.
Asad, Talal. 2020. "Thinking about Religion through Wittgenstein." *Critical Times* 3(3), 403–442.
Bakhtin, Mikhail. 1981. *The Dialogic Imagination: Four Essays*. Edited by Michael Holquist. Translated by Caryl Emerson and Michael Holquist. Austin: University of Texas Press.
Bakke, Odd Magne. 2012. "Black Critics of Lutheran Mission in Zululand and Natal in the 1950s, with Particular Emphasis on Socio-Political Issues." *Studia Historiae Ecclesiasticae* 38(1), 75–94.
Bandak, Andreas. 2015. "Exemplary Series and Christian Typology: Modelling on Sainthood in Damascus." *Journal of the Royal Anthropological Institute* 21(S1), 47–63.
Bandak, Andreas. 2022. *Exemplary Life: Modelling Sainthood in Christian Syria*. Toronto: University of Toronto Press.
Bandak, Andreas, and Jonas Adelin Jørgensen. 2012. "Foregrounds and Backgrounds—Ventures in the Anthropology of Christianity." *Ethnos* 77(4), 447–458.
Barad, Karen. 2008. "Posthumanist Performativity: Toward an Understanding of How Matter Comes to Matter." In *Material Feminisms*, edited by Stacy Alaimo and Susan Hekman, 120–154. Bloomington: Indiana University Press.

Bauman, Richard. 1983. *Let Your Words Be Few: Symbolism of Speaking and Silence among Seventeenth-Century Quakers*. Cambridge: Cambridge University Press.

Benussi, Matteo. 2022. "Ethical Infrastructure: Halal and the Ecology of *Askesis* in Muslim Russia." *Anthropological Theory* 22(3), 294–316.

Bialecki, Jon. 2011. "No Caller ID for the Soul: Demonization, Charisms, and the Unstable Subject of Protestant Language Ideology." *Anthropological Quarterly* 84(3), 679–703.

Bialecki, Jon. 2014. "Does God Exist in Methodological Atheism? On Tanya Luhrmann's *When God Talks Back* and Bruno Latour." *Anthropology of Consciousness* 25(1), 32–52.

Bialecki, Jon. 2015. "Affect: Intensities and Energies in the Charismatic Language, Embodiment, and Genre of a North American Movement." In *The Anthropology of Global Pentecostalism and Evangelicalism*, edited by Simon Coleman and Rosalind Hackett, 95–108. New York: New York University Press.

Bialecki, Jon, Naomi Haynes, and Joel Robbins. 2008. "The Anthropology of Christianity." *Religion Compass* 2(6), 1139–1158.

Bialecki, Jon, and Eric Hoenes del Pinal. 2011. "Introduction: Beyond Logos: Extensions of the Language Ideology Paradigm in the Study of Global Christianity(-ies)." *Anthropological Quarterly* 84(3), 575–593.

Bielo, James, ed. 2009a. *The Social Life of Scriptures: Cross-Cultural Perspectives on Biblicism*. New Brunswick, NJ: Rutgers University Press.

Bielo, James. 2009b. *Words Upon the Word: An Ethnography of Evangelical Group Bible Study*. New York: New York University Press.

Bielo, James. 2022. *Materializing the Bible: Scripture, Sensation, Place*. London: Bloomsbury.

Blom, Ida. 1990. "Changing Gender Identities in an Industrializing Society: The Case of Norway c. 1870–c. 1914." *Gender and History* 2(2), 131–147.

Blom, Ida. 2012. "Structures and Agency: A Transnational Comparison of the Struggle for Women's Suffrage in the Nordic Countries during the Long Nineteenth Century." *Scandinavian Journal of History* 37(5), 600–620.

Blommaert, Jan, ed. 1999. *Language Ideological Debates*. Berlin: De Gruyter.

Bost, Suzanne. 2008. "From Race/Sex/Etc. to Glucose, Feeding Tube, and Mourning: The Shifting Matter of Chicana Feminism." In *Material Feminisms*, edited by Stacy Alaimo and Susan Hekman, 340–372. Bloomington: Indiana University Press.

Brown, Hannah, Adam Reed, and Thomas Yarrow. 2017. "Introduction: Towards an Ethnography of Meeting." *Journal of the Royal Anthropological Institute* 23(S1), 10–26.

Bushnell, Katharine. 1921. *God's Word to Women*. Minneapolis: Christians for Biblical Equality.

Butler, Judith. 1993. *Bodies That Matter: On the Discursive Limits of "Sex."* New York: Routledge.

Cannell, Fenella. 2006. "Reading as Gift and Writing as Theft." In *The Anthropology of Christianity*, edited by Fenella Cannell, 134–162. Durham, NC: Duke University Press.

Cavell, Stanley. 1999. *The Claim of Reason: Wittgenstein, Skepticism, Morality, and Tragedy*. Oxford: Oxford University Press.

Chambon, Michel. 2020. *Making Christ Present in China: Actor-Network Theory and the Anthropology of Christianity*. New York: Palgrave Macmillan.

Chidester, David. 2020. "Already There: Categories, Formations, and Circulations in the Future of the Study of Religion." *Religion* 50(1), 40–45.

Coddington, Kate. 2017. "Voice under Scrutiny: Feminist Methods, Anticolonial Responses, and New Methodological Tools." *Professional Geographer* 69(2), 314–320.

Coleman, Simon. 1996. "Words as Things: Language, Aesthetics and the Objectification of Protestant Evangelicalism." *Journal of Material Culture* 1(1), 107–128.

Coleman, Simon. 2003. "Continuous Conversion? The Rhetoric, Practice, and Rhetorical Practice of Charismatic Protestant Conversion." In *The Anthropology of Religious Conversion*, edited by Andrew Buckser and Stephen D. Glazier, 15–27. Lanham: Rowman & Littlefield.

Coleman, Simon. 2006. "Materializing the Self: Words and Gifts in the Construction of Charismatic Protestant Identity." In *The Anthropology of Christianity*, edited by Fenella Cannell, 163–184. Durham, NC: Duke University Press.

Collins, Patricia Hill. 2000. *Black Feminist Thought: Knowledge, Consciousness, and the Politics of Empowerment*. 2nd ed., rev. 10th anniversary ed. New York: Routledge.

Coole, Diana, and Samantha Frost. 2010. "Introducing the New Materialisms." In *New Materialisms: Ontology, Agency, and Politics*, edited by Diana Coole and Samantha Frost, 1–43. Durham, NC: Duke University Press.

Dahle, Lars. 1911. *Grundforskjellen mellem den gamle og den moderne kristendomsopfatning*. Kristiania: Lutherstiftelsens Boghandel.

Das, Veena. 2015. "What Does Ordinary Ethics Look Like?" In *Four Lectures on Ethics: Anthropological Perspectives*, by Michael Lambek, Veena Das, Didier Fassin, and Webb Keane, 53–125. Chicago: HAU Books.

Das, Veena. 2020. *Textures of the Ordinary: Doing Anthropology after Wittgenstein*. New York: Fordham University Press.

Daswani, Girish. 2015. *Looking Back, Moving Forward: Transformation and Ethical Practice in the Ghanaian Church of Pentecost*. Toronto: University of Toronto Press.

Desai, Gaurav. 2001. *Subject to Colonialism: African Self-Fashioning and the Colonial Library*. Durham, NC: Duke University Press.

Diamond, Cora. 2004. "Criss-Cross Philosophy." In *Wittgenstein at Work: Method in the Philosophical Investigations*, edited by Erich Ammereller and Eugen Fischer, 201–220. London: Routledge.

Dilger, Hansjörg, Omar Kasmani, and Dominik Mattes. 2018. "Spatialities of Belonging: Affective Place-Making among Diasporic Neo-Pentecostal and Sufi Groups in Berlin's Cityscape." In *Affect in Relation: Families, Places, Technologies*, edited by Birgitt Röttger-Rössler and Jan Slaby, 93–114. London: Routledge.

Dolphijn, Rick, and Iris van der Tuin. 2012. *New Materialism: Interviews & Cartographies*. Ann Arbor, MI: Open Humanities Press.

Dons, Henny. 1914. "Kvinders arbeide for missionen." In *Norske kvinder: En oversigt over deres stilling og livsvilkaar i hundredeaaret 1814–1914*, edited by Fredrikke Mørck, 44–49. Kristiania: Berg & Høghs Forlag.

Dons, Henny. 1915. *Barnetro: Fortællinger til bruk i søndagsskoler og barneforeninger.* Kristiania: Norsk Søndagsskoleforbund.

Dons, Henny. 1919. *Stift barneforeninger for missionen.* Stavanger: Det Norske Missionsselskap.

Dons, Henny. 1920a. *Afrika venter: Barnebok om misjonen.* Stavanger: Det Norske Missionsselskap.

Dons, Henny. 1920b. *Kina venter: Barnebok om missionen.* Stavanger: Det Norske Missionsselskap.

Dons, Henny. 1922. *Madagaskar venter: Barnebok om missionen.* Stavanger: Det Norske Missionsselskap.

Dons, Henny. 1923a. *Hedningemisjonen i søndagsskolen: Raad og vink samt 52 fortellinger fra misjonsmarkene til bruk i søndagsskole og barneforeninger.* Stavanger: Det Norske Missionsselskap.

Dons, Henny. 1923b. "Kvindens oppgave og arbeide i missionen." In *Kvindens missionsarbeide,* by Henny Dons and Johanne Hoel Olsen, 3–10. Stavanger: Det Norske Missionsselskap.

Dons, Henny. 1925a. *Den kristne kvinne og hedningemisjonen: En historisk oversikt.* Oslo: Lutherstiftelsens Forlag.

Dons, Henny. 1925b. "Kvinders arbeide for missionen." In *Norske kvinder: En kort oversigt over deres stilling og livsvilkaar i tiaaret 1914–1924,* edited by Fredrikke Mørck, 165–167. Oslo: Berg & Høghs Forlag.

Dons, Henny. 1928. *Bibelens kvinner: Bibelstudier.* Oslo: Lutherstiftelsens Forlag.

Dons, Henny. 1933. *Liv og overflod: Bibeltimer for unge.* Oslo: Lutherstiftelsens Forlag.

Dons, Henny. [1937?]. *Vær med i Ungdomsmisjonen.* Oslo: Norges Kristelige Ungdomsforbund.

Dons, Henny. 1938. *Lærerinnenes Misjonsforbund, L.M.F.: Om L.M.F.s arbeide, oppgaver og mål.* Oslo: Hellstrøm & Nordahls Boktrykkeri.

Dons, Henny. 1945. "Lov og evangelium i forkynnelsen." In *Foredrag holdt ved kurset for kvinnelige sekretærer i Oslo 2.–8. januar 1945,* 3–14. Stavanger: Det Norske Misjonsselskap.

Dons, Henny. 1952. "Henny Dons." In *Hva livet har lært meg,* edited by H. E. Wisløff, 9–35. Oslo: Indremisjonsforlaget.

Droney, Damien. 2024. "Projects, Revisited: A Concept for the Anthropology of the Good." *Anthropological Theory* 24(2), 155–174.

Drury, Maurice O'Connor. 1973. *The Danger of Words.* London: Routledge & Kegan Paul.

Drury, Maurice O'Connor. 1981. "Conversations with Wittgenstein." In *Ludwig Wittgenstein: Personal Recollections,* edited by Rush Rhees, 112–189. Totowa, NJ: Rowman & Littlefield.

Dugan, Katherine. 2017. "Gendering Prayer: Millennial-Generation Catholics and the Embodiment of Feminine Genius and Authentic Masculinity." *Religion and Gender* 7(1), 1–17.

Duranti, Alessandro. 2003. "Language as Culture in U.S. Anthropology: Three Paradigms." *Current Anthropology* 44(3), 323–335.

Ebbell, Clara Thue. 1946. *På frammarsj: Bolette Gjør, misjonsvennen.* Oslo: Lutherstiftelsens Forlag.

Elisha, Omri. 2011. *Moral Ambition: Mobilization and Social Outreach in Evangelical Megachurches.* Berkeley: University of California Press

Engelke, Matthew. 2007. *A Problem of Presence: Beyond Scripture in an African Church.* Berkeley: University of California Press.

Engelke, Matthew. 2013. *God's Agents: Biblical Publicity in Contemporary England.* Berkeley: University of California Press.

Eriksen, Annelin. 2008. *Gender, Christianity and Change in Vanuatu: An Analysis of Social Movements in North Ambrym.* Aldershot: Ashgate.

Etherington, Norman, ed. 2005. *Missions and Empire.* Oxford: Oxford University Press.

Fader, Ayala. 2009. *Mitzvah Girls: Bringing Up the Next Generation of Hasidic Jews in Brooklyn.* Princeton, NJ: Princeton University Press.

Foucault, Michel. 1978. *The History of Sexuality, Volume 1: The Will to Knowledge.* London: Penguin.

Gad, Christopher, and Casper Bruun Jensen. 2010. "On the Consequences of Post-ANT." *Science, Technology, and Human Values* 35(1), 55–80.

Garriott, William, and Kevin Lewis O'Neill. 2008. "Who is a Christian? Toward a Dialogic Approach in the Anthropology of Christianity." *Anthropological Theory* 8(4), 381–398.

Gilligan, Carol. 1982. *In a Different Voice: Psychological Theory and Women's Development.* Cambridge, MA: Harvard University Press.

Gjør, Bolette [Margrethe, pseud.]. 1892. *Missionsbarnet.* Stavanger: Det Norske Missionsselskabs Bogtrykkeri.

Goffman, Erving. 1981. *Forms of Talk.* Philadelphia: University of Pennsylvania Press.

Griffith, R. Marie. 1997. *God's Daughters: Evangelical Women and the Power of Submission.* Berkeley: University of California Press.

Gullestad, Marianne. 2007. *Picturing Pity: Pitfalls and Pleasures in Cross-Cultural Communication; Image and Word in a North Cameroon Mission.* Oxford: Berghahn Books.

Hagemann, Gro. 2002. "Citizenship and Social Order: Gender Politics in Twentieth-Century Norway and Sweden." *Women's History Review* 11(3), 417–429.

Hagemann, Gro. 2004. "Norsk nyfeminisme—amerikansk import?" *Nytt Norsk Tidsskrift* 21(3–4), 275–287.

Halvorson, Britt. 2018. *Conversionary Sites: Transforming Medical Aid and Global Christianity from Madagascar to Minnesota.* Chicago: University of Chicago Press.

Halvorson, Britt, and Ingie Hovland. 2021. "Reconnecting Language and Materiality in Christian Reading: A Comparative Analysis of Two Groups of Protestant Women." *Comparative Studies in Society and History* 63(2), 499–529.

Handman, Courtney. 2017. "Walking like a Christian: Roads, Translation, and Gendered Bodies as Religious Infrastructure in Papua New Guinea." *American Ethnologist* 44(2), 315–327.

Handman, Courtney. 2018. "The Language of Evangelism: Christian Cultures of Circulation beyond the Missionary Prologue." *Annual Review of Anthropology* 47, 149–165.

Handman, Courtney. 2019. "A Few Grass Huts: Denominational Ambivalence and Infrastructural Form in Colonial New Guinea." *Anthropological Quarterly* 92(4), 1015–1038.

Haraway, Donna. (1985) 1990. "A Manifesto for Cyborgs: Science, Technology, and Socialist Feminism in the 1980s." In *Feminism/Postmodernism*, edited by Linda Nicholson, 190–233. New York: Routledge.

Hardin, Jessica. 2023. "Moving Materialities: Oceanic Epistemologies and Embodied Knowledge Production in Pentecostal Women's Health Mentorship in Samoa." *American Anthropologist* 125(2), 239–251.

Harding, Susan F. 2000. *The Book of Jerry Falwell: Fundamentalist Language and Politics*. Princeton, NJ: Princeton University Press.

Harkness, Nicholas. 2014. *Songs of Seoul: An Ethnography of Voice and Voicing in Christian South Korea*. Berkeley: University of California Press.

Haynes, Naomi. 2020. "The Expansive Present: A New Model of Christian Time." *Current Anthropology* 61(1), 57–76.

Hazard, Sonia. 2013. "The Material Turn in the Study of Religion." *Religion and Society* 4(1), 58–78.

Hekman, Susan. 2008. "Constructing the Ballast: An Ontology for Feminism." In *Material Feminisms*, edited by Stacy Alaimo and Susan Hekman, 85–119. Bloomington: Indiana University Press.

Hewitt, Nancy A. 2012. "Feminist Frequencies: Regenerating the Wave Metaphor." *Feminist Studies* 38(3), 658–680.

Hill, Patricia. 1985. *The World Their Household: The American Woman's Foreign Mission Movement and Cultural Transformation, 1870–1920*. Ann Arbor: University of Michigan Press.

Hirschkind, Charles. 2006. *The Ethical Soundscape: Cassette Sermons and Islamic Counterpublics*. New York: Columbia University Press.

Hoenes del Pinal, Eric. 2022. *Guarded by Two Jaguars: A Catholic Parish Divided by Language and Faith*. Tucson: University of Arizona Press.

Højer, Lars, and Andreas Bandak. 2015. "Introduction: The Power of Example." *Journal of the Royal Anthropological Institute* 21(S1), 1–17.

Hovland, Ingie. 2013. *Mission Station Christianity: Norwegian Missionaries in Colonial Natal and Zululand, Southern Africa 1850–1890*. Leiden: Brill.

Hovland, Ingie. 2016. "Christianity, Place/Space, and Anthropology: Thinking across Recent Research on Evangelical Place-Making." *Religion* 46(3), 331–358.

Hovland, Ingie. 2018. "Beyond Mediation: An Anthropological Understanding of the Relationship between Humans, Materiality, and Transcendence in Protestant Christianity." *Journal of the American Academy of Religion* 86(2), 425–453.

Hovland, Ingie. 2022. "Value Moves in Multiple Ways: Ethical Values, the Anthropology of Christianity, and an Example of Women and Movement." *Anthropological Theory* 22(3), 273–293.

Hovland, Ingie. 2024. "Feminist Cites: A Review of Feminist Relations to and Citations of the Canon." *Studies in Religion/Sciences Religieuses* 53(2), 207–226.

Høyer, Maria. 1925. *Kvinden: Fri eller træl*. Holte: Danske Kirkemissions Forlag.

Irigaray, Luce. (1977) 1985. "The Power of Discourse and the Subordination of the Feminine." In *This Sex Which Is Not One*, by Luce Irigaray, 68–85. Ithaca, NY: Cornell University Press.

Irvine, Judith T. 1989. "When Talk Isn't Cheap: Language and Political Economy." *American Ethnologist* 16(2), 248–267.

Irvine, Judith T., and Susan Gal. 2000. "Language Ideology and Linguistic Differentiation." In *Regimes of Language: Ideologies, Polities, and Identities*, edited by Paul V. Kroskrity, 35–83. Santa Fe, NM: School of American Research Press.

Irvine, Richard D. G. 2010. "How to Read: *Lectio Divina* in an English Benedictine Monastery." *Culture and Religion* 11(4), 395–411.

Jolly, Margaret. 1993. "Colonizing Women: The Maternal Body and Empire." In *Feminism and the Politics of Difference*, edited by Sneja Gunew and Anna Yeatman, 103–127. Boulder, CO: Westview Press.

Jordåen, Runar. 2006. *Helsebygg i Noreg: Ei historisk oversikt*. Oslo: Helse- og omsorgsdepartementet.

Jørgensen, Torstein. 1990. *Contact and Conflict: Norwegian Missionaries, the Zulu Kingdom, and the Gospel, 1850–1873*. Oslo: Solum.

Jouili, Jeanette S. 2011. "Beyond Emancipation: Subjectivities and Ethics among Women in Europe's Islamic Revival Communities." *Feminist Review* 98(1), 47–64.

Kaell, Hillary. 2020a. *Christian Globalism at Home: Child Sponsorship in the United States*. Princeton, NJ: Princeton University Press.

Kaell, Hillary. 2020b. "Renamed: The Living, the Dead, and the Global in Nineteenth-Century US Christianity." *American Historical Review* 125(3), 815–839.

Kalb, Don, and Herman Tak, eds. 2005. *Critical Junctions: Anthropology and History beyond the Cultural Turn*. Oxford: Berghahn Books.

Karpowitz, Christopher F., and Tali Mendelberg. 2014. *The Silent Sex: Gender, Deliberation, and Institutions*. Princeton, NJ: Princeton University Press.

Kartzow, Marianne Bjelland. 2009. *Gossip and Gender: Othering of Speech in the Pastoral Epistles*. Berlin: De Gruyter.

Kasmani, Omar. 2017. "Audible Spectres: The Sticky Shia Sonics of Sehwan." *History of Emotions: Insights into Research*, October. https://doi.org/10.14280/08241.54.

Keane, Webb. 2007. *Christian Moderns: Freedom and Fetish in the Mission Encounter*. Berkeley: University of California Press.

Keane, Webb. 2016. *Ethical Life: Its Natural and Social Histories*. Princeton, NJ: Princeton University Press.

Keane, Webb, and Michael Silverstein. 2017. "Curated Conversation: 'Materiality: It's the Stuff!'" In *Language and Materiality: Ethnographic and Theoretical Explorations*, edited by Jillian R. Cavanaugh and Shalini Shankar, 29–40. Cambridge: Cambridge University Press.

Keller, Eva. 2005. *The Road to Clarity: Seventh-Day Adventism in Madagascar*. New York: Springer.

Kielland, Gustava. (1882) 1996. *Erindringer fra mitt liv*. Oslo: IKO Forlag.

Kirsch, Thomas G. 2011. *Spirits and Letters: Reading, Writing and Charisma in African Christianity*. Oxford: Berghahn Books.

Klaits, Frederick. 2010. *Death in a Church of Life: Moral Passion during Botswana's Time of AIDS*. Berkeley: University of California Press.

Klassen, Pamela. 2018. *The Story of Radio Mind: A Missionary's Journey on Indigenous Land*. Chicago: University of Chicago Press.

Knott, Kim. 2010. "Religion, Space, and Place: The Spatial Turn in Research on Religion." *Religion and Society* 1, 29–43.

Laidlaw, James. 2014. *The Subject of Virtue: An Anthropology of Ethics and Freedom*. Cambridge: Cambridge University Press.

Landmark, Nils. 1889. *Det norske missionsselskab, dets oprindelse og historiske udvikling, dets arbeidsmarker og dets arbeidere*. Stavanger: Det Norske Missionsselskabs Forlag.

Larkin, Brian. 2013. "The Politics and Poetics of Infrastructure." *Annual Review of Anthropology* 42, 327–343.

Latour, Bruno. 1993. *We Have Never Been Modern*. Cambridge, MA: Harvard University Press.

Laugier, Sandra. 2013. *Why We Need Ordinary Language Philosophy*. Chicago: University of Chicago Press.

Lebner, Ashley. 2017. "Introduction: Strathern's Redescription of Anthropology." In *Redescribing Relations: Strathernian Conversations on Ethnography, Knowledge and Politics*, edited by Ashley Lebner, 1–37. Oxford: Berghahn Books.

Lebner, Ashley. 2021. "After the Medium: Rereading Stories on a String and the War at Canudos." *Journal of the American Academy of Religion* 89(4), 1290–1333.

Le Guin, Ursula K. 1993. "Loud Cows." In *The Ethnography of Reading*, edited by Jonathan Boyarin, vii–viii. Berkeley: University of California Press. https://doi.org/10.1525/9780520913431-001.

Lemons, J. Derrick, ed. 2018. *Theologically Engaged Anthropology*. Oxford: Oxford University Press.

Llewellyn, Dawn. 2015. *Reading, Feminism, and Spirituality: Troubling the Waves*. New York: Palgrave Macmillan.

LMF (Lærerinnernes Misjonsforbund). 1927. *Lærerinnernes Misjonsforbund 1902–1927, 25-årsberetning*. Oslo: Lærerinnernes Misjonsforbund.

Loustau, Marc Roscoe. 2022. *Hungarian Catholic Intellectuals in Contemporary Romania: Reforming Apostles*. New York: Palgrave Macmillan.

Lowe, Lisa. 2015. *The Intimacies of Four Continents*. Durham, NC: Duke University Press.

Lugones, María C., and Elizabeth V. Spelman. 1983. "Have We Got a Theory for You! Feminist Theory, Cultural Imperialism and the Demand for 'the Woman's Voice.'" *Women's Studies International Forum* 6(6), 573–581.

Luhrmann, Tanya M. 2012. *When God Talks Back: Understanding the American Evangelical Relationship with God*. New York: Vintage Books.

MacIntyre, Alasdair. 1985. *After Virtue*. 2nd ed. London: Duckworth.

Mahmood, Saba. 2005. *Politics of Piety: The Islamic Revival and the Feminist Subject*. Princeton, NJ: Princeton University Press.

Marsilli-Vargas, Xochitl. 2022. *Genres of Listening: An Ethnography of Psychoanalysis in Buenos Aires*. Durham, NC: Duke University Press.

Martin, Craig. 2014. "*Genealogies of Religion*, Twenty Years On: An Interview with Talal Asad." *Bulletin for the Study of Religion* 43(1), 12–17.
Massey, Doreen. 2005. *For Space*. London: Sage.
Mattingly, Cheryl. 2012. "Two Virtue Ethics and the Anthropology of Morality." *Anthropological Theory* 12(2), 161–184.
Mattingly, Cheryl, and Jason Throop. 2018. "The Anthropology of Ethics and Morality." *Annual Review of Anthropology* 47, 475–492.
Mauss, Marcel. (1938) 1985. "A Category of the Human Mind: The Notion of Person; The Notion of Self." In *The Category of the Person: Anthropology, Philosophy, History*, edited by Michael Carrithers, Steven Collins, and Steven Lukes, 1–25. Cambridge: Cambridge University Press.
Mayblin, Maya. 2010. *Gender, Catholicism, and Morality in Brazil: Virtuous Husbands, Powerful Wives*. New York: Palgrave Macmillan.
Mayblin, Maya. 2017. "The Lapsed and the Laity: Discipline and Lenience in the Study of Religion." *Journal of the Royal Anthropological Institute* 23(3), 503–522.
Meyer, Birgit. 2010. "Aesthetics of Persuasion: Global Christianity and Pentecostalism's Sensational Forms." *South Atlantic Quarterly* 109(4), 741–763.
Meyer, Birgit. 2011. "Mediation and Immediacy: Sensational Forms, Semiotic Ideologies and the Question of the Medium." *Social Anthropology* 19(1), 23–39.
Meyer, Birgit. 2020. "Religion as Mediation." *Entangled Religions* 11(3). https://doi.org/10.13154/er.11.2020.8444.
Meyer, Birgit, David Morgan, Crispin Paine, and S. Brent Plate. 2010. "The Origin and Mission of *Material Religion*." *Religion* 40(3), 207–211.
Michelet, Marie. 1946. *Minner og tidsbilleder*. Oslo: Dreyers Forlag.
Mikaelsson, Lisbeth. 2002. "'Kvinne, ta ansvar og ledelse i dine egne hender': Historien om Henny Dons." *Norsk Tidsskrift for Misjon* 56(2), 107–137.
Mikaelsson, Lisbeth. 2003. *Kallets ekko: Studier i misjon og selvbiografi*. Kristiansand: Høyskoleforlaget.
Mittermaier, Amira. 2011. *Dreams that Matter: Egyptian Landscapes of the Imagination*. Berkeley: University of California Press.
Mittermaier, Amira. 2012. "Dreams from Elsewhere: Muslim Subjectivities beyond the Trope of Self-Cultivation." *Journal of the Royal Anthropological Institute* 18(2), 247–265.
Moi, Toril. 2017. *Revolution of the Ordinary: Literary Studies after Wittgenstein, Austin, and Cavell*. Chicago: University of Chicago Press.
Mol, Annemarie. 2002. *The Body Multiple: Ontology in Medical Practice*. Durham, NC: Duke University Press.
Mol, Annemarie. 2015. "Who Knows What a Woman Is . . . On the Differences and the Relations between the Sciences." *Medicine Anthropology Theory* 2(1), 57–75.
Moore, Brenna. 2021. *Kindred Spirits: Friendship and Resistance at the Edges of Modern Catholicism*. Chicago: University of Chicago Press.
Mosevoll, Audun. 1992. "Norge." In *I tro og tjeneste: Det Norske Misjonsselskap 1842–1992*, Vol. 1, edited by Torstein Jørgensen, 146–313. Stavanger: Misjonshøgskolen.

Mosko, Mark. 2010. "Partible Penitents: Dividual Personhood and Christian Practice in Melanesia and the West." *Journal of the Royal Anthropological Institute* 16(2), 215–240.

Myhre, Knut Christian. 2018a. "Deep Pragmatism." In *The Mythology in Our Language: Remarks on Frazer's Golden Bough* by Ludwig Wittgenstein, translated by Stephan Palmié, edited by Giovanni da Col and Stephan Palmié, 95–113. Chicago: HAU Books.

Myhre, Knut Christian. 2018b. *Returning Life: Language, Life Force and History in Kilimanjaro*. Oxford: Berghahn Books.

Nash, Jennifer C. 2018. *Black Feminism Reimagined: After Intersectionality*. Durham, NC: Duke University Press.

Naumescu, Vlad. 2019. "Pedagogies of Prayer: Teaching Orthodoxy in South India." *Comparative Studies in Society and History* 61(2), 389–418.

Nielssen, Hilde, Inger Marie Okkenhaug, and Karina Hestad Skeie. 2011. "Introduction." In *Protestant Missions and Local Encounters in the Nineteenth and Twentieth Centuries: Unto the Ends of the Earth*, edited by Hilde Nielssen, Inger Marie Okkenhaug, and Karina Hestad Skeie, 1–22. Leiden: Brill.

Nome, John. 1943a. *Fra stiftelsestiden til Schreuders brudd*. In *Det Norske Misjonsselskaps historie i hundre år*, Vol. 1, edited by John Nome. Stavanger: Dreyers Forlag.

Nome, John. 1943b. *Fra syttiårene til nåtiden*. In *Det Norske Misjonsselskaps historie i hundre år*, Vol. 2, edited by John Nome. Stavanger: Dreyers Forlag.

Norseth, Kristin. 2002. "To alen av hvilket stykke? Tvillingsøstrene LMF og KMA i norsk, nordisk og internasjonalt perspektiv." *Norsk Tidsskrift for Misjon* 56(2), 91–106.

Norseth, Kristin. 2007. "'La os bryte over tvert med vor stumhet!': Kvinners vei til myndighet i de kristelige organisasjonene 1842–1912." PhD diss., Menighetsfakultetet, Oslo.

Nyhagen Predelli, Line. 2003. *Issues of Gender, Race and Class in the Norwegian Missionary Society in Nineteenth Century Norway and Madagascar*. Lewiston, NY: Edwin Mellen Press.

Oftestad, Bernt, Tarald Rasmussen, and Jan Schumacher. 2005. *Norsk kirkehistorie*. 3rd ed. Oslo: Universitetsforlaget.

Okkenhaug, Inger Marie, ed. 2003. *Gender, Race and Religion: Nordic Missions 1860–1940*. Uppsala: Studia Missionalia Svecana.

Oliphant, Elayne. 2021. *The Privilege of Being Banal: Art, Secularism, and Catholicism in Paris*. Chicago: University of Chicago Press.

Peirce, Charles Sanders. 1991. *Peirce on Signs: Writings on Semiotics by Charles Sanders Peirce*. Edited by James Hoopes. Chapel Hill: University of North Carolina Press.

Premawardhana, Devaka. 2018. *Faith in Flux: Pentecostalism and Mobility in Rural Mozambique*. Philadelphia: University of Pennsylvania Press.

Reinhardt, Bruno. 2014. "Soaking in Tapes: The Haptic Voice of Global Pentecostal Pedagogy in Ghana." *Journal of the Royal Anthropological Institute* 20(2), 315–336.

Reinhardt, Bruno. 2020. "Atmospheric Presence: Reflections on 'Mediation' in the Anthropology of Religion and Technology." *Anthropological Quarterly* 93(1), 1523–1553.

Reistad, Helen. 2014. "Fra rettferdiggjøring til fordømming? En sammenligning av fremstillingen av den nye imperialismen i Afrika i norske og britiske historielærebøker i perioden 1920–1990." Master's thesis, Høgskolen i Bergen.

Rettedal, Knut. 1951. *Kvinnens plass og rett i misjonsarbeidet belyst fra Skriften og historien.* Stavanger: Self-published.

Rhees, Rush. 1970. *Discussions of Wittgenstein.* London: Routledge & Kegan Paul.

Rich, Adrienne. 1994. "Compulsory Heterosexuality and Lesbian Existence." In *Blood, Bread, and Poetry: Selected Prose 1979–1985,* by Adrienne Rich, 23–75. New York: W. W. Norton.

Robbins, Joel. 2012. "Transcendence and the Anthropology of Christianity: Language, Change, and Individualism." *Suomen Antropologi: Journal of the Finnish Anthropological Society* 37(2), 5–23.

Robbins, Joel. 2013. "Monism, Pluralism, and the Structure of Value Relations: A Dumontian Contribution to the Contemporary Study of Value." *HAU: Journal of Ethnographic Theory* 3(1), 99–115.

Robbins, Joel. 2020. *Theology and the Anthropology of Christian Life.* Oxford: Oxford University Press.

Sæverås, Aud. 1986. *I samtale med Johanne Høeg.* Oslo: Lunde Forlag.

Scherz, China. 2017. "Enduring the Awkward Embrace: Ontology and Ethical Work in a Ugandan Convent." *American Anthropologist* 120(1), 102–112.

Schieffelin, Bambi B., Kathryn A. Woolard, and Paul V. Kroskrity, eds. 1998. *Language Ideologies: Practice and Theory.* Oxford: Oxford University Press.

Schielke, Samuli. 2009. "Being Good in Ramadan: Ambivalence, Fragmentation, and the Moral Self in the Lives of Young Egyptians." *Journal of the Royal Anthropological Institute* 15(S1), 24–40.

Seland, Bjørg. 2021. "Hauge-bevegelsens 'Prædikerinder': Kritisk blikk på forskning og formidling." *Norsk Tidsskrift for Misjonsvitenskap* 75(1–2), 111–132.

Shankar, Shalini, and Jillian R. Cavanaugh. 2017. "Toward a Theory of Language Materiality: An Introduction." In *Language and Materiality: Ethnographic and Theoretical Explorations,* edited by Jillian R. Cavanaugh and Shalini Shanker, 1–28. Cambridge: Cambridge University Press.

Simensen, Jarle. 1986. "Religious Change as Transaction: The Norwegian Mission to Zululand, South Africa 1850–1906." *Journal of Religion in Africa* 16(2), 82–100.

Skeie, Karina Hestad. 2005. "Pioneering Female Autonomy? Johanne Borchgrevink's Girls' School in Late-19th Century Madagascar." *Social Sciences and Missions* 16, 11–41.

Skeie, Karina Hestad. 2015a. "Gender, Mission, and Work: The Complex Relationship between Formal Rights and Missionary Agency in the Norwegian Lutheran China Mission Association." *Scandinavian Journal of History* 40(3), 332–356.

Skeie, Karina Hestad. 2015b. "Kjønn og åndelig lederskap: En analyse av kinamisjonæren Marie Monsens (1878–1962) transformasjon fra lærerinne til vekkelsestaler." *DIN: Tidsskrift for religion og kultur* 2, 31–59.

Skeie, Karina Hestad, and Seija Jalagin. 2017. "Inspirasjon, samarbeid og innflytelse: Et transnasjonalt perspektiv på Lærernes Misjonsforbund (LMF) i Norden 1899–2017." *Norsk Tidsskrift for Misjonsvitenskap* 38(2), 25–43.

Skeie, Karina Hestad, and Kristin Norseth. 2003. "Creating a Voice—Acquiring Rights: Women in the Norwegian Mission Society and the Process towards Formal Organizational Rights in 1904." *NORA: Nordic Journal of Women's Studies* 11(1), 5–13.

Slotta, James. 2023. *Anarchy and the Art of Listening: The Politics and Pragmatics of Reception in Papua New Guinea.* Ithaca, NY: Cornell University Press.

Spivak, Gayatri Chakravorty. 1985. "Three Women's Texts and a Critique of Imperialism." *Critical Inquiry* 12(1), 243–261.

Stanley, Brian. 2009. *The World Missionary Conference, Edinburgh 1910.* Cambridge: Eerdmans.

Stavem, Ole. 1915. *Et bantufolk og kristendommen: Det norske missionsselskaps syttiaarige zulumission.* Stavanger: Det Norske Missionsselskaps Forlag.

Strathern, Marilyn. 1988. *The Gender of the Gift.* Berkeley: University of California Press.

Strathern, Marilyn. (1991) 2004. *Partial Connections.* Updated ed. Oxford: AltaMira Press.

Strhan, Anna. 2015. *Aliens and Strangers? The Struggle for Coherence in the Everyday Lives of Evangelicals.* Oxford: Oxford University Press.

Tertullian. 1869. "On Female Dress." Translated by S. Thelwall. In *The Writings of Quintus Sept. Flor. Tertullianus, Vol. 1*, Vol. XI of *Ante-Nicene Christian Library: Translations of the Writings of the Fathers down to A.D. 325*, edited by Alexander Roberts and James Donaldson, 304–332. Edinburgh: T&T Clark.

Thorne, Susan. 1999. "Missionary-Imperial Feminism." In *Gendered Missions: Women and Men in Missionary Discourse and Practice*, edited by Mary Taylor Huber and Nancy Lutkehaus, 39–65. Ann Arbor: University of Michigan Press.

Thornton, Brendan Jamal. 2018. "Victims of Illicit Desire: Pentecostal Men of God and the Specter of Sexual Temptation." *Anthropological Quarterly* 91(1), 133–171.

Thornton, Brendan Jamal. 2019. Review of *Biblical Porn: Affect, Labor, and Pastor Mark Driscoll's Evangelical Empire*, by Jessica Johnson. *AnthroCyBib: The Anthropology of Christianity Bibliography Blog*, July 11. Edinburgh: University of Edinburgh.

Thorsnæs, Geir. 2022. "Norges befolkning." *Store norske leksikon.* https://snl.no/Norges_befolkning.

Thorsnæs, Geir. 2023. "Norge—befolkningsutvikling." *Store norske leksikon.* https://snl.no/Norge_-_befolkningsutvikling.

Tjelle, Kristin Fjelde. 1990. "'Kvinder hjælper Kvinder': Misjonskvinneforeningsbevegelsen i Norge 1860–1910." Master's thesis, Universitetet i Oslo.

Tjelle, Kristin Fjelde. 1999. "Misjonskvinneforeningsbevegelsen i Norge." *Norsk Tidsskrift for Misjon* 53(3), 175–190.

Tjelle, Kristin Fjelde. 2002. "Lærerinnenes Misjonsforbund gjennom 100 år." *Norsk Tidsskrift for Misjon* 56(2), 65–89.

Tjelle, Kristin Fjelde. 2013. *Missionary Masculinity, 1870–1930: The Norwegian Missionaries in South-East Africa.* New York: Palgrave Macmillan.

Tokheim, Marit. 1975. "Norske Kvinners Nasjonalråd 1904–16: Bakgrunnen for dannelsen av Norske Kvinners Nasjonalråd og organisasjonens utvikling under Gina Krogs ledelse." Master's thesis, Universitetet i Bergen.

Tomlinson, Matt. 2010. "Compelling Replication: Genesis 1:26, John 3:16, and Biblical Politics in Fiji." *Journal of the Royal Anthropological Institute* 16(4), 743–760.

Tomlinson, Matt. 2014. "Bringing Kierkegaard into Anthropology: Repetition, Absurdity, and Curses in Fiji." *American Ethnologist* 41(1), 163–175.

Tønnessen, Aud Valborg. 2014. *Ingrid Bjerkås: Motstandskvinnen som ble vår første kvinnelige prest*. Oslo: Pax Forlag.

Tremlett, Paul-François. 2021. *Towards a New Theory of Religion and Social Change: Sovereignties and Disruptions*. London: Bloomsbury.

Trible, Phyllis. 1973. "Depatriarchalizing in Biblical Interpretation." *Journal of the American Academy of Religion* 41(1), 30–48.

VanderMeulen, Ian. 2021. "Electrosonic Statecraft: Technology, Authority, and Latency on Moroccan Qurʾānic Radio." *American Ethnologist* 48(1), 80–92.

Vásquez, Manuel. 2011. *More Than Belief: A Materialist Theory of Religion*. Oxford: Oxford University Press.

Voksø, Per, and Erik Kullerud. 1980. *I trekantens tegn: Norges Kristelige Ungdomsforbund gjennom hundre år*. Oslo: Triangelforlaget.

Voll, Hilde Margrethe. 1977. "Fra oppdragelse til forkynnelse: Kvinner i Det Norske Misjonsselskap i Norge og på Madagaskar 1870–1920: Praksis og debatt." Master's thesis, Universitetet i Oslo.

Weber, Max. (1905) 2002. *The Protestant Ethic and the Spirit of Capitalism: And Other Writings*. New York: Penguin.

Webster, Joseph. 2013. *The Anthropology of Protestantism: Faith and Crisis among Scottish Fishermen*. New York: Palgrave Macmillan.

Wittgenstein, Ludwig. (1953) 2009. *Philosophical Investigations*. Rev. 4th ed. Translated by G. E. M. Anscombe, P. M. S. Hacker, and Joachim Schulte. Oxford: Wiley-Blackwell.

Wittgenstein, Ludwig. (1967) 2018. "Remarks on Frazer's *The Golden Bough*." Translated by Stephan Palmié. In *The Mythology in Our Language: Remarks on Frazer's Golden Bough* by Ludwig Wittgenstein, edited by Giovanni da Col and Stephan Palmié, 29–73. Chicago: HAU Books.

Wittgenstein, Ludwig. 1976. *Wittgenstein's Lectures on the Foundations of Mathematics: Cambridge, 1939*. Edited by Cora Diamond. Ithaca, NY: Cornell University Press.

Wittgenstein, Ludwig. (1977) 1998. *Culture and Value*. Rev. ed. Edited by Georg Henrik von Wright with Heikki Nyman. Revised edition by Alois Pichler. Translated by Peter Winch. Oxford: Blackwell.

Zwissler, Laurel. 2018. *Religious, Feminist, Activist: Cosmologies of Interconnection*. Lincoln: University of Nebraska Press.

INDEX

Abram, Simone, 34
actor-network theory (ANT), 145n24, 157n4
Adam and Eve. *See* Eve
affect, in Female Teachers' Mission Association (Lærerindernes Missionsforbund, LMF) meetings, 38, 40, 45, 148n5
Africa, 82–83, 85–86, 89–90, 97
agency, 105, 113; collective, 55; ethical, 29–30, 50–51, 54–55, 74, 152n5; individual, 75
Ahearn, Laura, 142n17
Alaimo, Stacy, 145n24
Amdahl, Einar, 121–22, 162n45
Anthony, Susan B., 153n32
anthropology, 142n14, 142n17, 144n22, 146n27; of Christianity (Protestant Christianity), 5–7, 14, 53, 80, 103, 118, 143n18, 146n29, 149n8, 152nn5–6; of ethics and morality, 146–47nn30–32, 157n6; and history, 12; linguistic, 29, 142n17, 144n22, 146n27, 151n3, 151n5; of religion, 14, 136, 142n17, 151n3
archive. *See* anthropology: and history; colonial archive; ethnography: in archive; liberal archive
Asad, Talal, 50, 144n22
Asker Seminar, 63
atherosclerosis, ethnography of, 19–20, 81, 147n31
authority, 15, 43–44, 49, 108–9, 124, 148n34; God's, 113

Bakhtin, Mikhail, 146n27
Bakke, Odd Magne, 158n18

Bandak, Andreas, 12–13, 118–19, 142n10
Barad, Karen, 16, 18, 23, 106, 127, 145n26. *See also* intra-activity; material-discursiveness
Bauman, Richard, 151n3
Bialecki, Jon, 143n18, 145n24, 146n29, 148n34 (intro.), 148n5 (chap. 1)
Bible, books of, 112–14, 119, 126; Acts, 149n9; Ephesians, 131; 1 Corinthians, 8, 28, 53, 60, 68, 73, 76, 108, 114–15, 142n13, 150n24; 1 Thessalonians, 112; 1 Timothy, 8, 34, 68, 108, 115, 123, 142n13, 150n24, 154n47; Galatians, 58, 116, 123; Genesis, 103, 108, 114–16; John, 15; Psalms, 119; 2 Corinthians, 125
biblical scholarship, feminist, 9
biblical words, 8–9
Bielo, James, 118, 142n15, 144n18, 151n4, 162n34
biography, 4, 142n10
Birkeli, Otto Emil, 121
Bjerkås, Ingrid, 77
Bjertnes, Carl Fredrik, 121
body, 6, 8, 17, 126–27, 128; as central to material religion, 60; as "material-discursive," 18, 106; multiple, 20–21, 81, 147n31; and reading, 104; separation of belief from, 136; speaking, 15, 54–55, 59–61, 73–74
body-soul unity, 119–20
body-word nexus, 50. *See also* throwntogetherness
body-word operations, 54, 137. *See also* operations: with words; woman-word operations

Borchgrevink, Johanna, 37
Bost, Suzanne, 158n23
British Empire, 4–5, 13, 24, 80, 87–91, 94, 97, 158n18
Brontë, Charlotte, *Jane Eyre*, 158n19
Bushnell, Katharine, 163n55
Butler, Judith, 106, 145n26

calling, 28–29, 36, 64, 72, 91, 93, 156n68. *See also* Norwegian Mission Society (Det Norske Missionsselskab, NMS): *Come Over and Help Us!*, painting
Catholic Christianity, 97, 105, 118, 143n18, 146n27, 148n35, 158n13
Cavanaugh, Jillian, 144n22
Chambon, Michel, 145n24
Chidester, David, 86
China, 1, 37, 41, 47, 50, 57–58, 84, 87, 97–98, 121, 163n55
"Christian globalism," 41, 89
Church of Norway (state church), 31–32, 57–58, 77
class, 158n23; in mission movement, 33–34, 70, 89, 149n19; in Norway, 36, 56, 62–63, 67, 117; in women's movement, 61–62, 65, 153n32
Coleman, Simon, 59, 144n18, 161n30
colonial archive, 87, 142n11
colonialism, 7, 88–90, 101, 158n18; and Christianity, 86, 88, 97. *See also* British Empire
colonial library, 86
Come Over and Help Us!, 31, 36, 41, 149n9. *See also* calling
conversion, 31, 45, 59, 93, 98
Coole, Diana, 145n24
crafts and crafting, 3, 23, 27–43, 49–52, 79, 82, 84, 92, 122. *See also* handcrafts
Crusades, 97
"cyborg," 146n27, 146n29

Dahl, Emma, 67–69
Dahle, Lars, 2, 4, 64, 66–69, 73, 88, 110, 152n26, 155n62, 155n68
Das, Veena, 5, 17, 73, 127, 142n12, 144n20
Daswani, Girish, 147n32

dematerialization, in Protestantism, 5–7, 14, 16, 25–26, 42, 53–55, 73, 136–37, 148n34
democratization, 7, 33, 62, 110
Desai, Gaurav, 86
Diamond, Cora, 148n33
Dilger, Hansjörg, 148n5
discourse, 9–10, 105–6, 145n26, 147n32. *See also* material-discursiveness
Dolphijn, Rick, 145n24
Dons, Henrikke Margrethe "Henny", 5–6, 8, 25, 27, 34, 40, 141n1, 141n8; *Afrika venter (Africa is Waiting)*, 79–80, 82–86, 88, 90, 93–94, 101, 158n17; at age ninety, 130–31; application to NMS to become missionary, 64–65; archival materials, 11–13; *Bibelens kvinner (Women of the Bible)*, 76, 114; as children's secretary for NMS, 78, 83, 102, 114, 120–22; committees and boards served, 65–67, 153nn30–31, 154n39; correspondence, 130, 157n2; death, 132; *Den kristne kvinne og hedningemisjonen (The Christian Woman and the Heathen Mission)*, 79, 90–94, 101; employment, 63, 107; and encountering Christianity, 63; as establisher and "chairman" of LMF, 36–39, 150n27; ethical project, 21–24, 56, 74, 79–82, 87, 98–101, 104, 127, 129, 137, 147n31; and founding Mission School for Women, 1–4, 15, 144n19; illness, 65, 163n52; interactions with Zulu Christians, 1, 47, 64–65, 88, 130; memoir reflections, 60; notes for talks and lectures, 76, 78, 95–96, 155n61, 156n2, 162n37; and Protestant life in language, 17–21, 131–33; published work, 156n2; racialized subjectivity, 94, 159n23; reading Eve, 103–7, 111, 114–17, 120, 124–28; retirement, 122; speaking in public, 72, 75–76; speaking on hillside, 55–57; speech at Mission Summer School, 53–54, 58–59, 72–73; speech at YWCA, 63; theological views, 76–77; travel to Scotland, 75; travel to South Africa, 47, 88, 120, 130; unpublished manuscript on mission history, 78–79, 95–98, 156n2; upbringing, 61–63; view of traditional crafting groups, 38,

42; voice, 55–56, 58–61, 67, 72; on women's right to vote, 110
Dons, Johanne Marie (née Fleischer), 62
Dons, Johannes Albrecht, 62
Droney, Damien, 147n31
Drury, Maurice O'Connor, 16, 101, 148n33
Dugan, Kate, 105
Duranti, Alessandro, 142n17

Ellingsen, Julie, 83–84, 122
enchantment, technology of, 45–46, 48
Engelke, Matthew, 29, 118, 143n18, 151n3
Eriksen, Annelin, 151n4
ethical project, 4–6, 21–22, 51, 74–75, 79–82, 87, 99–101, 104, 127, 129, 133, 147n31. *See also* project: ethics
ethics. *See* agency: ethical; anthropology: of ethics and morality; ethical project; project: ethics; Protestant ethic; values: ethical; virtue ethics; Wittgenstein, Ludwig: and ethics
ethnography, 9; in archive, 11–14
evangelical revivals, second wave, 13, 31–32, 41, 58, 97
Eve, 103, 109, 123, 128, 163n55; and order of creation, 108, 126

"fall," in Genesis, 115, 117, 123
Female Teachers' Mission Association (Lærerindernes Missionsforbund, LMF), 11, 23, 27, 36, 50–51, 65, 112–13, 122, 130, 148n1, 162n44; attention to their hearts, 31, 38–40, 42, 45–46, 50; donations to support women missionaries, 37; meeting format, 37–38, 43; *Missionshilsen* (*Mission Greeting*), magazine, 56–57, 59, 150n25, 157n2, 162n44; "Never bazaar," 27, 30, 49; number of attendees noted in minutes, 150n26
feminism, 7, 47–48, 66, 81–82, 87, 89, 101, 132, 134, 137; first wave (early women's movement), 4–5, 13, 61–62, 65–67, 70, 87, 89, 104, 110–11, 122, 128, 154n35; imperial, 89; liberal, 105; maternal, 117, 122, 161n33; modern, 4–5, 105; Protestant, 5, 21–22, 24, 51, 56, 79–82, 87, 90, 95, 100, 104, 127, 129, 133; religious, 104–5, 126, 132, 134; second wave, 122, 135; secular, 104–5, 128, 132, 134
feminism, mission. *See* mission feminist movement
feminist histories, 4–5, 47–48, 89, 104, 133–34
feminist movement. *See* feminism
feminist new materialism. *See* feminist theory: new materialist
feminist subject. *See* subject (subjectivity)
feminist theory, 54–55, 132–33, 158n23; difference, 151n5; intersectional, 151n5, 158n23; liberal, 17, 105, 151n5; new materialist, 16–18, 20, 23, 50, 55, 59, 74, 81, 105–7, 133, 143n17, 145n24, 145n27, 152n6, 156n27, 159n23; postintersectional, 143n17; poststructuralist, 105; Western, 104, 106
Føreid, Marie, 37, 71
Foucault, Michel, 147n32. *See also* self, Foucauldian technology of; subject (subjectivity)
Framnæs Christian school (Framnes), 56
Frazer, James, 16
Frost, Samantha, 145n24

Gad, Christopher, 145n24
Garriott, William, 111
Gislesen, Henriette, 92
Gjør, Bolette, 27, 32, 34–35, 64–67, 69–72, 92, 107, 110, 153nn32–33, 154n47
Goffman, Erving, 146n27
gossip. *See* speaking: women's talk (gossip)
Griffith, R. Marie, 105

Halvorson, Britt, 89, 93, 104
handcrafts: banned from LMF meetings, 27–30, 35, 37; produced at mission women's meetings, 27, 32–35, 42, 79, 82. *See also* crafts and crafting
Handman, Courtney, 79, 93, 144n18, 151n4, 157n4
Haraway, Donna, 145n24, 145–46nn2729
Harding, Susan, 118
Harkness, Nicholas, 146n27, 151n5
Hauge, Hans Nilsen, 31

Haynes, Naomi, 118, 148n34
Hazard, Sonia, 145n24
heathens, 3, 15, 27–30, 34, 36, 40–41, 46–51, 87, 89–94, 98–101, 116–19, 125–28
Hegel, Georg Wilhelm Friedrich, 101
Hekman, Susan, 145nn24–25
Herstad, Ida, 119
Hill, Patricia, 89
Hirschkind, Charles, 45, 160n2
Hoenes del Pinal, Eric, 143n18, 146n27
Højer, Lars, 13
homecrafts. *See* handcrafts
Home Crafts Circle of NMS (Det Norske Missionsselskaps Husflidsring), 37, 122, 150n29, 163n47
Home for Female Mission Students, 153n31, 157n11
Høyer, Maria, 161n32
humiliation thesis, 88

identity, 55, 59, 94, 143n17, 152n5, 158n23. *See also* subject (subjectivity); *and entries beginning with "self"*
ideology, 14, 16, 18, 142n17. *See also* language ideology
imperialism, 5, 7, 80, 88–89, 94, 101, 137. *See also* British Empire; colonialism
India, 37, 87, 97–98, 146n27, 159n41. *See also* Santalistan
individual, 30, 50, 55, 146n27, 147n31, 152n5. *See also* Protestant individualism
infrastructure, 79–81, 93–94, 98–101, 157n4
International Council of Women, 153n32
intimacy, in LMF meetings, 44
intra-activity, 6, 18, 21, 23–24, 106–7, 113, 126–27, 137
Irigaray, Luce, 9–10, 132
Irvine, Judith, 142n17
Islam, 45, 86, 104, 160n2. *See also* Muslims

Jensen, Casper Bruun, 145n24
Jews, 41, 91, 116–17, 119, 127
Jørgensen, Jonas, 12
Jouili, Jeanette, 105

Kaell, Hillary, 41, 49, 89, 104, 151n4, 158n22
Kasmani, Omar, 34, 148n5
Keane, Webb, 5, 53, 143n18, 144n22, 147n31, 148n34, 151n3
Keller, Eva, 118
Kielland, Gustava, 32, 92
Klaits, Frederick, 147n32, 152n5
Klassen, Pamela, 142n10
Kristiania (now Oslo), 61–62, 67

Ladies' Committee (Damekomiteen), 1–2, 65, 76, 91–92, 102, 150n29, 153n31, 157n11
Laidlaw, James, 147n31
Lange, Rachel, 38, 71, 85
language ideology, 142n17, 143nn17–18, 146n27, 151n3, 152n5. *See also* ideology; Protestant language ideology (Protestant semiotic ideology)
language use, 11, 16, 18, 21–23, 79, 132–33, 142n17, 146n27, 146n30. *See also* operations: with words; Protestant language use; Wittgenstein, Ludwig
lantern slides, 46–47, 79, 90
Latour, Bruno, 145n24
Lebner, Ashley, 151n44
Le Guin, Ursula K., 9–10
Lerheim, Lina, 37, 71
liberal archive, 87, 142n11
liberalism, 5, 7, 26, 62, 76, 89–90, 101, 134, 137. *See also* democratization; feminism: liberal; feminist theory: liberal; liberal archive; subject (subjectivity): liberal (Enlightenment, secular, self-liberating)
listening, 29–30; ethical, 45; genre of, 42; Protestant, 44–45, 49; Protestant, as a responsive relation to world, 49–51; responsive, 28, 30, 43, 46 (*see also* response); women's, 44–45; as world-enchantment, 44–46
Livingstone, David, 85
Llewellyn, Dawn, 104
Loustau, Marc Roscoe, 146n27
Lowe, Lisa, 87, 142n11
Luhrmann, Tanya, 44

Madagascar, 1, 8, 30, 36–37, 39–41, 50, 63, 67–69, 72, 84, 97, 118
Mahmood, Saba, 104–5, 160n2
mapping, 23–24, 148n33
marriage. *See* women: married; women: unmarried
Married Women's Property Act, 62
Marsilli-Vargas, Xochitl, 30, 42
Massey, Doreen, 55, 61, 152n6. *See also* thrown-togetherness
material-discursiveness, 6–7, 16–18, 22, 25–26, 43, 50, 61, 74, 80, 100, 106–7, 126–27, 130–32, 137–38, 147nn31–32
materiality, 5–6, 14–18, 21, 42–43, 106, 118, 131, 135–38, 143n18, 144n22, 148n34 (intro.), 148n5 (chap. 1), 156n24. *See also* dematerialization, in Protestantism; material-discursiveness
Mattes, Dominik, 148n5
Mauss, Marcel, 14
Mayblin, Maya, 151n4, 160n2
mediation, 29, 149n6
meetings: "conjured context" of, 34, 39, 49; ethnography of, 28, 34
Meyer, Birgit, 6, 29, 60, 142n16, 143n18, 149n6, 151n3
Michelet, Marie, 161n33
Michelsen, Anna, 83, 122
Mikaelsson, Lisbeth, 65, 80, 87, 141n8, 148n3, 152n15, 153n30, 156n68, 162n37
"missionary imperial feminism," 89
mission bazaars, 27, 33, 37, 79
mission feminist movement, 2–4, 9, 13, 41, 47–48, 71–72, 74, 80, 90, 110–11, 141n8
mission groups. *See* mission women's groups; Norwegian Mission Society (Det Norske Missionsselskab, NMS): mixed-gender mission groups
mission histories, 78–80, 82, 86, 88, 91, 95–100, 102
mission organizations, in Norway, 31–32, 36–37, 41, 58, 153n30
mission revivals. *See* evangelical revivals, second wave

Mission School (Stavanger), 1–2, 4, 11, 32, 79, 99, 102, 134–35
Mission School for Women (Kristiania/Oslo), 1–3, 7–8, 15, 65, 75, 78–80, 91–92, 95–100, 112, 134–37, 157n11, 159n24
mission societies, women's, 80, 91, 94, 98, 108, 153n30
Mission Study Council (Norges Missionsstudieraad), 56, 67, 91
Mission Summer School, 53, 56–61, 67, 72–75, 91
mission women's groups, 32–35, 69, 72–73, 80, 92, 94, 98, 101, 111, 149n13, 160n16; and class, 33, 149n19; meetings, traditional, 38, 51, 71; as source of income for NMS, 32–33, 92, 108; today, 52
Mission Workers' Circle (Missionsarbeidernes Ring), 66–67, 153n33, 154n36
Mittermaier, Amira, 30, 105, 149n8, 160n2
modernity, Western, 5, 7, 14, 26, 136–37, 148n34
Moi, Toril, 5, 17, 74, 142n12, 144n20
Mol, Annemarie, 16, 19–21, 23–24, 81–82, 101, 132, 145n24, 145–46nn27–28, 147n31. *See also* multiplicity
Monsen, Marie, 87
Moore, Brenna, 158n13
Morgan, David, 60
Mosko, Mark, 146n29
motherhood, 87. *See also* women: married
motherliness. *See* feminism: maternal
Muhammad, 86
"Muhammedan," 41, 90, 93–94, 98, 101, 116–17, 119, 127. *See also* Islam; Muslims
multiplicity, 6–7, 19–22, 25–26, 50–51, 75, 81–82, 101–2, 106–7, 126–27, 130–32, 137–38, 145n24, 145n27, 146n29, 147nn31–32
Muslims, 85–87, 105. *See also* Islam; "Muhammedan"
Myhre, Knut Christian, 17, 144n22

Naumescu, Vlad, 146n27
needlework. *See* handcrafts
new materialism. *See* feminist theory: new materialist

Nielssen, Hilde, 87
Nissen's School for Girls (Nissens Pigeskole), 63
Nome, John, 102, 149n10
Norseth, Kristin, 34, 75, 110, 141n8
Norway, population of, 149n18
Norwegian Association for Women's Rights (Norsk Kvindesagsforening), 61–62
Norwegian Association for Women's Right to Vote (Kvindestemmerettsforeningen), 61–62
Norwegian Mission Society (Det Norske Missionsselskab, NMS), 1–4, 27, 31–33, 56, 58, 67–69, 78, 130, 134–35, 149n10, 158n18; *Barnebladet* (*Children's Magazine*), 84, 121, 157n2; children's groups (children's work), 83–85, 121–22, 163n45; *Come Over and Help Us!*, painting, 31, 36, 41, 149n9; communal living and working space for women, 84, 96, 103; female traveling secretaries in, 70–71, 85, 113, 156n2; general assembly, 35, 39; grassroots, 32, 68–69, 71–73, 79, 107–10; *Missionslæsning for Kvindeforeninger* (*Mission Reading for Women's Groups*), women's magazine, 64, 66, 69–70, 72, 107, 149n12; mixed-gender mission groups, 32–33, 69–70, 72, 107, 160n3, 160n16; *Norsk Missionstidende* (*Norwegian Mission Tidings*), magazine, 31, 33, 35; women's groups, 32–33 (*see also* mission women's groups)
Norwegian Women's National Council (Norske Kvinders Nasjonalråd), 39, 66–67, 153nn32–33, 155n68
Nyhagen Predelli, Line, 67–69, 110, 141n8, 152n15, 160n3, 161n33
Nylænde (*New Frontiers*), feminist women's magazine, 75, 109

Okkenhaug, Inger Marie, 87, 89
Oliphant, Elayne, 148n35
Olsen, Louise, 92
Olsen, Ragna, 63
Olsen, Theodor, 68
O'Neill, Kevin Lewis, 111

operations: embodied, 159n23; ethical, 21 (*see also* ethical project; project: ethics); with words, 6, 19, 103, 104, 106, 144n22, 145n26 (*see also* body-word operations; language use; woman-word operations)
ordinary language philosophy, 144n20
Orthodox Christianity, 143n18, 146n27

Paine, Crispin, 60
patriarchy, 104–7, 132–33
Paul (the apostle), 8–9, 28, 53, 58–60, 73–77, 108–9, 112–16, 123–25, 142n12, 149n9, 155n67
Peirce, C. S., 144n22
Pentecostal Christianity, 44, 59, 111, 118, 143n18, 146n29, 147n32, 148n34 (intro.), 148n5 (chap. 1)
performativity, 106, 127
Pharo, Sophie, 63
place. *See* space, and place; woman's place
Plate, S. Brent, 60
power, 105–7, 132–33, 143n17, 147n32
prayer and prayer meetings, 56–57, 73, 86, 92, 105
preaching, 46; women's, 58, 75, 109, 152n15, 155nn67–68 (*see also* speaking: women's, as forbidden in churches; women: as pastors)
Premawardhana, Devaka, 146n29
project, 21–22, 146n31; ethics, 22, 81, 107, 133, 147n32 (*see also* ethical project); gender, 111, 128; modern, 7, 137–38
"Protestant bias," 6, 14–15, 25, 136, 142n16
Protestant ethic, 5, 22, 26, 136
Protestant individualism, 5, 7, 14, 22, 25, 53, 148n34
Protestantism, 25–26, 134–38; anthropology of, 5–7, 14, 22, 143n18; and Western modernity, 7, 134–38, 148n34
Protestantism, and colonialism. *See* colonialism: and Christianity
Protestantism, and feminism. *See* feminism: Protestant; mission feminist movement
Protestant language ideology (Protestant

INDEX

semiotic ideology), 5–6, 14–15, 25, 53–54, 74, 136–37, 143n18, 151n3
Protestant language use, 5–6, 17, 26, 53, 73, 79, 106, 136–37, 143n18
Protestant listening. *See* listening: Protestant
Protestant missions (mission movement), 31, 87–90. *See also* evangelical revivals, second wave; mission histories; mission organizations, in Norway
Protestant reading. *See* reading: Protestant
Protestant self. *See* Protestant individualism; Protestant sincerity (sincere self)
Protestant sincerity (sincere self), 5–6, 14, 22, 25, 53–55, 73, 133, 137, 143n18. *See also* speaking: and sincerity
Protestant speaking. *See* speaking: Protestant
Protestant writing. *See* writing: Protestant

Quakers, speech, 151n3

race, 86, 89, 158n23. *See also* subject (subjectivity): racialized
Ramabai, Pandita, 159n41
reading: as arranging, 118–19; Bible, 44, 103, 107, 111–14, 118; in children's groups, 84–85; as cognitive act, 118; as dwelling, 118–19; as iterating, 126; and materiality, 118–20, 127; in mission women's groups, 69, 71; Protestant, 103–4, 106; Protestant, as material-discursive intra-actions, 126–27; as receiving, 111–14, 129, 161n30; women's, restricted, 111
Reformation, 97
Reinhardt, Bruno, 44, 149n6
response, 23, 28–30, 42–43, 45–46, 49–51; ethics of, 30. *See also* listening
Rettedal, Knut, 57, 60
Rhees, Rush, 100
Rich, Adrienne, 84
Robbins, Joel, 80, 143n18, 147n32, 148n34, 149n7, 157n6, 160n2

salvation, 40, 116, 119
Santalistan, 37, 40–41, 50, 58, 121. *See also* India
Satan, 6, 103, 116–17, 123–25, 127–28
Schielke, Samuli, 160n2
Second Great Awakening, 31. *See also* evangelical revivals, second wave
Seland, Bjørg, 152n15
self, Foucauldian technology of, 44. *See also* feminist theory: poststructuralist; subject: poststructuralist
self, sincere. *See* Protestant sincerity (sincere self)
self, singular. *See* Protestant individualism
self-cultivation, 22, 26, 44–45, 105–6, 120, 127, 132–33, 147n31, 160n2. *See also* virtue ethics
self-silence, 10–11
"seriation," 118
Sewall, May Wright, 153n32
silence, women's, 8, 34–36, 43, 49–50, 53, 60, 72–73, 76, 108
Silverstein, Michael, 144n22, 147n31
Simensen, Jarle, 88
Sinding, Marie, 63–64, 75
Skeie, Karina Hestad, 34, 47, 87, 110, 141n8
slavery (transatlantic slave trade), 84–85, 92, 97
Slotta, James, 29
snake, in Genesis, 116, 123–24
sounds and silences ("sonic-scene"), in meetings, 28, 34, 38, 42, 49, 52, 73
South Africa (Natal), 1, 36–37, 46–47, 65, 85, 88, 92, 97, 158n18, 162n38. *See also* Zululand; Zulus
space, and place, 54–55, 59–61, 75, 152n6. *See also* woman's place
speaking, 29, 146n27; body, 15, 55–56, 60–61, 73; in mission women's groups, 71; Protestant, 53–55, 73–74, 151n3; Protestant, as thrown-together voice, 73–75; and sincerity, 14, 54; and space, 54, 59–61; women's, 8–10, 68–70, 72; women's, as forbidden in churches, 53–54, 57–58, 60, 67–68, 71, 75–76; women's talk (gossip), 70. *See also* preaching; voice
Spivak, Gayatri Chakravorty, 158n19

state church. *See* Church of Norway (state church)
Strathern, Marilyn, 50, 81, 142n14, 145n24, 145–46nn27–29, 147n31, 151n44
Strhan, Anna, 44–45, 161n30
study circle, 91–92, 94
subject (subjectivity), 4–5, 131–34, 145n24; circuit, 21, 105, 107, 120, 147n31; and class, 153n32 (*see also* class); feminist, 104–6, 133; gendered (woman), 21, 54, 94, 158n23; imperial, 158n19; liberal (Enlightenment, secular, self-liberating), 45, 104–5, 132, 134; material-discursive, 106–7, 113, 127, 132, 147n31 (*see also* material-discursiveness); momentary (instantiated), 56, 74–75; multiple (collective, composite, distributed), 6, 26, 50, 74–75, 106–7, 127, 131, 137, 146n29 (*see also* multiplicity); new materialist, 105, 147n32 (*see also* feminist theory: new materialist); poststructuralist, 44–45, 105, 133, 147n32; racialized, 94, 159n23; religious (self-cultivating), 105, 120, 127, 132, 134; and space, 54. *See also* body; identity; Protestant individualism; *and entries beginning with "self"*

Tertullian, 125
third figure, 90, 94, 98–99, 101. *See also* heathens; "Muhammedan"
Thorne, Susan, 89
Thornton, Brendan Jamal, 111, 128
throwntogetherness, 55, 61, 75
Tjelle, Kristin Fjelde, 33, 36, 111, 141n8, 149n13, 149n17, 149n22, 154n35
Tokheim, Marit, 154n35
Tomlinson, Matt, 126

values: ethical, 80, 82, 101, 106, 146n30, 147n32; hierarchy of, 80–81, 101, 157n6
van der Tuin, Iris, 145n24
Vårt Land, Christian newspaper, 130, 156n68
VID Specialized University. *See* Mission School (Stavanger)
virtue ethics, 22, 45, 105, 107, 127, 133,

146–47nn30–32, 157n6. *See also* self-cultivation
voice, 54–55, 61, 67, 73–75, 151n5. *See also* speaking

Weber, Max, 14
Webster, Joe, 45–46, 144n18, 151n4, 161n30
whiteness, 83, 90, 94, 97, 101, 158n23. *See also* subject (subjectivity): racialized
Wittgenstein, Ludwig, 5, 16–20, 50, 73, 101, 118, 131, 134, 142n12, 143n17, 144n20, 146n30; crisscross method, 20–23, 25, 143n17, 147n33; and ethics, 146n30; in feminist scholarship, 17, 144n23; form of life, 16–18, 50, 74, 86, 133, 144n22, 145n25; language, idea of, 16–17, 19–20, 100, 144n22, 145n25; language-games, 17, 30, 145n26; and new materialism, 145n25; "surveyable representation," 147n33. *See also* language use; mapping; material-discursiveness; multiplicity; operations: with words; ordinary language philosophy
woman, 22, 99, 105–6, 115–17; creation of, 111, 114, 126 (*see also* Eve)
woman's place, 2, 60, 74, 86, 120, 122–23, 128; in mission work, 60
woman-word operations, 6, 15, 18, 20, 25, 31, 43, 50, 74, 102, 106, 127, 131–32. *See also* body-word operations; operations: with words
women: education, 1–3, 8, 37, 48, 63, 91–93, 135, 159n41; employment, 33, 36, 41, 48, 62–64, 67, 70, 89, 92, 128; legal rights, 62, 66; married, 62, 64, 85, 87, 89, 108; as missionaries, 15, 43, 80, 94, 98–99, 101, 141n8, 153n30 (*see also* mission societies, women's); as pastors, 48, 77, 129, 135, 155n68; right to vote in national elections, 3–4, 61–62, 66, 104, 128; right to vote in NMS, 72, 107–11, 160n3; unmarried, 36, 56, 62–63, 67, 70, 84, 153n13
women's groups, in mission movement. *See* mission women's groups
women's mission societies. *See* mission societies, women's

women's movement (early). *See* feminism: first wave (early women's movement)
women's ordination. *See* women: as pastors
World Missionary Conference: Edinburgh (1910), 88; New York (1900), 93
writing: and circulation, 79–80, 93; Protestant, 78–79, 81, 94; Protestant, as productive but partially connected infrastructure, 81–82, 100–102; and subjectivity, 94; women's, 99–100

Young Women's Christian Association (YWCA), 63–65, 91, 114; *Vort Blad (Our Magazine)*, 63, 72, 157n2

Zululand, 1, 11, 37, 50, 85, 88–89, 98, 130. *See also* South Africa (Natal)
Zulus, 1, 4, 85, 87–90, 94
Zwissler, Laurel, 105

www.ingramcontent.com/pod-product-compliance
Lightning Source LLC
Chambersburg PA
CBHW022012290426
44109CB00015B/1146